Making Short Films

Jim Piper

ALLWORTH
PRESS
NEW YORK

10   09   08   07   06   5   4   3   2   1

Published by Allworth Press
An imprint of Allworth Communications, Inc.
10 East 23rd Street, New York, NY 10010

Cover design by Derek Bacchus
Page composition/typography by SR Desktop Services, Ridge, NY
Cover photo by Lianne Neptune

ISBN: 1-58115-444-5

Library of Congress Cataloging-in-Publication Data
Piper, Jim.
    Making short films / Jim Piper.
        p.   cm.
    Includes indexes.
    1. Short films—Production and direction.   I. Title.

 PN1995.9.P7P53   2006
 791.4302'3—dc22   2006003317

Printed in Canada

This book is for
DAVE HALL

For his skill, his craft, his art, and his friendship.

CONTENTS

Acknowledgments

Allworth editors rule, as my students would say. Nicole Potter-Talling is a terrific first scrutinizer, advising me to take this out, expand that, clarify over here, watch my language over there—with unfailing good judgment. Nana Greller deftly kept the whole enterprise on schedule, nailing down blurb writers, gently bugging me about deadlines, bringing everything together. And then Monica Lugo at the end of the line—Monica the patient! I can't tell you how many last minute changes I asked of her. Monica is a genius at making everything fit and look right, too. What kind of editor spends all afternoon helping me find a good picture of a consumer DV camera? A good one.

And profuse thanks goes to Joachim Shirmacher here in Fresno. He took the thirty films I wanted readers to see and created the wonderful DVD that comes with the book.

Nobody does a good book alone. In my case, I not only had helpful editors and a great DVD author, but also 122 students whose films I proudly describe in the pages ahead.

1

About Short

I ask you: Why do you want to make short films at all? There's no money in short films, let me tell you that from the start. Why not just jump right into making features, and skip the whole short film step? I assume you've given this question some thought. I am going to try to read your mind now. Maybe you want to make short films for these reasons:

> - Short films cost much less to make than feature films.
> - Short films take less time to make.
> - Short films require less control than long films.
> - Short films probably require less expertise, less know-how.
> - Beginners can learn a lot making short films before trying their hand at features.
> - Short films are minor investments of commitment. If you make one that doesn't work out, it's no big deal. You pick yourself up and make something else, also short.

And here is a reason you probably have not thought of: Short films have the potential to be much more expressive and creative than feature films.

You say, wait a minute. How can that be? We usually associate feature films with Hollywood product. Surely Hollywood people have the money, talent, and resources to be expressive and creative. Or if not Hollywood, then the independent film scene. How is it possible that a short film made by a beginner like me might turn out more original than a feature film produced by pros? The answer lies, almost magically, in length.

THERE IS NOTHING LIKE ABOVE ALL ELSE

Let me tell you about Anoush Ekparian, who makes only short films. Anoush does things like take her camera to a busy intersection in San Francisco, stop pedestrians, and ask them to look at the camera and recite this line: "Above all else, guard your heart, for it is the wellspring of life." She gets a few dozen people to do this as she films them in close-up. All sorts of people: old people, young people, bohemians, suits, Asians, African Americans, and so on. Then she imports this footage into a computer editing program and tightens the shots. She puts a title on the front end—*Above All Else*—and credits at the end. No music. Five minutes.

From *Above All Else* by Anoush Ekparian.
This film is on the DVD.

Anoush meant *Above All Else* to be a kind of spoof. The line she asked the people to give is, after all, a bit corny. She was interested in how people gave the line and what they revealed about themselves as they spoke, knowing they were being filmed. Some people gave the line perfectly straight, some smirked, some were impressively theatrical, some satirized the line by hamming it up, some were shy and self-conscious, and some were, like, give me a break. So *Above All Else* turns out to be a film about how people comport themselves on camera. Think of it as a film poem, or a kind of documentary without surface commentary. Or a film about film. Of course, Stephen Spielberg would not make such a film. But Anoush's film has more creativity about it—or at least it makes audiences pay more attention to what is going on—than most five-minute segments of a Spielberg film or anybody's feature film. In this way, it is more expressive and creative than a feature film.

This book, then, explains how to make meaningful and expressive short films, not exactly like *Above All Else* because there is only one *Above All Else*, but films that capture the independence and daring spirit of *Above All Else*. You don't have to spend a lot of money making films like these. You don't have to prepare a lot. And above all, you don't have to imitate Hollywood. Why reinvent Hollywood? Who says films have to be two hours long? Short films free you.

I can't explain to you exactly how to make art, but I do give you many examples of how applying the craft of filmmaking will lead you into film art, often without being aware of it. All those close-ups in *Above All Else* have tremendous power to make viewers feel and think. That is what doing art is, making something that has a good effect on a person's heart and head.

A CASE IN POINT: DENNIS DUGGAN

For years before his death in 1988, Dennis Duggan was San Francisco's leading super 8 filmmaker. His first film was called *Endangered Species,* and it ran ninety minutes. In other words, it was a feature. It was a pretty good film for a beginner. Then Dennis started going to film festivals, where, he discovered, virtually all the films were short. I met him at a festival in Palo Alto. "I love these films," he told me. "If I had known it was okay to make short films, I would have made them before I made *Endangered Species.*"

We've been brainwashed to not pay attention to short films. The film industry wants to sell you on features, not on arty short films. At any rate, Dennis started making short films. All of them were more inventive than *Endangered Species*, which had pretty much stuck to the standard beginning-middle-end structure of most features. He never made another feature, so happy was he making shorts. There is a second moral to this story: Public awareness of the potential of the short film is practically nonexistent in this country.

So you don't have to feel deprived making short films. I take that back. You are deprived of one thing: money. You won't get rich making short films. You have to keep your day job. But most poets and artists are like this. They have to work at 7-Eleven or teach or drive cabs or sell used cars or do brain surgery to support themselves while they paint or sculpt or write or edit film at night or on their days off.

Most people who make feature films do not, in fact, become millionaires. Instead, they often go into debt and live out their lives in obscurity. They end up borrowing from friends and relatives to make films that may not be any good in the first place. And even if they do make good films and get them into distribution, their films probably won't be profitable. It usually takes two years to finish a feature film. The time spent is filled with frustration. Actors quit on you. Your only camera breaks down. No one wants to pick up your film for distribution, and even if they do, it plays for only a week in Omaha then closes forever. Chances are it will never go to video. The Spielbergs are very rare indeed, and so are the successful low-ball indie features like *Napoleon Dynamite*.

However, when you make short films you endure none of this. Nobody shuts you out. You get an idea on Thursday, prepare on Friday, shoot on Saturday and Sunday, edit on Tuesday, have a local band do music for it on Wednesday, promote it around town on Thursday and Friday, and exhibit it at a film jam at a local coffeehouse the next Saturday night. Then it's on to the next film. You work alone like a poet or a painter. Or you might collaborate with two or three of your film friends. Or you might work alone again. Short is pleasant.

There is no law that says you can't later "move up" to making features after a period of making shorts, if you are so inclined. ("Move up"! Ugh! To me, it's usually an artistic move down.) You will have learned so much about all aspects of film production, making serious short films on your own. Most film schools don't provide enough experience to allow students to really learn production. Practically all serious young film students therefore find themselves making films on their own in addition to the exercises they complete in film school.

If you hanker to eventually leave short filmmaking and go into big-time filmmaking, understand this: Most feature films are mired in commercialism, stuck in formula, restrained by box-office prospects, and compromised from the day the scriptwriter writes "Scene 1." The director of a Hollywood movie isn't any kind of artist. He's just the chief audio-visual engineer of a marketing entity. He was hired to make everybody, including himself, a lot of money.

Even so-called independent production is fraught with compromise. Always, always, always you have to think about the market. Should the film "end happily"? Say you don't really want a happy ending. To make your point, your film has to end on a somber, tragic, or bittersweet note. Then someone—maybe your distributor or agent—informs you that nobody wants to see downer films. If you want people to like your film, you'd better turn it around and make sure everything comes out just fine at the end, you are told. What to do? Makers of short films never have such conflicts. People who make short films are truer to themselves. They answer to no one. Short makes it possible. Short unleashes creative potential. Short is better than long.

SCHOOL YOURSELF

Watch *Mistress*, a film about a young indie filmmaker desperate for funding. He has to sell out at every turn in order to get the money he needs.

EMPHASIS ON CREATIVITY

This is not a highly technical book. Half of the remaining chapters have to do with understanding equipment and technique, while the other half offer you hundreds of ideas and approaches for making short, doable films. The idea chapters emphasize communication and art—the art of the short film. This is a separate thing, just as the short story is a separate art form from the novel. Throughout the book, I have emphasized creativity over technical matters like mouse clicking.

MAINLY ON YOUR OWN

Most books on filmmaking, and most classes too, stress that making films is a collaborative enterprise. You are supposed to go in with four or five people and pool your talent, equipment, and money, and make a film sort of by committee. This way of working excludes many potentially good filmmakers out there who just don't have the social skills necessary to lead or fit into a communal work ethic. This way of working robs the individual of his or her unique vision. I have always felt that filmmaking should be as lone-wolf and individual as writing fiction or taking pictures.

Or the Film Commune

On the other hand, the collaborative aspect of making short films could lead you into the formation of deeply satisfying, lifelong relationships with people you enjoy working with, people with good ideas and a passion for cinematic expression, people who relish the care, art, and thought that go into the production of even a short film. You stay the boss—most of the time—but your merry little band of helpers is always at the ready. This is how Dave Hall worked. He made highly original short, spoofy films, in both super 8 and just about every video format that came along, and always kept his people close to him. Dave, Phil, Dennis, Brad, Donna, and the rest hung out with each other, lived together, married each other—in effect forming a filmmaking commune which endured from the 1960s, when Dave was a student of mine, until his death a few months before this book was published. The commune lives on.

MINIMALIST FILMMAKING

This book also favors what I call *minimalist filmmaking*. It means deriving much from little. It means preferring understatement and suggestion to explicitness. I didn't invent this term, but I'd like to resurrect it. Of course, I swim upstream on this issue. I hope you will want to follow. Like salmon, we are bound for spawning grounds. Because restraint frees you. Short frees you and restraint frees you. All poets are minimalists. The whole idea of poetry is economy of language. As I will say so often in this book, short filmmakers are more like poets than any other kind of artists.

A Minimalist Story Film

Kathy Verzosa's film about abortion, called *Little Star*, is stripped to the bone. You find nothing unnecessary in it. You do not listen in on the couple discussing abortion. You

From *Little Star* by Kathy Verzosa.
This film is on the DVD.

don't know whether they are married or not or why it's not right to go ahead and have the baby. There is no backstory, no setup. You don't see a doctor or a nurse or a procedure room. All you see is the couple rising in the morning and driving to the clinic. The camera does not follow the woman into the procedure room. Instead, it stays with the father, who worriedly paces the hall. Time passes. The woman comes out. The two enter an elevator, where a young woman and a man are just coming out. The woman holds an infant. The couple looks on fondly as the mother and child pass by.

No matter what your opinions about abortion, you can't help but feel for this couple. The film "says": Abortion is hard. You sense this in the faces of the couple.

From *Food Not Bombs* by Sarah Hernandez.

A Minimalist Documentary Film

Food Not Bombs is a nine-minute documentary film by Sarah Hernandez about an organization that picks up food from restaurants and markets—good, edible food, not garbage—and distributes it to the poor. The film could have featured a heavy narration about the plight of the poor and our responsibility to do whatever we can for them. It could have interviewed both workers and recipients and gotten into the politics of hunger. This would have been fine. But the film doesn't include any of that. Instead, it's about the workers themselves simply interacting with others as they prepare the food for distribution. The film, then, is more about a kind of blessedness the volunteers radiate as they do their good works. Short films are particularly well suited for bringing out such subtle, unexpected moods, which can get lost in long films.

A Minimalist Art Film

An art film is offbeat, unconventional, and unpredictable. This art film runs only two minutes and at first seems to be nothing more than rather lovely footage of low hills in silhouette against a purpling sundown. Then it changes—or I should say, the film doesn't change, *you* change. You begin to see the hills not as hills but as the curves of a woman. She lies prone. In successive shots, you make out, in silhouette, her buttocks and hips, her waist, her breasts and nipples, her neck and chin. It's a remarkable transformation of perception—*your* perception. The guitar music is hymn-like. This is a hymn of praise to woman. In fact, that is the title, *Woman*. You begin to associate the hills and the sundown with Mother Earth, with natural, earthy female qualities. Travis Leeper made this film, and he must have been in love when he did it. (Flip ahead to page 238 for more about this film as a special effect.)

From *Woman* by Travis Leeper.
This film is on the DVD.

PROSUMER FORMATS

The filmmaking formats on which this book is based are often called *prosumer* systems. Prosumer joins a syllable from *professional* and two from *consumer* to suggest the blending of serious intent with everyday, low-cost consumer equipment. These formats include:

> Super 8 film equipment (flourished from 1965 to 1985).
> Consumer-grade analog video equipment (1975 to 1995).
> Consumer-grade digital video equipment dates from the mid-1990s and is best utilized in conjunction with computers.

I use the terms *film* and *filmmaking* for all of these formats. They are the older, primal designations, and I think we ought to honor them.

Super 8 is a lovely, real-film format, and not video, but it's in the sunset of its life. Once you work in video, you may find super 8 limiting. Actually, some young people really want to make super 8 films to return to the celluloid roots of filmmaking and reconstruct the good old days. Many Web sites are devoted to super 8, and the medium has thousands of devotees worldwide. Super 8-ists want to hold the film in their fingers. They want to cut it with scissors, not a with a mouse click. At any rate, when appropriate, here and there in the book, I give you some information and pointers about super 8.

ABOUT THE FILMS DESCRIBED IN THIS BOOK

Most of the 100-plus films I describe in this book were made by rank beginners—my students. I made a few. Five or six were originally produced in super 8. Not all are so hot technically; the point of the book is not to make you a film smoothie, but to make you a film artist, for which technical perfection is not a requirement. A small number of the films I describe have not actually been finished. They were started and abandoned, for various reasons. One or two exist only as notes, screenplays, script conferences, or ideas. All the same, I believe it's useful to describe them. You need not know which is which. The important thing is to give you good models for craft and art.

All the frames in the book have been reproduced with the kind permissions of the filmmakers.

THE SIDEBARS

You'll also find hundreds of *sidebars*, or brief lateral excursions, in the book. These sidebars fall into two categories.

Try This

These sidebars are meant to get you outside and shooting. I have concocted many filming exercises, some of which lead to finished short films, for reinforcing important points I make through hands-on experiences. You can do most of these exercises by yourself, or with friends and classmates.

School Yourself

These sidebars are intended to broaden your historical and theoretical knowledge of film. Each School Yourself sidebar invites you to see a few films or read about something I just explained. Taken together, these sidebars are meant to be a kind of course, a "Film 101."

SCHOOL YOURSELF

Watch short films online. Some sites include *www.atomfilms.com*, *www.ifilm.com*, and *www.omnishortfilms.com*. Search Google by "Short Films" to hit other sites. The shorts you'll find on these sites, though, are primarily slick, professional films by experienced filmmakers or graduate students with lots of money. Most run longer than the films described in this book—too long, in fact, to be very distinctive. (Remember: the longer the film, the less likely that it will turn out authentically artistic.) Also, the sites themselves are decidedly commercial with many ads, especially ads that want you to download movie players for $29.95. Plus, you have to watch these movies on a little screen about the size of a business card with the possibility of the film stopping to "buffer" many times. All the same, these films are instructive. See as many as you bear.

THE DVD: A FESTIVAL OF SHORT FILMS BY BEGINNERS

Included with this book is a DVD of 30 films described in this book. These films run the gamut from mere off-the-shelf exercises to intriguing documentaries, thoughtful story films, and innovative art films. Some are crude and amateurish, while others are quite polished. All are meant to deepen your understanding and appreciation of the short film. This is the first and only filmmaking book aimed at students and beginners to include such an illustrative DVD.

ABOUT YOUR AUTHOR

I've taught filmmaking to beginning students at the college level for several decades. I've also taught film study, literature, and writing.

I teach in the humanities division of Fresno City College in California. This means I value matters of creativity and expressiveness over technical things like upgrading RAM to 512. A colleague over in computer graphics teaches Final Cut Pro, an advanced computer editing program. He does a good job at this. I do not teach Final Cut Pro. I teach editing.

Your author.

I've also made a number of short films myself, which have taken awards in places like Redding, Palo Alto, Hollywood, Toronto, Glasgow, Brno (in the old Czechoslovakia), and London. Some years ago, I published a book about super 8 filmmaking, called *Personal Filmmaking*, with information and ideas that apply equally to video. And three years ago, I wrote a book (also published by Allworth Press) called *Get the Picture?* about the close viewing of films.

PART I:

Getting Started

2

Equipment Systems

*F*irst, you'll need to put together a complete equipment system. Compatibility is essential. Instead of trying to cobble together a system with reluctant components, fitting square pegs into round holes, I urge you to think the whole system through. You'll have an easier time of it, technologically speaking, if you do.

TWO TAKEOVERS

But first, a little technical history in the form of the media wars of the last half of the twentieth century.

When Film Ruled the Earth

For decades and decades, film held sway. Physically, film—real film I'm talking about here, not videotape—is a ribbon of an organic substance called *celluloid*, which has been coated with light-sensitive chemicals, or emulsion. When light hits the emulsion, it changes. Millions of tiny gels of color explode (silently and harmlessly) and mix in a fraction of a second. But they don't just explode and mix randomly. A lens in the camera organizes light and focuses an image on each passing frame of the film with its emulsion.

Essentially there are three extant celluloid or film formats: 35 mm, 16 mm, and super 8 mm. The *mm* refers to the width of the film in millimeters. The most expensive film to buy and process is 35 mm, which is why only large studios or rich graduate students can afford it. All Hollywood films and most independent, or "off-Hollywood," films are shot in 35 mm. Low-line independent or industrial filmmakers used to favor 16 mm; digital video has largely taken over these functions.

Super 8 came out in 1965 and replaced the older "regular 8" film, which was 16 mm sliced in half. It had to be threaded in cameras. Super 8, the main home movie format for a time, is cartridge loaded and is called super 8 because Kodak made the sprocket holes smaller, thereby increasing the frame size. In 1970, Kodak came out with a sound version of its film, and home movies learned to talk.

The Video Takeover

Then in the late 1970s, video moved in and gradually took over from film on many levels. Video is an electronic, not a photochemical, medium. It also uses ribbons of film, but it's called tape because it works more like audio recording tape than like film. Like film, it uses a lens to corral light falling on sensors in the camera, which in turn record images and sound on tape.

Video has four main advantages over film:

1. You can rewind the tape and instantly look at what you just shot. You don't have to take the tape to a lab and have it processed, as you do with film.
2. You edit the tape by pushing buttons, not by physically handling it, as you do when you edit film.
3. Minute for minute, videotape is much cheaper than film. You can get one or two hours of sound and images on most videotape cartridges. Meanwhile, a fifty-foot cartridge of super 8 film gives you less than four minutes of "content."
4. If you have the right equipment, you can add numerous effects while editing video—effects which before you had to pay a lab to do.

There are many video formats, ranging from consumer-grade VHS and video 8 tapes and cameras to professional Beta tape and cameras for fully professional documentary and TV work.

About the only place that video has not taken over completely is in the making of feature films, where 35 mm still rules, but even that is changing as . . .

DIGITAL TAKES OVER

Digital video (or DV) is videotape processed by a compact, dedicated computer inside a camcorder (camera), which is attached to a lens—the presence of the lens is what all these formats have in common. *Dedicated* means that the computer does just one thing, which is to record moving images and accompanying sounds. The dedicated computer and the lens, combined, are called a "camcorder," which I have always thought was a dumb term, so from now on in this book I crabbily insist on calling it a *camera*.

Digital filmmaking began in the early 1990s. It hasn't completely taken over. But we need a new name for the old, pre-computerized video, and so we now call that *analog*. Analog means continuous, curving, blending—just the way the world is. Digital means no curves, no blends. With digital, which is the adjective form of digit or number, it's either off or on, 1 or 0, yes or no. Digital means stair steps instead of diagonal lines. This might make it seem like analog, with its ability to capture the curves and shadings of the real world, would be the superior video system. And, in fact, better analog cameras in the right hands do produce images equal to or better than digital images. But the stair-step changes of digital have by now become so refined that they don't look like stair steps any more. We don't perceive them as stair steps. We resolve them into continuous curves and diagonal lines.

Moreover, because digital is computer based, it yields to wondrous processing that analog can't match. I'll just mention three things digital can do that analog can't:

1. Digital cameras offer many features for image processing that go way beyond the realm of analog. For example, digital cameras have "image stabilizing," which smoothes out handheld footage that otherwise would appear jerky.
2. You edit digital video in a computer and increase your technical and creative options a thousand percent. This is nonlinear editing, which means that you edit sound and image as you would edit words with a computer word processor.
3. Each time you make a copy of an analog tape, you lose a "generation." The image is duller and softer, and the sound loses fidelity. But there is no loss of quality when transferring digital sight and sound.

QUICK TOUR OF DV CAMERAS

DV cameras come in two forms: consumer cameras and professional cameras.

Consumer DV Cameras

Your Uncle Jack used a consumer DV camera to film your sister's wedding last June. Ninety-nine percent of consumer DV cameras are used for filming home movies. The other 1 percent is used by people like you and me to make serious short films. The four films I described in the last chapter were shot with consumer cameras.

DV consumer cameras start at about $400 for model closeouts and go up past $1,000.

Two Consumer DV Camera Formats: High 8 and MiniDV Formats

Consumer DV cameras come in two formats: high 8 and miniDV. High 8 is the older, slightly larger format; miniDV may yield slightly sharper images, but you will be very pleased with the quality of the images you get with high 8. Most models of professional cameras are based on the miniDV format. High 8 is fast becoming obsolete. I still see closeouts in discount stores.

Canon Optura consumer camera with liquid crystal screen that can be rotated to face the subject or the camera operator.

Professional DV Cameras

Professional cameras are differentiated from consumer cameras by the fact that they use three receptor chips (*CCDs* or charge-coupled devices) to record images. Consumer cameras have just one. Pro cameras with three chips produce sharper, truer images than do consumer cameras, but don't feel that you have to run out and buy one tomorrow. You will love the images you get with a consumer camera. In time, as you grow as a filmmaker and develop a keen eye, you may want to "move up" to a professional-grade camera. I put "move up" in quotes because as a film artist, you want to make sure that purchasing a pricey pro camera is truly an aesthetic move for you and not just some keep-up-with-the-Joneses thing to do.

Canon XL 2.Pro cameras start at about $2,000 and go up into the stratosphere.

SCHOOL YOURSELF

Watch these feature films, which were shot mainly or entirely in digital:

➤ *Star Wars: Episode III—Revenge of the Sith*: Director George Lucas had special, ultra-high-end DV cameras made especially for him, to more easily integrate the many computer-generated backdrops.

➤ *Sin City*: All of the settings, locations, and backdrops are digital.

➤ *Time Code*: An amazing experimental film featuring not just one ninety-minute uncut take but four, all seen on the screen at the same time.

➤ *The Gleaners*: A wonderful, underappreciated French documentary about the alternative lifestyles of scavengers.

➤ *What Dreams May Come*: One of the first films with lots of digital effects.

➤ *The Celebration*: An ultra-realistic film from Denmark of the Dogme 95 school. There's a family reunion as the patriarch turns sixty and dark doings emerge. Dogme

95 filmmakers believe in no brought-in lights, no tripod, no special costuming, no makeup, and lots of improvising.

➤ *Troy*, *Kingdom of Heaven*, and *The New World*: These historical films, originally shot in 35 mm, are loaded with digital effects.

Professional cameras have, in addition to a full array of automatic features, many manual settings. Professional cameras have better built-in microphones and may feature interchangeable lenses. Many nonprofessionals use pro cameras because they like to be seen with them. Some very green, aspiring filmmakers spend a lot of money on professional cameras, thinking they will make better films if they do. These people seldom really want to make films. They want to play around with expensive cameras—not the same thing.

Web Sites to Visit to Learn About Models

I am not going to get into current models or try to compare them. Here are some Web sites to visit to learn what is on the market at the time you read these words:

➤ *www.dealtime.com*
➤ *www.canondv.com*
➤ *www.crutchfield.com*
➤ *www.multimedia.com*
➤ *www.sonystyle.com*

Or simply search by "DV camcorders." Educate yourself.

The zooming range of DV cameras varies from 10:1 to 25:1. For an old super 8 guy like me, that's a lot of zooming. I never felt disadvantaged using a super 8 camera with a 6:1 zoom. And the size of the lens on a modern miniDV camera is remarkably compact. Old super 8 hands can't believe that lenses with such long zoom aren't fatter and heftier.

Probably the most remarkable feature of modern DV cameras is how well they perform under low-light conditions. You can shoot practically anywhere, even in near darkness, and be assured of getting some kind of viewable image, albeit probably grainy and colorless.

COMMON FEATURES OF DV CAMERAS

Better DV cameras also have the following:

➤ Auto and manual focusing.
➤ Auto and manual setting of exposure (brightness and darkness).

- Jacks for extension microphones.
- Jacks for earphones.
- Many imaging-altering digital features.
- Two ways to view subjects, through a traditional viewfinder and through a swing-out liquid crystal display (LCD) screen.
- Portability: The modern DV camera is remarkably palmable. It fits nicely, lightly, in the palm of your hand, and invites mobile, handheld, spontaneous shooting.

(Flip ahead for a longer discussion of these features: to page 100 for auto/manual exposure, to page 111 for auto/manual focus, and to page 236 for digital features.)

ENTRY-LEVEL EDITING PROGRAMS

The entire process of editing, as well as the equipment needed, changed completely during the evolution from real film to analog to digital. Here's how.

Dinosaur Editing

In the old real-film days, you edited *physically* with viewers and cranks. You cranked actual film through the viewer (which resembled a small TV set). You handled either the same film that ran through the camera or a copy called a work print. You physically cut it with scissors. To make a splice, you taped the tail (end) of the last shot to the head (beginning) of the next shot. All this physical contact with the film meant that you risked scratching or otherwise damaging the film.

With this contraption, you edited one picture track and no sound, unless the sound was on the film.

Analog editing was nearly as clumsy. You worked with a kind of computer, primitive by today's standards. You did not deal with the tape that came out of the camera reel but with images from the tape. By pressing buttons, you shuttled the tape back and forth, studied it on a monitor, determined edit in and edit out points, and pressed a few more buttons. A cut was then made by copying a part of the shot from the original. Copying meant that you lost a little image quality and sound. You had to edit *in sequence* or linearly. If you made a mistake, you had the choice of doing the entire sequence over or copying the good parts to drop into your reedited sequence. Again, you lost some fidelity in the copied part.

Digital editing started out in the early 1990s using expensive dedicated computers and way-up-there editing programs. Then the industry got it all down for amateurs and prosumers so they could edit using their $1,000 computers that either came with an editing program or could be bought for $100 or so. Because of this cost reduction and the development of simplified editing programs, now anyone can make DV films. Sometimes I think everyone is.

iMOVIE HD6

iMovie is the simple, powerful editing program that comes with all new Macintosh computers. The "HD" stands for high definition. Nearly all the films described in this book were edited with iMovie because that's the program that comes with the Mac computers used in my classes. Truly, iMovie is wondrous. With it, you can cut footage, rearrange it, change colors, create special effects, add music or narration, and create titles. I like to say that you can't really appreciate iMovie unless you have edited super 8 or 16 mm, which actually give you a backache, but young people don't like to hear that.

Main components of the iMovie screen. You store shots you import on the *shelf* (upper right); you view shots and edited sequences in the *monitor* (upper left); you edit in the *clip pane* (bottom), which also converts to the *timeline* for editing sound.

STUDIO MEDIA SUITE VERSION 10

No less wondrous than iMovie is Studio, an entry-level editing program by Pinnacle Systems. iMovie is only for Macs. You can't install it in a PC machine. A few PCs come with editing programs preinstalled, but I have not worked with any I could live with. Better to buy a "third-party" editing program for your PC for about $100. I like Studio. The latest version is number 10. Studio is the equal of iMovie, though it's not identical. I am not going into a feature-by-feature comparison. iMovie does a few tricks that Studio can't do, and vice versa. The competition has been good for both programs. Studio may be a little harder to set up since it's not "dedicated," as iMovie is. But dozens of my students have made nifty films with it.

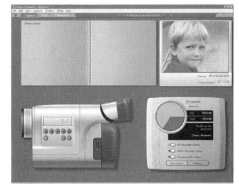

Studio has a separate capture screen. You control your camera with the controls on the camera icon. You also get to see the shot that you are capturing (importing), and the pie icon keeps you informed about how much hard drive space you have left. iMovie does all this too, but not as elegantly. (Flip ahead to page 146 for another view of the Studio and iMovie screens.)

Generations, an iMovie Film

This seven-minute film by Irvin Benut has to do with two generations of spousal abuse and a suggestion of a third. Man gets home from work, demands his dinner, wife says it's not ready yet, man slugs her. Meanwhile a kid of about ten watches this from the next

Irvin shot his film with a Sony DV (digital video) camera. With the Sony, as with most digital video cameras, you can set exposure (lightness/darkness) manually. You can dial the look you want. Irvin wanted a dark look.

This film is on the DVD.

From *Revenge* by Chris Housepian and Dan Huffman.

room. He goes outside in the rain and broods. Then the film says "Twenty years later." The kid has grown up, and now he abuses his wife. Another kid, the son of the second man, watches. He's hurting inside, too. The film ends by implying that he'll grow up to abuse, too, no matter how despondent he might have felt about it as a child.

(Flip ahead to page 99 for more about lighting film.)

Revenge, a Studio (PC) Film

This is a chase film, made with Studio. It was something of an exercise, and a fruitful one, in directing action and editing it. It's about a scumbag guy who steals another guy's wallet in a parking structure. But the victim catches on and gives chase. They run and run, across sidewalks, through yards, over fences, down alleys—on and on. The film cuts back and forth between the victim and the robber. You can tell that the thief is gradually pulling away because of how Chris Housepian and Dan Huffman, who made the film, set up the action, filmed it, and edited it. They show the chaser and chasee running lateral to the camera, coming at the camera, and moving away from the camera. The victim finally gives up, goes back to his car, drives off, then, on seeing the thief crossing a street, steers toward him, and—poetic justice, I guess.

EDITING WITH iMOVIE AND STUDIO: AN OVERVIEW

It's pretty awesome:

First: you import your film into iMovie or Studio. You do this with a *firewire cable* that transmits sound and image in real time. The shots go into something called a *shelf* or *clip pane* in iMovie or an *album* in Studio. We used to call these *film bins*.

Second: you drag all the separate shots of your film down to something called the *timeline*. This is a horizontal space at the bottom of both the iMovie and Studio screen, which shows all your shots. Each shot is represented by a *thumbnail*, or the first frame of the shot.

Third: you edit. You trim shots. You rearrange them. And you do this by pointing, clicking, and dragging.

Fourth: you add special effects, such as fades and dissolves. You create titles.

Fifth: you create a soundtrack. You get to select among live sound, music, narration, and sound effects. You can also mix music and other sounds.

Sixth: you export your finished film to new, clean tape or, if your computer is so equipped, burn a DVD of it.

(Flip ahead to pages 145–49 for a more complete list of things you can do with iMovie and Studio.)

EXHIBITING

You have two ways to show your finished film. If your film ends up on tape, you project it with your camera by means of cords running from your camera to inputs on the front of your TV or to a video projector for big-screen playback. Or you make a DVD of your film and project with a DVD player.

Young filmmakers prefer, I believe, to make DVDs of their films, if they can. That way they can give their films to cast and crew and play them back on any consumer DVD player, or take their films to any venue that has a DVD player, and exhibit. Of course, to make a DVD of your film, you need a DVD burner. Often, this is built into high-end computers and is included in single all-purpose drives that not only play and burn CDs but show commercial DVDs as well. If your computer doesn't have a DVD burner, you can purchase an exterior or outboard burner for a few hundred dollars.

It's hard to damage a DVD if you handle it with care. Tape has moving parts and can snag or break, even if you do handle the cartridge with care.

ADVANCED EDITING PROGRAMS

You may find no reason at all to move into an editing program more sophisticated than iMovie or Studio. Either program may suit you for many years. As I say in chapter 7, which is about editing, some filmmakers—called *mise-en-scène filmmakers*—just don't see editing as a big deal. They don't need very fancy editing programs. On the other hand, you may want to explore one of the advanced editing programs. Many prosumer filmmakers do. Two of the best known are Final Cut by Apple and Premiere by Adobe.

Final Cut for Macs

Final Cut is an editing program for experienced editors. It leapfrogs over iMovie, giving you ninety-nine picture tracks and ninety-nine sound tracks to work with! When would you need so many picture tracks? You need them for creating *double exposures* and for *compositing,* or the layering of images. Double exposing, a term from 35 mm filmmaking, means superimposing one image on another, as you probably already guessed. You can't do this with iMovie. Compositing has to do with building up a complex image fashioned from a number of separate images superimposed or occurring sequentially or simultaneously in separate windows. This is the kind of thing you see, for example, at the start of *Monday Night Football*. The logo is crowded with multiple images of quarterbacks dropping back, linebackers swatting down passes, tight ends dancing in the end zone, cheerleaders strutting their stuff, worried coaches on the phone—all while the title MONDAY NIGHT FOOTBALL spins and zooms up from the background. You can never do anything like this with iMovie or Studio.

Final Cut also includes very professional sound editing options. You can convert tracks into waveforms and look for spikes as editing points, allowing you to cut on the beat. You can equalize sound to filter out wind rumble. You can edit image precisely to sound. It's okay to use copyrighted music in your iMovie film, as long as you don't plan to make money with the film; otherwise, you have to use uncopyrighted music or you may get into legal trouble. Current versions of Final Cut include a complete array of music loops that are not copyrighted—canned music, to be sure, but imminently useful.

Final Cut has dozens of so-called effects and filters or ways of rendering images. Many effects look just like those of iMovie but are accomplished with much greater control and grace. There are many all-out professional filters included in Final Cut that you can't get with iMovie, including color correction, which is necessary when you shoot under different lighting conditions.

Upper left is the browser, where you gather all your shots, stills, and sounds. Upper center, is the viewer, the monitor for editing. Upper right is the canvas, the monitor for previewing in real time. Below, the timeline, combining all video and audio tracks.

The Final Cut screen brings more information up front for you. The *browser* (upper left) is a pane for storing all your separate *clips*—and not just film clips, but clips representing still photos, sounds, and music. They are easily pulled to the timeline. Another pane, the *viewer* (upper center), is where you look at your separate clips and decide how you want to edit them. The *canvas* (upper right) is for looking at finished sequences. Most editing is done in the timeline, the horizontal bands at the bottom of the Final Cut window. The timeline shows both your picture tracks and your sound tracks and how they relate to each other—when they start and stop, and how long the separate tracks run. This is a lot of information for one screen, and each component is rather small. But you can magnify any of this with a mouse click.

Final Cut comes three ways: Express, Pro, and Studio. Studio, at well over $1,000, costs the most and includes lots of plug-ins and assorted programs. The cost of Pro, only slightly less loaded up than Studio, hovers just under $1,000 and, as I've indicated, is used by advanced amateurs and professionals all the way up to those making films commercially released in theaters. Express is a reduced version of Final Cut, costing $300. Aimed at advanced amateurs rather than professionals, Express drops some features the amateur isn't likely to need.

No version of Final Cut can be installed in PC computers. It is strictly for Macs.

Advanced Editing Programs for PC

There are many advanced editing programs for PCs. Liquid by Pinnacle Systems and Premiere by Adobe Software are just two. Premiere works in both PCs and Macs.

These programs are complex and expressive in a special-effectsy kind of way. Both are roughly the equal of Final Cut. Final Cut will have the edge in one aspect; Liquid in another; Premiere the edge over that other thing. Back and forth. Some filmmakers swear by Final Cut, some by Premiere. Ford and Chevy. More taste, less filling. This book is no place to go into comparisons, which can be very technical. My advice: Learn your craft with iMovie or Studio. You can pick up *all* of the art with these starter programs, too. Either Liquid or Premiere will certainly extend your *technical* knowledge of editing, but they offer little to help you grasp the *art* of short filmmaking.

Premiere makes a hundred-dollar editing program, called Elements, that has been favorably compared in the computer magazines with Studio.

Plug-ins for Both iMovie and Studio

You can hot rod both iMovie and Studio with little programs called *plug-ins*, which are like buying a low-ball car and tricking it out with spoilers, mud flaps, and foxtails. You don't end up with a Lexus, but you feel better about what you drive. Apple sells many plug-ins for iMovie, and so do a dozen other outfits. You can buy plug-ins that give you more special effects, plug-ins for fancier titles, or plug-ins for animation.

Pinnacle Systems, which makes Studio, offers a multiplicity of plug-ins for Studio and makes several deluxe versions of Studio. One even gives you multiple picture tracks.

You can see what these plug-ins strive for—they want to transform you from a Civic filmmaker to an Acura filmmaker; that is, they want you to feel that you have approached the nirvana of Final Cut or Premiere.

The best plug-in is your brain.

ADDITIONAL EQUIPMENT

In addition to a DV camera, a computer, and an editing program, you will need a few pieces of relatively low-cost and low-tech gear. They are:

> An off-camera *unidirectional* microphone and a twelve-foot extension cord.
> A boom for the off-camera mic.

- One or two long-life camera batteries, especially if you'll be shooting a lot of documentaries.
- Some white sheets of posterboard for reflecting light.
- An inexpensive three-fixture set of lights with stands.
- A tripod.

(Flip ahead to page 164 for more about microphones, to page 164 for booms, and to page 99 for more about lighting.)

THE SUPER 8 OPTION

This is the authentic film option—not virtual film, not video, but film with real sprocket holes running along one edge.

Super 8 offers that one true advantage of real film: It looks like film. I don't mean the ribbon you hold in your fingers; I mean the image projected on the screen with a projector. My younger readers won't know what this means, so thoroughly has the digital

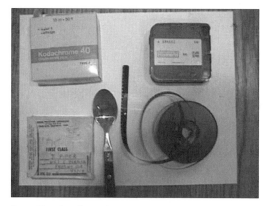

Super 8 reel and spool.

look settled into the national consciousness. But when you project super 8 with a projector, you may be struck with the warmth and realness and *photographic* look of it. You go, "Oh, so that's what true film looks like." By comparison, video looks, well, different. At least people used to talk like this ten years ago when video was first making real headway against film. People talked about the look of film versus the look of tape. It's an analogous to the vinyl versus CD wars in music. Supporters of vinyl records swear that vinyl is warmer and richer than CD. Even the scratches on vinyl are claimed to be more "authentic." So many people are sentimental this way that Apple has included an effect in iMovie called "old film," which actually lays down scratches on the "film" (video) and makes it jump randomly every few seconds to simulate damaged sprocket holes.

Equipment for Super 8

If you go super 8, you'll need the following equipment:

- Camera
- Tripod
- An editing contrivance called a *viewer*

- Super 8 splicer
- Super 8 splicing tape
- Three-fixture set of photographic lights
- A better tape recorder, preferably a DAT (digital audio tape) recorder

This camera by GAF takes both silent and sound film.

You don't need a special tripod for making super 8 films, since the thread size for the bolt that secures the bottom of the camera to the platform of the tripod is identical for all film and video formats. Lighting kits start at about $150. Viewers are inexpensive, low-tech affairs made of plastic and about the size of a portable DVD player (but differently shaped). They used to sell new for under $100. Splicers could be hard to find. Go on eBay for both viewers and splicers. Like super 8 cameras, super 8 projectors come in silent and sound versions. Super 8 film can be sound stripped—that is, narrow bands of iron oxide are applied to the film's edge. Try to obtain a stereo sound projector because super 8 sound film has a recordable balance stripe (also iron oxide) to give you two tracks to mix.

Super 8 sound projector and sound camera, both by Elmo.

School Yourself

Visit www.super8sound.com or www.pro8mm.com. Either address takes you to the same place, Pro8mm of Burbank, California, an outfit that has taken super 8 seriously since the 1960s. It used to call itself Super8Sound. It makes special deals with Eastman Kodak and German film suppliers to package professional film stocks in super 8 cartridges. It also sells new and used super 8 cameras and editing equipment.

Pro8mm is the first place to look to for transfers of super 8 to DV video so you can gain all the advantages of computer editing. It's just a lot easier to edit super 8 in a computer editing program than on a super 8 editing bench and with a super 8 sound projector. The biggest advantage of working in digitized super 8 is that you retain the film look of the original super 8 camera stock.

You can pick up good, scarcely used super 8 equipment from swap meets, yard sales, and pawn shops. Generally, the condition of the exterior of the equipment is a guide to how much it has been used.

Two Drawbacks to Super 8

There are two major drawbacks to using super 8:

1. You will have to shell out about $30 to shoot and process one roll of film. Running time: three minutes, twenty seconds.
2. You can't look at your footage immediately after you shoot it. You have to drop the cartridge off at a film lab for processing. Mail is more like it. All this, the mailing, the processing, the mailing back, could take several weeks.

3

Planning Short Films

*M*any people who make short films hardly plan at all. They just have a glimmer of something or other in their heads, so they round up a small cast and a helper or two, or go out to where they'll shoot say, a documentary, like Earth Day goings-on at a regional park in their town, and shoot with little thought about how they'll later edit or what sounds to use. And you know what? They often make fine films with an appealingly loose and improvisational style.

On the other hand, some makers of short films feel the need to plan, plan, plan. This chapter is mainly for them.

THE FILM IDEA

At the very least, you need an idea for your film, a clothesline of the mind you can hang everything on. I really don't know where these ideas come from. Maybe just out of the blue. Or maybe as the fruitful result of tuning in. I mean tuning in to life or to art and being able to pry out a nugget of truth as a starting point for a film.

Tuning in to Life

Life is full of small, meaningful moments you might turn into films. You have to see the truth of the moment. You have to open it up; it's an oyster with a pearl inside. Suppose you are in an inner-city park. You see what appears to be a homeless woman. You wonder about her. You set aside your revulsion or feeling of superiority and try to see life through her eyes. What might be going through her mind? How might you turn her life, as you see it, into a short film? You don't have to bother her. You could interview her and make a documentary about her, or you could make a story film with someone you know playing the homeless woman.

Love in the Park

I'm guessing that Rosemary Aguinaldo worked like this when she got the idea for her *Love in the Park*, a film about a homeless woman. In this analog video film, the homeless woman sits on a park bench with her shopping cart next to her, filled with her life belongings. Another apparently homeless person, a man, comes up to her, and tries to befriend her, but she is distant and preoccupied, or maybe just in a deep funk. The man goes to a trashcan and digs out a partially eaten sandwich for the

From *Love in the Park* by Rosemary Aguinaldo.

woman. She doesn't want it. She seems scarcely aware of his existence. The man goes back to the trashcan and finds a rose in pretty good shape, which he tries to give to the woman. She declines that, too. Finally, the man finds an unopened bottle of beer, which she is happy to accept.

Most people watching this film laugh at this point, but a few understand its serious intent. In rejecting food and the rose, the woman rejects life itself and the possibility of love. Only the beer interests her. Seen this way, the film is very sad.

Rosemary made a long leap from simply sighting a homeless woman in a park to coming up with a complete film idea, and from there to a finished film. You might have to do something like this, too. You can train yourself to look at life in such a way and pluck out ideas for films.

Tuning in to Art

In my classes, I don't just insist that students make minimalist films. Most of them are relieved by this. To them it feels like less work. Anyway, I let them decide. But one semester, the minimalist approach really caught on. I don't know how these things happen. For some reason, every other student was making a minimalist film, most pretty good. This was fine with me.

Before this, Rachel Irvin could not come up with an idea for a film. Nothing came together for her. This is what she told me. Also, I think she was afraid of making any kind of ambitious film. She didn't want to work with a lot of people or embark on anything complex. Then she tuned in to the art of minimalism. Soon after—*click!*—it occurred to her that she didn't have to make a long or complex film. Other students were making bare-bones yet artful films. Why couldn't she? Rachel had some experience writing short poems. The experience of making a minimalist film might be something like that.

Some Mornings I Smoke

The film Rachel came up with, *Some Mornings I Smoke*, compresses an entire life into ninety seconds. A woman emerges from a sliding door into the backyard of a tract house. She sits on a cement step before a leaf-strewn yard, reaches for matches, then lights up. She opens a textbook. She's dressed in a robe. Her hair isn't too neat. One ankle sports a tattoo. No music. Only outdoor sounds.

From *Some Mornings I Smoke* by Rachel Irvin. *This film is on the DVD.*

This film brims with meaning. It's about starting a school day when you don't want to, or starting any kind of day you don't look forward to. It could be about the relentless restarting of life all of us have to do every morning. It's about dread, boredom, banality, sameness. The title adds an extra dimension: Not all mornings are like this. The patio is covered with a layer of leaves, suggesting neglect. The tattoo suggests more playful, even rebellious times. Where have they gone?

Finally the point: Rachel responded to art—namely, what I had taught about minimalism and the eight or ten minimalist films students made—to find the idea for her film.

PLANNING

Planning may take several forms:

Mulling and Brooding

The bare idea takes root in your mind and flourishes into a full-blown film idea, if you let it, if you hang on to it. Stay with the idea. Mull it over in your mind. Give it time to mature. Days. Weeks, maybe. Just don't let go of it. Think about it when you are alone.

Or it may take shape—from idea to a finished film-in-your-head—almost instantly. Filmmakers vary.

Visualizing

It's also helpful to start *visualizing* your film as soon as possible. What images, what symbols, what places will dominate? Rosemary's film may have started to come together for her when she *saw,* in her mind's eye, the man, the sandwich, the rose, and the can of beer. Her mind leapt from her recollection of the homeless woman to these additional images that drive the story. Then her narrative sense took over and worked out the fable-like tale. How do I know this? I asked her. Rachel may have lived at the house she filmed at. Middle-class. Neglected. Plain. Unfulfilled. Like the life of the character.

CONSIDERING SPOKEN WORDS

Modern DV cameras pick up dialogue, or any kind of spoken word, with the greatest of ease, plus editing programs make adding narration a breeze. But too many words ruin a film. They especially ruin a short film because better short films are based primarily on images. Words tend to make images explicit. Still, used in moderation, there are times when you can't get by without some kind of talking. The type and quantity of spoken words will figure in your planning.

From *Bonsoir My Love* by Hannah Rae.
This film is on the DVD.

For example, in chapter 10, I describe a cute little film called *Bonsoir My Love*, by Hannah Rae. It's about making oneself pretty and desirable for guys, and the rigmarole females have to go through to achieve this. How do you get this idea across? Hannah decided that she would need both visuals—trying on outfits; getting dressed, undressed, and dressed again; applying makeup just so—*and* words in the form of a kind of flow of thoughts filled with frustration, fear, and hope, and meant to be private, of course, but kindly shared with viewers. The words enhance the visuals and vice versa.

Hannah told me how the two parts of the film, the visual and verbal, came to her in a flash. She said, "I knew the stuff about getting dressed wouldn't stand by itself, so I came up with the idea of revealing my thoughts." You hear, "What am I gonna wear? What am I gonna wear?" as Hannah, herself the star, rummages like mad through her closet. Words explain visuals; visuals explain words. (Flip ahead to page 200 for more about narration. Also, turn to page 240 for a discussion of how fast motion enhanced this film.)

ESCHEWING HOLLYWOOD

I don't use the word *eschew* very often, and when I do, I am very serious. Eschew means don't, leave off, stop, desist. I didn't write this book to have you imitate Hollywood. Make one or two chase films or drugs-going-down films, and get them out of your system. Then tune in to the kind of artful and original films I am trying to induce you to make. If you can't do this, and insist on being a slave to Hollywood, you aren't ready for my book. Come back next year.

WRITING A SCREENPLAY

Or maybe you are the type of person who likes to write your thoughts out, completely, before embarking on a film. Okay, you may want to write a screenplay then. Here is a segment of a screenplay, which is found in its entirety in chapter 9. It has far more dialogue than I'd like, but it's not a minimalist film. I have withheld the name of the filmmaker, on her request.

PARTIAL SCREENPLAY FOR *BOMB READY TO EXPLODE*

1. A rural road. We see a sign by the side of the road that says "The New Rock Lompoc Federal Correctional Facility." A car speeds away from the facility, pulling the camera to the right, revealing a cluster of one-story buildings in the background surrounded by a chain-link fence.

2. Cut to car. Woman drives. Man is buoyant, happy. He looks like a man who's just been given his freedom. She is Vera; he is Thomas. Vera pats him on the leg.

                         Vera
                 Okay, Thomas. So all that's
                 behind you now.

   Thomas nods. He wants to agree. He really does. But the slightest shadow of uncertainty clouds his face.

3. A parole office. Institutional, official, a little bleak. A parole officer and a psychologist interview, or rather lecture, Thomas. The parole officer is Philips, the psychologist Santini. Vera is present.

                      Philips
                 You understand, Thomas, what we
                 have here. One slip-up and back
                 to Lompoc you go. I mean, you so
                 much as look at a kid for over
                 two seconds, and I find out, I
                 send your ass back to the slammer.
                 You got that?

   Thomas nods. But it's that same conflicted nod he gave in the car.

```
                    Santini
                 (to Philips)
        Hey, Dan, back off. It's going
        to be fine. I've arranged for
        Thomas to interview for a job. I
        mean, it's not a great job, but it's
        a job. Right, Thomas?


   Thomas nods again, tries to smile.


                    Santini
                 (to Thomas)
        We're all on your side, Thomas.


   Thomas smiles weakly at Santini.
```

Writing a screenplay always makes you feel better prepared. You know your story better; you know your characters better. Also, a screenplay helps you with pacing—how long the various parts or scenes should be.

The format of this screenplay—spacing, indents, and so forth—is a good one. It's not far off the format that professional screenwriters follow. (Flip ahead to page 180 for the complete screenplay.)

THE HALFWAY WRITING OPTION—DOING NOTES

An option halfway between no writing and screenplay writing is to simply take a lot of notes about the film that is still in your head. You can do this like keeping a journal, day by day. Buy yourself a nice notebook to do this in. Here are some possible notes for a film called *Macho Walk*, which is described in chapter 4.

Dec. 12. Just make sure we get the two extreme long shots of the guys walking toward the camera. They have to be way off, like dots. Then we get tighter shots of them, looking macho, determined, not willing to give up an inch. When they collide, we'll film that three or four times—a long shot, a medium shot, a couple of close-ups. Then they get into an argument about who's right. Just make this up. Shoot it three or four different ways. Then get some wide shots of them crossing and going on.

Writing, though always hard, is a great taskmaster. It forces you to concentrate, to solve problems, to see your project through to the end.

SETS AND LOCATIONS

A set is an interior space for filming, whereas a location is exterior. Hollywood builds sets; you find them. Hollywood goes to great lengths to control locations. As a minimalist filmmaker, you are more philosophic.

First, you want to find sets and locations that resonate with your film. Don't film in your backyard or family room simply because they're handy. Find a location that communicates just as much as do your film idea, your shooting, your editing, and your sound. Make all five equal partners.

Finding Sets

To find good sets, you look and look. You are observant and patient. You visit the apartments of your friends or houses of relatives. You look around, noting where windows are located relative to the sun. You note the furniture, the stuff on the walls, the color of carpets, the overall look and feel of the place. You imagine how the space will work in your film.

You'll want to hold out for just the right interior. You ask acquaintances if you might poke around their places. You hold out and hold out, and finally you find just the right dining room or living room or kitchen.

SCHOOL YOURSELF

Watch the following feature films for their extraordinary sets: *Metropolis, Modern Times, The Apartment, Psycho, Juliet of the Spirits, 2001: A Space Odyssey, Blade Runner, City of Lost Children, Being John Malkovich, The Ninth Gate, The Matrix, Fight Club, Antitrust, Panic Room.*

Yes, these are big, big films and hardly minimalistic. But they can teach you a lot about how sets, in and of themselves, communicate.

Finding Locations

You burn up a tank of gas just driving around town, or out to the country or to another town, scouting around. You visit shopping malls, back alleys, river banks, junk yards, abandoned buildings, modern churches, venerable old cathedrals, cluttered alleys, college campuses, fields, streams, bridges, freeway interchanges—looking, looking, looking for that right backdrop or location.

Surrendering to Outdoors

When you film outdoors, you control almost nothing. The filming doesn't always go smoothly. Imagine this: You are trying to get four simple lines of dialogue out of two borderline actors. It's hard enough to work with them, but then a train goes by a block away and ruins the sound of the take. You, your helper, and the cast of two have to sit on the curb and wait for the damn thing to go by. You don't have a producer to contact the railroad and pay to reroute the train for the day. So the train finally passes, and you jump up and get all ready to shoot again—until the world's slowest, loudest airplane drones by directly overhead.

But you are fine with this. It's just part of working minimalist. You would much rather have the delays than be a big-time director with lots of power and money to delay trains and airplanes. You are happy working small. (Flip ahead to page 164 for information and ideas about mic booms and other matters pertaining to recording dialogue.)

$CHOOL $YOURSELF

Watch American Movie. This is a great documentary about a low-ball filmmaker. He's not a minimalist filmmaker—he's too ambitious for that—but a lot of what he goes through is typical of enthusiast filmmaking. Overall, though, he lacks the serenity, the surrender, the zen of what I am trying to get across in this chapter. The film is very poignant and meaningful in its own right, and I shouldn't ask it to be something it isn't. I hope you see it.

Also, read Monster, screenwriter John Gregory Dunne's frustrating account of what it's like to work with Hollywood moguls and assorted egoists (Random House, 1997).

Marcelo's Nightmare Building

Marcelo Moriega needed a nightmare location. He figured out how to break into the old, long-locked-up administration building at Fresno City College. The building, which was erected in 1910, had to be closed down in the 1970s because it didn't meet California earthquake standards. It was one of the last remaining examples of California Norman-

From *Nocturne* by Marcelo Moriega.

esque mission architecture. Marcelo gazed at the building's seemingly impenetrable brick exterior and yearned to make a film inside. It was taboo to be inside at all. If the cops had found him, they would've chased him off.

But to Marcelo, the inside of the old administration building was like being inside the head of someone having a bad dream. He managed to get in the building and was drawn to the haunted, pigeon-infested spaces where janitors and stagehands hung out decades earlier.

He found cramped, airless rooms, dungeon-like cells, steep cement stairways, windowless back rooms, and low-ceilinged basements. In those places, he set his film. It was the perfect location for a film he called *Nocturne*. In fact, the location alone could have suggested the film.

Tale to Tell: How a Library Worked for Me

The Age of Reason is a narrative super 8 film I made about the end of a relationship between a young woman college student and a young man, a dropout. The only thing that bound the couple together was addictive sex that lingered like a bad cold. What the woman really wanted was to finally break off the sex and return to her studies and the disciplined life. But the young man just kept hitting on her and hitting on her.

I set this film in a library where the woman was trying to study. The library, designed and built in the 1930s when libraries looked like libraries, offered the perfect backdrop with its vaulted ceilings, stained-glass windows, busts of dead white geniuses, and hard, echoing rooms. Passion was not welcomed there.

TRY THIS

Scout sets and locations for a film or two you have in mind. For sets (interiors), check out apartments, condos, homes, workplaces, and garages (which might be decorated to look like something else). For locations (exteriors), drive around town with an eye to the right place for filming—that is, the location will actually expand the meaning of your film.

An Album of Sets and Location

Library reference room where I shot *The Age of Reason*.

Rooftop location for *Sparkle*, a music video about finding out who you are, and soaring. I can't think of a better location for that particular theme.

Downtown alley in *November Apparition*, by John Neeley and Katherine Jose.

Films about being out in the middle of nowhere automatically evoke loneliness and desperation.

Proud Warrior, an Asian martial-arts-themed *Macho Walk*, is a very formal film with carefully composed shots and choreographed action. The filmmaker, Sam Gill, was just as picky about his locations. This lake is located in the Sierra Nevada about an hour east of Fresno.

This film is on the DVD.

This untitled, kick-ass poker film by Byron Watkins looks like it was set in some dark, back-alley dive. Actually, it was shot in the dining room of an ordinary tract house. Byron just fooled with the existing overhead light a little and underexposed to get this noirish effect.

From *Photo Finish*. I had trouble getting this super 8 film about a suicide off the ground until I found this junkyard. Wrecked cars and trucks, wrecked lives.

WHEN THE LOCATION IS SENSITIVE

There aren't many places in town where you can just set up and shoot without getting permission or without fear of being thrown out. City streets, alleys, parks, playgrounds—that's about it. But you may require other kinds of locations, owned or controlled by people you have to deal with—namely, property owners and managers of corporate space. Here are some pointers for dealing with this situation.

Shooting on Private Property

If you will be shooting on private property, you will have to get permission to do so. Usually this is not a problem, but the matter depends on how you present yourself. Act flaky, and the owner will tell you to stay off his property. Act responsible, and chances are good you will get your permission.

Explain your film to the owner. Take him into your confidence. Don't hold anything back. Kind of soft-peddle the risks. You'll get permission this way.

You work from an unburdened frame of mind when you have permission. On the other hand, work without permission and you are always afraid that the owner will show up and shoo you off. You don't do your best work this way.

Shooting on Corporate Property

If you want to shoot on corporate property, like in a supermarket or shopping mall, you can count on a security guard or a manager saying no. It's just the corporation's policy not to allow the likes of you to do any photography on its property. The corporation might feel liable if anyone were to get hurt and simply won't want to take chance. Or the corporation might feel that your messing around with a camera, helpers, and cast would cause a disruption and drive business away.

But some managers are cool. Just because one supermarket manager said no, you can't film in my store, that doesn't mean that another supermarket manager will say no. Keep trying.

Shooting Guerrilla

By this I don't mean that you take a gun to a large primate. I mean that you move into a private space and shoot fast, before anyone catches on, without permission. You work like guerrilla fighters who hit and run before anybody can react.

I really can't condone guerrilla filming, but students, amateurs, and low-budget filmmakers do it all the time. If anybody asks me, I will disavow your behavior, like the *Mission Impossible* director. But my students have shot guerrilla countless times and Lord knows I've done it. My advice: Be exceedingly well-prepared so you can move in and out fast. Rehearse in your backyard or in a park. Be all ready. Then move into the unauthorized location, set up fast, film fast, and get out.

When Do You Shoot Guerrilla?

You shoot guerrilla when you:

➤ Absolutely must film at a particular location
➤ Can't get permission or think it won't be granted
➤ Can pull it off quickly and cleanly, without a lot of props, activity, or extras

SIMPLE PROPS AND LOW-BALL EFFECTS

The making of meaningful props doesn't have to be expensive or complicated, as these two films illustrate:

From *Penetration*.

Penetration

In a minimalist super 8 film about how we worship the dollar and the things it can buy, the filmmaker had a woman kneel against a backdrop of a colorful stained-glass window. It feels like Catholic confession or the recitation of catechism. The scene is played to a Gregorian chant and feels churchy. But as you watch, you realize that you are in a satire. You notice that the stained-glass window contains the Chevrolet logo. Careful lighting and the placement of the stained-glass window turn this scene into a satire on consumerism as a kind of religion. The stained-glass window, which in my opinion makes the whole film, was put together in about an hour with some pieces of translucent colored acetate, available from any art supply store, held together with black electrical tape. The whole assembly then was taped to a south-facing window in the laundry room of an ordinary house. The stained-glass window prop cost less than $10 to make.

The Deserter

Many years ago, a student of mine, Larry Foster, made a film called *The Deserter*, which is about a soldier doing time in a stockade. Larry wanted to show the guy in a gloomy, bare, cement cell. He located a building with cement block walls and had the prisoner sit in front of it toward a late afternoon sun. Before this, Larry cut some strips of corrugated cardboard and taped them to another piece of cardboard that was like a window frame. He had a friend show up with a piece of plywood cut to look like a rifle. The actor playing the prisoner slumped gloomily against the wall. An assistant steadied the cardboard with

38   MAKING SHORT FILMS

the strips on a stepladder. The guy with the plywood rifle walked back and forth like a guard. The cardboard strips threw shadows like bars onto the prisoner, and the other guy pacing with the rifle on his shoulder threw shadows like a sentry on duty.

After I saw the film, I walked Larry to his truck. I asked him about how he did the jail-cell scene. Did he talk someone at the Fresno County Jail into letting him shoot there? Larry laughed. He reached into his pickup and got the cardboard out of the back and held it up for me. I laughed, too.

From *The Deserter* by Larry Foster. Sorry, I couldn't work in the shadow of the rifle.

TRY THIS

Contrive a really important prop or easy special effect for your film. Make it meaningful. But don't get too fancy. Don't let the prop or the effect intrude and call too much attention to itself, unless you are avowedly doing an art film. Just think over the props and materials you'll need for your shoot, and endeavor to make one thing more meaningful than the others.

PLANNING DOCUMENTARIES

Planning documentaries all depends on how much you can control. If you can control nothing, then arrive at the site with lots of tape and a long-life battery or two, and shoot everything. Try to come with some kind of overall idea in mind, and shoot stuff pertaining to that. If you have some control or much control, then set up your shooting the way a theatrical filmmaker would, with rehearsing, controlled movement, and the like. Make sure you get lots of interviews. Get the camera in close for best sound or use an outboard microphone with a boom. (Flip ahead to page 79, which bears on planning documentary films. Also see page 164 for information about microphone booms.)

YOUR PEOPLE

A lot of my students have made films entirely by themselves with no help at all, and you know from reading the book so far that I have no problems with that. But every now and then you may need a helper or two, or it might just be your style to work collaboratively. Both approaches have their rewards.

If you work with other people, choose them carefully, as carefully as choosing your locations.

Your Cast

Most makers of short films recruit their cast from among their fellow students or friends, if they can act and are dependable. If they can't or aren't, you have to do something else. For example, visit your local college and ask the person who runs the theater arts department whether you might place a notice on the casting callboard for actors for your film. In the notice, describe your film in a few sentences and make a list of the parts you need. Also, speak to a professor of acting and work it out to visit his or her classes. Pitch your film to the class and pass out information about it. Provide specific role information—age, male or female, and so forth.

Every drama department always has more students who want to act than there are parts in plays. Moreover, college-age actors often like being in films more than stage plays. There is almost no chance the college will be producing a film. Your film project could be very popular among drama majors who yearn to act in films.

Working with Drama People

You should also make your drama department–recruited cast aware that acting for film is not like acting for the stage. Never does the cast have a chance to act uninterrupted for ten or twenty minutes, as they would on stage. Instead, as you doubtless are realizing, films are made in little chunks, thirty seconds for this shot, ten-second follow-up shot, fifteen-second close-up. Plus, it's certain that you, the director, will call for retakes, either because something about the performance did not please you or because you just want to try a new camera angle. Some drama majors may not like these conditions and quit on you.

Age-Specific Parts

One common failing of student-made short dramatic films is that the cast looks too young for some parts. Somehow, casting an eighteen-year-old as a lawyer or someone in charge just isn't very convincing. So hold out for older persons for those kinds of roles, if you can.

Above all, don't cast someone in his twenties to play an old guy. Gray hair on a kid may cut it on the stage, which is more stylized than film, but it's just not convincing on film. Go out and find a willing old guy to play the role.

Your Crew

Crew is the nice, short word for all the people who work for you "behind the camera." Hollywood uses too many of these people—dozens and dozens, in fact. As for you, you might get along just fine with a single helper. Often, working small is cozy and intimate.

What the Crew Does

Any film in the making, even a minimalist film, has a number of technical matters to be attended to—camera, lights, props, and so forth. The director should not have to fuss with this stuff. Her mind should be focused on shooting, on the art of the thing, on performance, on meaning, and how the camera brings these things out. The crew takes care of the many little things leading to a take. In fact, a good crew—maybe just one helper—works like the techy part of the mind of the director. He anticipates what she needs and provides it when she needs it. She doesn't have to turn around and go, "Where's that damn music box?"—or whatever. The techy says, "Right here." The director says, "You read my mind."

The Helper as Sound Recordist

You might make your helper responsible for recording sound, especially if you use a microphone boom and an external microphone. A *boom* is a pole that the microphone is attached to, which the sound person holds up over the heads of the actors. (Flip ahead to pages 164–65 for information about microphone booms and related matters.)

Is One Helper Enough?

You be the judge. Maybe you want a helper just to do sound while another person does things like set the camera on the tripod, make sure tape is cued, set lights, set out props, and so on.

What Do You Do?

Probably, you direct and shoot. Your cast rehearses. Your helper helps. A nice division of labor. But doing the directing and the filming may be too much for you. So you turn the running of the camera over to someone else, hopefully a person with some visual smarts.

GETTING READY FOR THE TAKE

Here is a procedure you might follow to get ready for a take of a story film.

First: Discuss the roles that your cast will be playing. Explain their psychology, as you see them, the good and the bad. Go way beyond (or beneath) the actual screenplay to create a *back character*—that is, explain how the character might be in the world beyond the confines of the script.

Second: Discuss aspects of the screenplay bearing on character. Solicit questions from your cast about what specific moments in the screenplay mean for character. At this point, you are not talking about acting specifically, but instead are establishing character in the minds of your cast.

Third: Now run lines with your cast. This means repeated readings for the purpose of learning lines. Bring the cast along until they are almost polished.

Fourth: After this, block the scene. This means figuring out how, where, and why the cast will move. Movement is very important. You don't want people to just stand like tree trunks and give lines. Figure out realistic but also meaningful moves. (For example, someone turns his back to someone else = rejection.)

A minimalist shoot. Cameraman, right, is also the director. Microphone boom held high out of frame.

Fifth: Now is the time to oblige the cast to polish their lines—know them cold.

Sixth: Bring it all together—giving lines, blocking.

Insert: Rehearse the camera. Where you insert this step will vary. If it takes a long time to get the camera ready, then get it ready first. You don't want an eager cast to wait while you perfect a complicated camera move. Or check out camera moves just before you shoot.

Seventh: Shoot.

Eighth: Assess. Look at what you just shot in the camera's LCD screen, if you have such a camera, and if the sun doesn't wash out the image. Or just discuss what happened during the take.

Ninth: Retake, as needed, if needed, if someone gets a bright idea.

(Flip ahead and back to the following pages where film dialogue is discussed: pages 30, 51, 159, and 192.)

RETAKES

I keep saying, tape is cheap. If you don't like the way the taping of a scene went, do it again. And do it right away, before the actors forget their lines. But discuss before you retake. Make sure that the cast knows what to do differently, and why. If you anticipate retaking a lot, it might be wise to "slate" each shot—that is, noting shot number and take with big pad and a thick felt tip pen. This will help you make a shot log and decide on a best take.

THE DIRECTOR AS CAMERA OPERATOR

Truly, only the director can judge the quality of the performance as the camera captures it. This is why I urge all minimalist filmmakers to be their own camera operators, if possible. This means that the director has to know something about framing, composition, angle, optics, perspective, and focus. Accordingly:

Framing has to do with how we see a character in the film frame—in close-up, as a medium shot, in long shot. Frame matters. Find the one that's best for the dramatic moment.

Composition is the functional and artful placing of objects in the frame so that the frame has balance, is pleasing to the eye, works everything in, and is actually meaningful.

Angle—there are essentially three: eye level, low, and high. Most shots are taken at eye level. You really need a good reason to go low or high. Don't just go low or high because it feels cool. Have a good reason.

Optics is about perspective. Wide-angle shooting makes things seem farther off; telephoto brings them closer.

Focus, too, is important. You have a choice between setting the camera back and shooting in telephoto, which could blur backgrounds, or moving the camera closer to the subject and keeping everything from foreground to background in focus. Also, you can focus manually. (Flip ahead to chapter 5, where all of these matters are taken up in detail.)

HONORING THE SUN

One last technical point: If you are shooting outdoors, strive to set up your shooting angles to have the sun at your back. Avoid shooting into the sun. If you shoot in the morning, try to shoot toward the west; if in the afternoon, east. Never decide on an exterior without first visiting it during the hours you'll be filming and noting where the sun is.

4

The Starter Film

The starter film is your first film, your training-wheels film. Make one or two or all five of the off-the-shelf scenarios described in this chapter, and I guarantee that you will learn much about the basics of filmmaking.

SCENARIO 1: LUCKY GUY

Here is the story:

The setting is a country road. Traffic is very sparse. We see a hitchhiker, a young man, trying to catch a ride. He has a bulging backpack by his side. A car approaches. The hitchhiker sticks out his thumb. The car passes him by. Another car appears, the hitchhiker sticks out his thumb, but again the car just whizzes by. Same with a third car—no luck. Now the hitchhiker looks discouraged. He sits down by the side of the road and hangs his head. He does this for several long seconds. Then he looks up, sees another car coming, gets to his feet, and sticks out his thumb. This time the car slows and stops. The driver is an attractive young woman who smiles at the hitchhiker. He returns her smile, grabs his backpack, swings it into the car, and gets in. She drives off.

From a version of *Lucky Guy* by Dave Bletz.

Sexist? Maybe. If you don't like this ending, you can change it. A few pages later, I suggest some alternate conclusions to this scenario. In fact, all five scenarios can be changed to suit you. The main thing is that each of the scenarios present instructive filmmaking opportunities. *Lucky Guy* is about space and how it affects people. If you choose to make it, you'll get a little experience in filming in a desolate location, and showing, through facial acting, how the hitchhiker feels about being out there all alone.

SCENARIO 2: THE END

A young man and a young woman sit together on a picnic table in a park. They look distant, sad, as if they are not getting along well. It's like the end of the relationship. The

man turns around and looks at the woman, but she is looking away. Then the man looks straight ahead. Then the woman turns and looks at the man, but he is looking away. Their faces can't find each other, and maybe this is indicative of their relationship—their hearts can't find each other either. Then the woman sighs, gets up, and walks away.

The End is about editing. The entire unfolding of the story is determined through editing. You can edit so that he looks at her, but she is looking away—to suggest that he is

From a version of *The End* by Onesta Francis.

willing but she is not. Or the opposite: She looks at him, but he is looking away. He's not willing.

Darom Southichak made this version of *Snatch*. Darom had the snatchee give chase herself since she couldn't recruit a third person.

SCENARIO 3: SNATCH

This is an action scenario premised on a purse snatching. A woman with a purse is walking down a sidewalk or talking to someone on a mall. The snatcher sneaks up on her, grabs the purse, and runs off. But another guy sees the whole thing and starts running after the snatcher. He catches up with him, wrestles him to the ground, and gets the purse away from him. He then returns the purse to the appreciative woman.

SCENARIO 4: GOTCHA!

This scenario has a kind of trick ending. The setting is a modest apartment. The door opens, and a woman comes in. She holds up a pair of long scissors, which she snips noisily. She's mean-looking, suspicious, pissed. But she's also poised and in control. She keeps snipping the scissors ominously open and closed. She looks around the room, then spots something just a few feet into the apartment. It's a woman's blouse on the carpet. She picks it up and inspects it contemptuously. She advances across the living room and spots something else, a man's tie, also on the carpet. She looks around. She finds more

clothing, alternating between women's and men's. Finally, she comes to a hall and spots a pair of women's thong underwear and a pair of men's boxer shorts. She grinds her heel into the thong underwear and her toes into the boxer shorts. She picks the boxer shorts up. Then she deliberately takes her scissors and makes a big cut in the shorts right at the crotch. Immediately, the film cuts to a man and woman in bed. The man bolts upright, howls, and grabs his groin. The scissors woman appears at the bedroom door, holds up the scissors and the shorts triumphantly, and says, "Gotcha!"

Veronica Roscoe's *Gotcha!* More stills from this film on pages 49 and 55.

Gotcha! is an exercise in a very basic editing technique called the point-of-view sequence. In three quick clips, we see someone look, then we see what the person sees, then the person reacts. This is repeated for most of the articles of clothing the woman finds. More on point of view later.

SCENARIO 5: MACHO WALK

Macho Walk is about two men who happen to be walking directly toward each other in a vast and empty field. They approach each other at a great distance. They spot each other

but don't seem to know each other. They start walking on a collision course. They get closer and closer, but neither yields to the other. The closer they get, the more determined they look. They clench their fists. They set their jaws. Finally, they bump into each other—then act like a couple of babies, holding their noses and rubbing their foreheads.

This film isn't very "realistic," of course, but it isn't meant to be. It's an art film story. I described an art film on page 7 called *Woman*. Art films are stylized, which means that they

Doug Crutchfield made this version of *Macho Walk*.

are based on an extension or distortion of a technique, story, or setting—some aspect of the film that calls attention to itself. The photography is very washed out, or the editing overlaps action. In this case, it's probably not the photography that is so different but the idea of the setting, which turns the film into a metaphor for silly male ego. The field represents the whole wide world of compromise, generosity, and step-asides. Men don't really have to bump into each other and hurt each other. They can just step around each other, get along, and cooperate willingly.

When the guy wakes up, he finds that an old couple had stopped for him. This film has a big cast: Four girls in the car, the seniors, and the hitchhiker.

This film is on the DVD.

Another version of *Lucky Guy* described on page 50 uses a female hitchhiker, but it lacks the creepy quality of Julie's film.

CUSTOMIZING THESE SCENARIOS

Now here are those alternate conclusions I promised.

It Was Only a Dream

The babe in the car in *Lucky Guy* is only a dream. You set it up so that between cars the hitchhiker falls asleep. Or the hitchhiker could wake up to find that the person in the car is actually super ugly, maybe wearing one of those scary latex monster masks. Courtney Fontes made a version of *Lucky Guy* with a carful of willing cuties stopping for the hitchhiker. Alas! It was only a dream.

Julie Klieber made a *Lucky Guy* that grows sinister by (a) making the hitchhiker a female and by (b) shooting the last half of the film from inside the car. We never see the driver or what he might be up to.

The End

As I've already suggested, you can communicate solely through editing who wants to keep the relationship going: he, she, neither, or both. Here is a working out of the fourth option: As the woman walks away from the man on the park bench, you could have her stop, appear to reconsider, then turn and look at the man. The man, meanwhile, lifts his head and looks at her. He gets up from the bench. He walks a few feet toward her. She walks a few feet toward him. Then—the old standby—each runs toward each other. Finally they reach other and embrace.

Snatch

My class and I did this film many years ago in super 8, with the girl studying on the grass outside a college building. Snatcher snatches purse, second guy gives chase. Meanwhile, the girl, lost in her book, is oblivious to everything. Second guy gets the purse and returns it to the girl, thinking she'll appreciate what he did and let him come on to her. But the girl thinks he stole it and yells for the police. We called this film *Heroism Will Get You Nowhere.*

Gotcha!

One of my students made the woman seem very much in love with the guy—she hugs his pictures and so on. So she decides to drop in on him without warning. She enters the guy's place and sees various garments, male and female, on the floor. She looks horrified—but not as horrified as when she finally opens the bedroom door and finds the guy dressed up as a girl, in a dress, with makeup and all. Veronica Roscoe made this version of *Gotcha!*

Just before the discovery.
This film is on the DVD.

Macho Walk

Do the same story but with women. How would they react to each other out in the middle of nowhere? Or do a man and a woman. Or have the two guys actually fight.

More Variations

My students are endlessly creative in varying these basic scenarios. Here are some examples:

Train as a Metaphor

In Grayson Soenke's version of *Macho Walk*, the tough guys walk toward each other on train tracks. They can't just step aside. They have to run into each other. But just before they collide, Grayson cuts to a train going in one direction then to a second train going in the other direction. With some tricky editing, it looks like the trains have to collide. Then quick cut to the tough guys actually colliding. Train = unyielding mass = masculine ego.

From *Lucky Guy* by David Lennon.
This film is on the DVD.

From Brennan Miller's cosmic *Macho Walk.*

They go at it again. From *Happy Endings* by Andy Kith, Dustin Fults, and Sean Cates.

Gender Change

Another student of mine, David Lennon, made *Lucky Guy* with the hitchhiker as a girl, not a guy. The clever thing about this film is how David hides the gender of the hitchhiker by having her stuff her hair up under her hat and never filming her from the front. The driver of the car is a nice-looking young man just out to do a favor. He's pretty pleased when the girl, coming up to the open window, takes off her hat and lets her long locks fall to her shoulders. Pure male fantasy.

Good and Evil

For his *Macho Walk,* Brennan Miller made one walker God and the other the Devil. A preacher appears and marries them!

Expansion

A few of my students take these exercises very seriously and expand them into much more complicated stories than I've suggested. For example, three of my students—Andy Kith, Dustin Fults, and Sean Cates—pushed *Macho Walk* out to a ten-minute film with a story that goes like this: Nerd offends tough guy on a city street. Tough guy beats up nerd. Nerd gets martial arts training from a master. Nerd returns to scene to find tough guy and challenge him. But—this is not a Hollywood movie—tough guy beats up nerd again! Ha! Ha! So Andy, Dustin, and Sean stand our expectations on their head. The simple, stripped-down *Macho Walk,* renamed *Happy Endings,* becomes a statement about how life doesn't always turn out the way it does in a Hollywood movie.

Snatch as an Art Film

Bob Warkentin couldn't make a straight *Snatch*. He contrived a preposterous situation in which a studious type is playing chess with himself in a parking lot. Along comes a guy on a skateboard who snatches one of the queens off the board and skates off with it. I call this kind of film a "miscellany." It has this and that, but nothing connects. Or maybe it does connect on a deeper level than we can perceive. Or it's just absurd, and that's all it is. It makes audiences laugh.

From *Snatch* by Bob Warkentin. I discuss absurdity as an art-film option on page 228.

NO DIALOGUE BUT MAYBE MUSIC

None of these films, except *Gotcha!*, requires dialogue—on purpose. And *Gotcha!* has just one word. You'll learn much more about filmmaking if you communicate as much as you can through moving images instead of through words. Add music, if you want.

Just itching to write some dialogue and get some good actors to deliver it? Fine, but save it for your second film.

TRY THIS

Make one of these off-the-shelf films. Customize it. Change it around. Expand it. Make it arty. However, I would like you to retain the original premise, at least, as a challenge. Keep the film short.

LEARNING SOME FILMMAKING BASICS

I set these ready-made movies up to be potentially rich in basic, actually *classic*, shooting and editing techniques that apply to nearly all forms of filmmaking. If you make these films my way, you'll just naturally learn the techniques to help you communicate better and produce a smoother film.

These techniques are not only useful; they're historical. If you employ them, you'll be participating in a grand cinematic tradition that goes back to about 1915. You'll also learn the basics of film communication. The techniques are:

- ➤ The master shot
- ➤ Follow-up shots
- ➤ Cross-cutting
- ➤ Cut-ins

- The POV (point-of-view) sequence
- Match-cutting
- Cutaways

The Master Shot

The master shot is a wide and long-running shot that records a complete action or a unified part of a story or a documentary subject. If the film is short, as are these five off-the-shelf films, the master shot might embrace the entire story. People are seen from head to foot; you also get a good idea of the setting.

Though tightly framed, this master shot served Eric Hoskins well when he made his version of *The End*.

The purpose of a master shot is to *establish*—characters, personality, acting technique, facial expression, movement, and setting. The way people appear in the master shot is the way they should appear in all shots that derive from the master shot. So if a guy is standing with his hands on his hips in the master shot, he'd better be standing with his hands on his hips in the next shot.

Master shots, then, depend on thorough, technical rehearsing of both the cast and the camera. When you take a master shot, you'll let the camera run for a relatively long time—a minute, maybe longer, maybe two or three minutes. Your cast has to know what to do and how to appear and act for the entire running of the shot. This means, as I said, that you have to work everything out in advance. The advantage of doing this is that you'll be all rehearsed for what I call your follow-up shots.

Skip the master shot in your starter film, if you want. Actually, Hollywood uses far fewer master shots today than it did forty or fifty years ago. But master shots can be especially instructive for beginners because they teach the value of thorough thinking and rehearsing. You become a real filmmaker if you can set up a master shot, rehearse and film it, then make sure that subsequent shots honor it.

Follow-Up Shots

You may think that master shots are pretty complete films in their own right, covering entire actions as they do. So why bother taking other shots at all? You are partly right. Master shots ought to be *dramatically* complete. But they aren't *cinematically* complete. They are only outlines. They need filling in, which is why experienced filmmakers always take a few follow-up shots after they get their master shots down.

Master shots can't do it all. They are great for establishing setting and showing gross action, and are nearly indispensable for guiding a cast through a rehearsal. But they are poor for isolating important details. So the usual pattern is to follow up with closer, tighter shots—namely, medium shots and close-ups:

➤ Medium shots show two people from about the waist up.
➤ Close-ups show just a face, or a pair of men's shorts on a hallway carpet.

A medium and a close-up shot from *Proud Warrior* by Sam Gill.
This film is on the DVD.

The job of follow-up shots, then, is to break down a master shot into more specific, better-seen components.

Understand that follow-up shots don't depict new action; they don't advance the story past where the master shot went. Instead, they *duplicate* action of the master shot, but at closer range. Excess footage is cut out during editing.

Cross-Cutting

Cross-cutting consists of two (or more) long-running shots that are cut up during editing and alternated. Cross-cutting could have been employed in all of the off-the-shelf scenarios—in *The End* as the film cuts back and forth between close-ups of guy and girl; in *Macho Walk* with cuts back and forth of each of the men getting closer and closer to each other.

Lucky Guy has one or two places where cross-cutting might be useful. Hitchhiker looks down road. Cut to car coming. Cut back to hitchhiker sticking out his thumb, a hopeful look on his face. Cut back to car whizzing by. Cut back to hitchhiker now looking discouraged. This sequence was originally two longer takes. Editing turned them into five separate clips (pieces of shots).

Cross-cutting in Nick Kitchen's *Snatch*. Bad guy, victim, bad guy, victim—back and forth.
This film is on the DVD.

This version of *Macho Walk* by Tim Tsurda comes down to a yo-yo contest. Here's a cut-in of the loser's yo-yo.
This film is on the DVD.

Cut-Ins

Cut-ins are close-ups or extreme close-ups of small but vital things in a story. They are spliced into the main line of action. For example, you could shoot the purse in *Snatch* all by itself at the woman's side, with nothing else in the frame. In *Macho Walk*, just before the two men converge and as they start to feel territorial and combative, you could cut in the balled fist of one of the men. Cut-ins contribute important details and create mood and drama.

POV (Point-of-View) Sequences

POV sequences show what a character sees and how he reacts to what he sees. The sequence is created during editing and consists of three shots:

First: A character is seen in close-up, appearing to look at something.

Second: We see what the character sees, from the exact same position and angle, as if through the eyes of the character. If the character is moving as he looks, the clip of what he sees should also move.

Third: We see the character again in close-up, reacting to what he sees.

Girl looks.   Cut to guy girl sees.   Girl responds.

From Veronica Roscoe's *Gotcha!*
This film is on the DVD.

Match Cuts

All professional movies have dozens and dozens of match cuts. A match cut joins two shots of the same action from different angles. The action across the cut is smooth and continuous. Usually, the shots have quite different frames, from long shot to close-up, for example. Thus, the hitchhiker in *Lucky Guy* looks wistfully down the road in the long shot. He slumps to the ground and hangs his head. Cut to a close-up, the better to see discouragement on his face. His head should be in the same position it was before in the long shot.

Match cut from Joe Doyle's *The End*. The position of the girl's finger is matched from the close-up to the medium shot.

Shooting for Match-Cutting

Sometimes, while you shoot you have to look ahead to editing. If you think you'll be match-cutting two shots, then overlap the action. Have your hitchhiker sit down twice, first at the end of the long shot, then again at the start of the close-up. This will give you many places to match the cut.

In this westernfilmization of *Macho Walk* by Doug Crutchfield, a wife looks on worriedly as men start to duke it out.

Cutaways

This is a cut to a secondary subject on the edge of the action. The cutaway should color or lend meaning to the main action. Imagine a fistfight. You cut away to someone who looks very afraid. This makes the fight serious. However, if you cut away to someone who merely smirks or looks like, "Here we go again," viewers know not to take the fight very seriously.

If you want to employ a cutaway, and I hope you do, you'll need to recruit a third actor, who won't have much to do until it's time to shoot the cutaway. None of the five scenarios mention cutaway figures.

Possible Cutaway for The End

Say you make a version of *The End* that takes place in a park. Some kids are playing nearby. You recruit one of them to look wistfully at the couple in close-up. You direct the kid: "Pretend they're your parents and they're breaking up." The younger the kid, the better. You cut this in near the end. The cutaway could represent the child the couple never had.

TRY THIS

Make a film that includes all seven of these basic techniques. Base your film on one of my five off-the-shelf premises, modified, if you like, or base it on a completely different premise. Keep it short and simple. If the technique isn't really needed, force it anyway and create humor.

SCHOOL YOURSELF

Watch old movies for these basic shots and cuts. This film grammar—master shots, follow-up shots, cross-cuts, cut-ins, sequences, match-cuts, and cutaways—is found in nearly every film made after 1915, when the American D. W. Griffith and a few other global film figures pretty much codified these techniques for the whole world of filmmaking to emulate. Films made this way are said to exhibit "classic style" or "classic Hollywood style."

Watch new movies, too, for these basic shots and cuts. Practically all new movies, no matter how flashy, tricky, arty, or weird they try to be, will still have to fall back on these seven venerated basics of shooting and editing at one time or another.

SCHOOL YOURSELF

Watch *Mad Hot Ballroom*. This is a documentary about kids learning to dance and competing with each other in the New York City public school system. The cutaways, especially near the end, are hilarious and entirely purposeful, as well. You could get no better education in the art and craft of cutaways than from this film.

SHOT LIST AND MORE

A *shot list* is something you write out the night before shooting. It's a list of all the shots you think you need to cover your story well. Call it a wish list because for one reason or another you won't be able to get everything you think you need. Below is a shot list for *Lucky Guy*. The notes in italics refer to the seven basics of shooting and editing I mentioned before. ELS stands for extreme long shot; LS stands for long shot, MS for medium shot, and CU for close-up. HH stands for hitchhiker.

Shot List for Lucky Guy

1. ELS. HH stands by side of country road trying to get a ride. He sticks out his thumb. Three cars go by. No luck. He sits down by the side of the road, looking discouraged.
   This is a master shot. The HH is seen from head to foot. In fact, he's smaller than that. He's less than half the height of the frame. The rural setting dominates.

2. MS. HH looking from left to right, watching a car speed by.
   This is a follow-up shot. It also sets up the first and third shots of a POV sequence.

3. ELS. Car in distance getting closer. It speeds by HH.
   After editing, this will be the middle shot of the POV sequence.

4. MS. Shot 2, pretty much repeated with the HH looking a little discouraged now.

5. MS. Angle behind HH as another car speeds by.
   The story needs at least three cars that don't stop to make the hitchhiker really discouraged.

6. CU. HH sitting beside the road, looking very discouraged. Then he looks to left, apparently sees a car, gets up.
Another follow-up shot to master shot. This shot also sets up another POV sequence.

7. LS. Car in distance, angle down highway.
Second shot of POV sequence.

8. MS. HH looking at car, extending thumb, hopeful.
If after editing, this shot follows shot 6, it will have to be match-cut.

9. ELS. Car in distance, angle from a short distance down the road, car approaches, slows, stops. HH looks inside, appears to talk a little to the driver, then gets his backpack, climbs in car, and car drives off.
Another master shot.

10. MS. Car and driver. The driver is a young woman. She's pretty and flirtatious. We see face of HH in window. He goes out of frame to get his backpack, then gets in car. Woman drives off.
Follow-up shot. This shot will have to be match-cut to the master shot. Also cross-cutting: This shot will be cut up and alternated with snippets of the next shot.

11. MS. HH looks in car window, sees driver, sees how pretty and flirtatious she is, gets in car, woman drives off, camera pans with departing car.
To be cross-cut with 10.

As I said, a shot list like this is a shopping list you take to the supermarket to get the ingredients for that tuna casserole your wife likes. If you go to the supermarket without a list, you might forget that all-important ingredient, the green pepper. Same for shooting: If you go out shooting without a shot list, you might forget to take that all-important shot from between the legs of the hero as he guns down the bad guy in the alley.

From Shot List to Shot Log

If a shot list is wishful thinking, representing the footage you'd like to get, a *shot log* is reality. It's a list of all the shots you actually came back with, including all bad takes and all those extra shots your hotshot actors made you take.

I strongly urge you to make a shot log. Sit down with your tape or film, look at it, give each shot a name or title, and jot down info and notes on frame, counter numbers, action or what is seen, and the usefulness of the shot, like this:

TAKE	FRAME	ACTION	NOTES	COUNTER
1	LS	Tom picking himself up from ground	Can't use this. Tom moved too fast. Lousy acting	4:56
2	LS	Same	Can't use this either. Tom didn't look in enough pain	5:24
3	LS	Same	Ah! This is the keeper.	5:49

Get the picture?

Tip: Write the shot log at your computer. You can toggle back and forth between your film imported into an editing program like iMovie or Studio to a word processor program like AppleWorks or WordPad. Look at the shot in the editing program, then toggle back to the word processor to write comments about it.

From Shot Log to Cutting Continuity

But you are not through writing yet. You should now write something called an edit decision list (EDL) or cutting continuity, from the old celluloid days. This is like a paper movie, the final sequence of shots to be assembled by the film editor. It's the shots all cut up into clips and put in proper order. To help you understand the difference, I have cut up *Lucky Guy* (on paper) on the following page.

SHOT	LIST/FRAME	DESCRIPTION	NOTES
1	1 ELS	HH trying to thumb a ride	Cars go by
2	2 MS	HH looking at cars	First shot of POV sequence
3	3 ELS	Car in distance	

WHAT HH SEES; MIDDLE SHOT OF POV SEQUENCE

SHOT	LIST/FRAME	DESCRIPTION	NOTES
4	2 MS	HH looking to right, car goes by, HH looks discouraged	Third shot of POV sequence
5	1 ELS	Another car goes by	Clip from the master shot
6	2 MS	HH looking at car, even more discouraged	
7	4 LS	Car speeds by	
8	5 LS	HH watches another car speeding by. Things are really looking bad.	This is the new angle
9	4 LS-MS	Another car speeds by	These are all the shots of cars speeding by
10	1 ELS	HH sits down, discouraged	Another clip from the master shot
11	6 CU	Still discouraged, sits for a time, then sees a car, gets up	Another POV sequence starts This shot has to be match-cut with shot 10
12	9 ELS	Car in distance	Middle shot of POV sequence: what HH sees
13	10 MS	HH looking at car, extending thumb, hopeful	HH reacting to car: shot of POV sequence
14	9 ELS	Car pulling over, HH walks to passenger door	Second master shot
15	11 MS	Angle through passenger window. The driver is a pretty young woman.	This is what HH sees
16	11 MS	HH smiles	
17	10 MS	Girl smiles back	
18	11 MS	HH gets in car	Shots 15–18 are cross-cut
19	9 ELS	Car drives off	From second master shot Shots 18 and 19 are match-cut

Thus, the original eleven uncut shots of the shot list (see page 57) become nineteen clips in the finished film.

OTHER APPROACHES TO YOUR FIRST FILM

Don't care to make any of my off-the-shelf films? Fine. Here are a few more approaches to making your first film. All are pretty basic.

Make a Short Documentary Film

Documentary films are not fictions. They are not "theatrical." They are not based on a made-up event of a babe picking up a discouraged male hitchhiker or a disgruntled woman magically getting back at an unfaithful lover. They are about some real person, place, or event. Those are your main choices.

Heavenly Light

For some comments about artistic control of this film, see pages 208–9.

Heavenly Light is about a woman who makes stained-glass windows. The film is only six minutes long, so it can't convey a lot of information. In fact, it has no words at all. But it does show several distinct stages of creating a stained-glass window. It's played to a CD of a Gregorian chant. The whole enterprise feels churchy, holy. You get enough information visually to kind of understand what goes into the making of a stained-glass window. But the information is not as important as the feel of the film, which is that the woman is working in an ancient craft. Peter Chang made this film.

My Zone

Anoush's "zone."

My Zone is a reverse home movie, a documentary about an ugly neighborhood in which Anoush Ekparian once lived. But this is not a film about flowers, sweet children, and lovely houses. Instead, we see more ugliness than beauty, or plainness—graffiti, trashcans, mean-looking kids. Anoush does not care to prettify her neighborhood. Instead, she wants to be honest about it. Anoush would make a terrible real estate agent.

Start Walking

Start Walking is a fortuitous documentary by Bob Warkentin that records a fight that took place at Fresno's Fulton Mall. In technique and style, it's the opposite of Peter Chang's

Flip ahead to page 116 for how Bob used his zoom lens to good advantage.

This film is on the DVD.

carefully controlled and planned *Heavenly Light*. Bob controlled nothing. He didn't even know that a fight was going to break out when he strolled down Fulton Mall with his camera at the ready. He just happened to be in the right place when some young people—women, actually—started to brawl. Bob's camera has a long zoom lens. He just stood back and zoomed in and out to frame and reframe the action, as well as the ensuing police mop-up.

Bob didn't interview anyone or get the facts of the fight. He let that part go. Instead, after editing, he put some funky, that's-the-way-it-is music with the visuals. The music trivializes the fight. Interviews and the like would have blown it up to be a big thing, which would have been an entirely different film. It was just one of those things, a slice of life. Perfect for the short film. Bob's film runs five minutes.

TRY THIS

Make a film about a person who does something visually interesting. Interview the person. During editing, slide the interview under shots of her doing the thing. Keep it visual; keep it moving. Do not make a starter film about a guy who repairs watches. Not visual.

Or, Make a starter film about a place you love or hate or have some strong feelings about. Try to communicate mainly through images. Interview people. Have someone narrate what visuals don't communicate. Use music to channel viewers' reactions and feelings. You don't have to base a starter documentary on a lovely thing. Base it on something ugly or disagreeable.

Or, make a chance documentary. Go to an event where stuff is likely to happen, where there is a lot going on, where people are free and open. Have your camera ready. Get lucky.

(Flip ahead to page 204 for pointers about avoiding making a documentary that is without form or purpose.)

Make a Music Video

Music videos amount to putting images to music. If you want to make a music video, you have two main choices: *Either* do a literal film so that when the singer says, "I'd climb the highest mountain for you," we actually see some guy huffing and puffing up the side of

62   MAKING SHORT FILMS

a mountain. The images repeat the words. The images may be cleverly produced, but they don't really add anything to what the words say or what the music suggests. *Or* do a film with oblique or ironic images. This means that the images do not duplicate the words. They go somewhere else. They do their own thing. But together, the words, music, and images create a new thing.

Whichever, strive to have some connection—literal, ironic, fun-poking, or informational—between the song and the visuals.

Sparkle, a Straight Music Video

Ryan Hoverman has a band. He's also a film-maker. His band wrote the song "Sparkle" and Ryan made the music video, which is about a nerd who finally breaks out, learns how to dress and act, and becomes a cool guy. The trouble is, the cool guy looks and acts like millions of other cool guys, so he's not at all unique. I think Ryan intended this.

This is a straight music video in that the images just duplicate, in a sense, the words. If the band says, "He was a nerd," we see Ryan as a nerd; if the band says, "He got cool," we see Ryan all cooled out. Nothing oblique or ironic.

From *Sparkle* by Ryan Hoverman.

Project 454, an Ironic Music Video

I made this film a number of years ago in analog video. I edited it by ganging two VCRs and using one as the input unit and the other as the recording unit. This procedure is called *crash editing*.

Actually, I swiped the idea from a student, Dennis Boos, who had made the film about ten years before this in the super 8 film format. It was a terrific film that always got laughs from audiences. But somehow it got lost. Dennis gave me permission to remake the film.

Project 454 tells a story about a guy who buys a VW bug, runs it through a car wash, then drives it to a vacant lot to give it a wax job. At this point, the film gets weird. The guy goes sexual. He runs his hands over the curves

Dennis called his film *Project 454*. I never learned why.

of the bug as he might caress a curvaceous woman. Soon, he is kissing a headlight and fingering a tire valve stem. His passion mounts. He strips down. At the end, he raises the hood of the car, which is the trunk, climbs inside, and pulls the hood down over him.

I think Dennis was saying something about our pathological love affair with automobiles. What I haven't said yet is that both Dennis and I cut our films to go with the pop song, "You've Got a Friend." No other sound was used. Dennis cut the film to run the length of the song, which is about three minutes and sixteen seconds. I did, too; it was a real challenge working "crash." I transferred the song to the edited tape by means of an audio dub feature on an old VCR. I could just as easily have played "You've Got a Friend" on a separate CD player while running the film. When audiences get into the film—and they always do—they don't care whether the song is on the tape or being played separately.

The visuals mean one thing, and the music throws an ironic light on the visuals.

Another Ironic Music Video: Silent Night

Silent Night, by Gilbert Anthony, strikes a strong tone of satire. It's about the crass commercialism and greediness of Christmas shopping. It was shot in a K-Mart at the height of the shopping season. We see lots of hands, stacks of merchandise, price signs, and the zombified faces of shoppers in their own auto-pilot consumer worlds. I don't know how Gilbert pulled this off without getting thrown out. And while viewers see this, they hear "Silent Night." The visuals, then, comment on the music, and the music comments on the visuals. I don't know of any more effective way to get at the hypocrisy of Christmas shopping—in only three minutes.

TRY THIS

Make a music video. I'd prefer you go the oblique or ironic way. It's usually more interesting than the literal way.

Or, go beyond music videos. You don't have to base your film on just pop songs. You can create images to accompany a piece of classical music, jazz, a poem, or a prose excerpt. You might even write the poem or prose yourself. If you go this way, you can lay in additional sound, like music, to extend meaning.

Poem Video

Meghan Apper was so moved by a poem by Ani DiFranco that she used it as the backbone of a film. The poem, called "Self Evident," amounts to an angry interpretation of social and political events that surrounded 9/11, written soon after the event, like, we should have seen this coming. Meghan went out and shot stuff around Fresno—churches, homeless men, streetwalkers, affluent homes in the suburbs, trains and train tracks. She also shot 9/11 footage from her TV. Sometimes Meghan's images add force to DiFranco's anger, sometimes they say, No, I don't feel that way at all. For example, as we see the following image:

We hear these lines from the poem:

> cuz take away our Playstations
> and we are a third world nation
> under the thumb of some blue blood royal son
> who stole the oval office and that phony election

What did Meghan mean, pairing religious imagery with a jab at people who play video games and a rant against George Bush? That religion can't save us? That *only* religion can save us? Your mind works constantly when you attempt to attach the meanings of images and words in Meghan's film.

THE HOME FILM
This kind of film is a "home movie," only it is better shaped and more thoughtful. Also, it is edited, usually with a computer editing program, and the filmmaker adds sound beyond mere live ambient sound. The result is not a movie; it's not a home movie; it's a bona fide film.

In Search of Zoey
In Search of Zoey is a home film by Hamp Skellwigger about the five pets of his household. It could have been just a home movie—that is, random, unshaped, unedited, unplanned. It could have been like thousands of home movies about pets made by Americans every day across the country. But thanks to iMovie, Hamp made it a film.

From *In Search of Zoey* by Hamp Skellwigger.

The film has a little drama. Its whole purpose is to find Zoey, the elusive family cat. Mere home movies are not shaped like this. Hamp edited the film to insert Zoey fleetingly or way in the background at strategic points. He also shot the other four animals that have no inclination to hide, and he shot his stepson Kyle appearing to look for Zoey. Hamp directed Kyle to look a little sad or concerned. When Kyle does find Zoey, out in the back of the property, he smiles. She's a very beautiful calico cat, and the wait is worth it.

As for sound, Hamp retained most of the live sound, automatically recorded with the camera's microphone, as he filmed. Hamp also added narration with iMovie to impart information about his animals and the way Zoey keeps to herself. And to further enhance the soundtrack, Hamp used a piano solo by Bela Bartok to give the film a little class. To top things off, Hamp added a little fanfare when the film finally cuts to lovely Zoey sunning herself in the eaves of a storage shed. Hamp did all this with iMovie, which includes the fanfare as one of the audio effects in its library of sound effects.

The "Realistic" Home Film

One variant of the home film that my students have made with some success is what someone has called the "realistic" home film, which means it aims to show someone's family as it really is, not just the kind of smiling, waving, public-relations home movie most people make.

So the realistic home film captures family members being crude, indifferent, bored—even cruel or hurtful—in other words, just the way they are in real life. This kind of film, then, is a documentary about the banality of family. It usually has to be shot secretly, since people seldom want to look stupid or ugly on camera. It's a great blackmail film: Dad, buy me a new car or I'll show Mom this movie.

TRY THIS

Make a home film. Base it on pets, siblings, or some family activity like a birthday party or camping trip. Next, edit it, pare it down, sequence the footage meaningfully. Get interviews and edit them to pair well with images. Add music, titles, and credits. Strive to make a real film, not just a home movie.

PART II:

Deeper into Technique

5

Deeper into Shooting, One

*T*his chapter and the next, both of which are about shooting, aren't just about how to do close-ups or find the zoom rocker arm on your camera. They are also about the *art* of cinematography, or videography, if you like. And they suggest how, by applying the best-choice craft I describe, you can create engaging visual art and render the subject of your film more meaningful for your viewers.

COVERAGE

Coverage is your very first consideration. Coverage is about coming home from shooting with all the shots you need to edit effectively. To do this, you have to think about editing as you shoot. For example, you are filming a situation where a guy is parked outside a house and wants to know what is going on inside. You might take these shots:

1. Guy sitting in car.
2. Guy looking.
3. View of house—the guy sees a scroungy guy coming out.
4. Reaction of the guy—he's disgusted at the sight of the scroungy guy.

If you think of your shots as an edited sequence, you'll be all set to edit.

Or consider this: Instead of taking four shots, you take just two by combining shots 1, 2, and 4, and maybe by zooming a bit into the face of the guy behind the wheel. As you shoot, you know that you will later edit the two shots to produce the four clips of the sequence above. But you have to cover yourself first.

Think of obtaining good coverage as shopping for a big meal. You have two choices. You can meticulously write down everything you need in advance, then go to the store and pick up all the things on the list. Or you can show up at the grocery store without a list and just wing it, aisle by aisle, hoping your memory will be jogged by the parade of products you see. If you go the second way, you're almost guaranteed to forget something and have to go back. Filming is like this.

Refining the Shot List

I explained a shot list in the last chapter. Now for a refinement: You want to try to combine some of the shots, especially those of the same subject. This is what we just did in the little sequence about the guy outside the house. You'll end up with a smoother film if you can combine shots.

Sample Shot List for The End

Here's the shot list for a scenario I described in the last chapter called *The End.* The seven shots of the shot list below could be consolidated to five.

1. Wide shot of a man and a woman sitting on a bench in a park. They look glum, as if their relationship is coming to an end. He looks at her, but she is looking away. Then he looks away. Then she looks at him, sees he is looking away, and looks away herself.

2. Tighter shot of the man, morose, finally looking at the woman, then looking away.

3. Wide shot of the woman, who gets up, walks away. Camera pans; she keeps walking for 100 feet. We see her from behind. Then she stops, becomes very still, looks at the man.

4. Same as shot 3 but from the front. Camera moves backward as the woman walks (cameraperson walks backward). Camera moves in close, so we can see her face. She seems undecided. Then she seems like she's making a mistake. Turns to look back at the man.

5. Woman, as she turns and looks hopefully at the guy.

6. Man. He looks at the ground, then he looks up, sees the woman stop, keeps looking, then smiles when she looks back at him.

7. The couple run toward each other, fall into each other's arms, spin around, laughing joyously.

Thus the whole film might have been shot with just seven runs of the camera.

Now for the consolidation: Shots 3, 4, and 5, all of the woman, might have been just one take, a single running of the camera—but only if the actress playing the woman is well rehearsed. Also shots 2 and 6, of the man, might have been combined into a single take. Finally shots 5 and 7 might have been combined. The result is improved *continuity* from shot to shot.

So the point here is this: Prepare the night before. Write a shot list to make sure that you get all the coverage you need to edit. Then study the list to see whether you might consolidate some shots. The more you consolidate, the more rehearsed your subjects will need to be. (Flip back to page 60, where you'll find a shot list for a hitchhiking scenario.)

Not a Screenplay

Understand this: A shot list is not a screenplay. It's just a list of reminders. *Don't forget to take the shot of the guy looking under the car. Don't forget to take the close-up of the exhaust pipe.* These are the shots the filmmaker thinks he or she needs to make a film at the computer, with an editing program. All the shots on the list are much longer than they will be in the finished film. You will also have many more *clips* in the finished film than you had shots in the shot list. As I have indicated, many shots will be cut up into several pieces or clips. Many will be cross-cut and match-cut, terms I discussed in the last chapter. (Flip back to page 59 to see how a shot list is broken down into a clip-by-clip screenplay or guide to editing.)

Coverage for the Bathroom Scene in The Silence Between Us

Sarah Hagey and Katherine Jose made a film about a woman leaving a man. One scene in the film takes place in a tiny bathroom as the woman makes herself up before leaving. Many filmmakers, beginning and otherwise, would do the bathroom scene in just one shot, but not Sarah and Katherine. They did *eight* shots (see below and following page).

Why so much coverage? It gave the filmmakers lots of editing options. They like editing as much as shooting. They feel editing can be just as expressive as shooting, so they set themselves up.

This film is on the DVD.

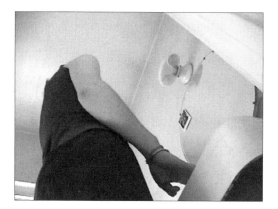 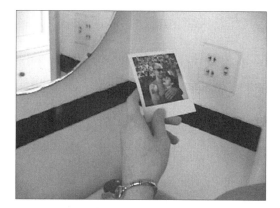

Coverage for Documentary Films

If you can control what is going on, then make a shot list or even write a complete screenplay. If you can't control the goings-on, then about all you can do is make a list of the things you think (or hope) will turn up. Then you just shoot everything. You bring a spare long-life battery and lots of tape. You shoot and think, think and shoot. Always, you ask, how might I use this in my film; how might I edit this? You should come back with far more footage than you could ever use, but you never know how it will all turn out in the editing. Since you've shot so much, you'll be well-covered.

Children of the Sky

Children of the Sky is a super 8 documentary by Bob Riding about hang gliding in Yosemite National Park. This was a number of years ago, before such activities were prohibited. The people took off from Glacier Point, 3,000 feet above the Yosemite Valley floor. Okay, put yourself in Bob's shoes: What kind of coverage would you need? Below are stills from three clips to show, in part at least, how Bob decided to cover his subject.

Taking off from Glacier Point, 3,000 feet above the valley.

But Bob didn't just shoot from safe ground. He also mounted the camera on a glider, set it to Lock Run so the glider guy wouldn't have to fool with it, and got spectacular coverage of the valley floor from way up there.

And landing.

Bob also covered spectators on both Glacier Point and in the valley, and he got shots of the people putting their gliders together at the start and taking them apart at the end.

If you work in super 8, you'll have to substitute for camera or computer editing features that your super 8 system lacks. This is a credit from *Raku*, Lori Woodruff's fine super 8 film about a Japanese method of pottery that depends heavily on natural elements. Lori prepared the credit on a sheet of clear acetate and taped it to her car window. Then she positioned the car to frame wild-flowers in the background and took the shot.

Coverage for Super 8 Films

As I said back in chapter 2, super 8 film is expensive to shoot because you get only three minutes and twenty seconds of film per cartridge. Naturally, you will not want to shoot fast and loose too much. You have to be very sure of what you want to do in the finished film and go after only that. The shot list or a list of hoped-for coverage looms very important.

Shooting this way is hard. You feel constrained if you are coming to super 8 from video. But videographers are often profligate. You shoot stingy in super 8. You strike a compromise between how much you can spend on film stock and how thoroughly you want to cover events. In my experience, thoughtful super 8 filmmakers don't cover their subjects any less thoroughly than do filmmakers who work in video. They just plan better and think twice before they shoot. I used to talk to Bob Riding about his filmmaking. He never complained about the "short" runs of super 8 cartridges. He just went ahead and made films.

FRAMES AND FRAMING

Frame is about how large or small your subject is, as seen in the viewfinder of your camera and later shown in your finished film. Frame is a noun and a verb. As a noun, it refers to five common ways of sizing subjects, like this:

1. **Extreme long shot:** The subject is seen very small, a mere dot or stick. This is because it's the setting—mountains, cityscape, seaside, inner city—that dominates, not people.
2. **Long shot:** This frame characteristically shows two people from head to foot, with the setting clearly seen but not dominating.
3. **Medium shot:** Two people in the frame, but tighter now, from the waist up.
4. **Close-up:** The face or head of a subject.
5. **Extreme close-up:** An eye, the face of a watch, a bullet hole.

I might add: *Medium close-up* and *medium long shot*. The list of frames is stretchable. Actually, frames blend into each other, as twilight blends into night. We give them names for our convenience.

When frame is a verb, we talk about "framing a subject." We look in the viewfinder, move back or move up, or zoom in or out, and get the subject to be just the size we want. Or we change the angle, which I discuss in more detail later.

Size (of the subject) really does matter. Consider these common uses and effects of the various frames.

Extreme Long Shots (ELS)

You'd want to use an extreme long shot (ELS) to:

➤ Establish a big, important setting like a mountain meadow, an empty parking lot, or a forest of tall buildings.

➤ Show a person overwhelmed and insignificant in the setting.

➤ Do both.

ELS from *Canal Banks* by Robin Stein. You can barely see a figure on the right bank and the reflection of another figure on the left bank. Mainly, though, the canal itself dominates.

Another ELS from *Lucky Guy* by Courtney Fontes.

ELSs aren't just rural. If you get back far enough, you can photograph people in the city to make them look somewhat overwhelmed or cut off. In this shot, the hard buildings contribute. From *The Job* by Adam Klusener.

Long Shots (LS)

LSs are good frames for showing subjects from head to foot performing continuous action. Space or spacing is important.

An ATM robbery goes bad. The LS is a good frame here for capturing stuff going on in the foreground and the background. From John Neeley's *Blood Money*.

Carol Piper and Stephanie Brown made this documentary called *Save the Canal* about a beloved canal in their neighborhood that a flood control district wanted to pave over. They took a lot of long shots, the better to show people and the canal—the whole point of the film.

Medium Shots (MS)

Medium shots are wide enough to contain a little action, but not so wide that facial expressions can't be seen.

From Irvin Benut's *Generations*. Man is pissed off because his wife does not have dinner on the table for him when he gets home from work. He eventually slugs her. The MS is the perfect frame for this unhappy bit of action. *This film is on the DVD.*

From *The Day Is Long* from Katherine Jose and Sarah Hagey. Filmmakers often employ medium shots when they want to show a lot without making subjects too small to be seen well. Katherine and Sarah used this frame to show the picture taker, the boy asleep, plus the mall.

Close-Ups (CU)

Close-ups of faces do three things:

1. Close-ups have potential to reveal a person's emotions. The actor does not have to say much or act much. In fact, too much talking or gnashing of teeth spoils the effect. A slight downturn of the mouth or darting of eyes can say a lot. Film is terrific this way and superior to any other form of narrative in conveying inner states. It would take a page to write what we perceive instantly in CU.

Two CUs from Doug Crutchfield's *Macho Walk*. It's refreshing to see older faces in short films.

2. CUs isolate. If MSs integrate, CUs separate. We look at only the face; nothing else is in the frame to distract us. The filmmaker won't let us see anything else. She insists, Look at this woman's face. Read her character. The person is isolated not just for our viewing convenience, but because the story probably calls for isolation at this point.
3. CUs involve and engage viewers. ELSs and LSs tend to disengage viewers emotionally from the action. CUs work just the opposite. They pull viewers emotionally into the drama or into the personality or predicament of the character. You can't help it. It's like you are standing right next to the actor in the film, who is not an actor to you for the moment but a real person. Maybe you'd like to pull back, get away, but for the time being the filmmaker will not let you. You have to plunge into the life and feelings of the character.

There's quite a story behind this close-up. The girl has dropped by the pizza parlor where her ex works. She hopes to get back with him. But the guy saw her coming and makes a pizza for her that includes crunched-up cockroach parts. Ah, look at her expression! So innocent! Such is the power of the close-up to involve you.

A film about tattooing and body piercing just has to have an abundance of ECUs.

Films with a lot of CUs are often driven more by character than by plot. Characters framed often in CU have complex, arresting personalities. If they don't, what's the point?

(Flip ahead to page 127 to see how Annette Marin used the CU at left in her film *Was a Good Boy, Was a Bad Pizza*.)

Extreme Close-Ups (ECU)

You don't need to take very many ECUs, unless your story has a lot of teensy details that have to be seen. Mike Gomez's *Inksanity*, a documentary about a tattoo and body-piercing shop, uses lots of ECUs—not only to show the procedures clearly, but to make the audience wince.

Frames for Documentaries

The documentary filmmaker ought to be just as conscious of her framing as the story filmmaker. ELSs are for establishing settings and are indispensable for documentaries with a strong sense of place or event, like a concert or an endangered place in nature. LSs might frame a couple of people who have to be seen from head to foot, like they're dancing, while also retaining a sense of setting. MSs are good frames for showing people doing something at closer range, like soldering together the frame for a stained-glass window. You might also conduct interviews in MS, which leaves room for something else important to be seen.

CUs—you have to be careful about these when you are making a documentary. You don't always want to shove the camera in too close. You might offend the person you are filming or make him nervous or shy.

TRY THIS

Make a film in which frames are important. For example, do a lot of close-ups, because it's a film that tells a story about characters with complex lives and feelings.

Or, make an outdoor film with lots of long shots or extreme long shots.

CONTINUITY

The film medium—celluloid or video—is a contradiction. Though it is composed of many separate and discrete *clips*, it flows smoothly, fluidly—good films do, that is. This *visual continuity* is achieved in two ways, through filming and later through editing. Sound, too, may contribute. Here are some things you might keep in mind as you film to assure good visual continuity in your finished film:

Rehearse thoroughly, technically as well as artistically. Make sure people do the same thing or stand the same way through all the takes of the same action. If a girl has her hand on her hips in one shot and her arms at her side in the next, you will not be able to cut those shots sequentially. The result will be a jump cut.

Strive to shoot on one side of the action. Pretend there is a line extending through the main area of the action. Film only in a 180-degree arc on one side of the line. This will assure that people move and face in expected ways.

Overlap action from separate shots that will later be cut together. So if a guy sits down at the end of a long shot, have him also sit down at the start of the next shot. During editing, you cut out the overlapping action.

Make sure people move their eyes or their heads in expected directions. If a woman looks at a man to her right, and later you cut to the man, he had better be looking to his left, if you want them to make eye contact. If she looks right, and in the next shot he is also looking right, you can't cut those shots together because she will seem to be looking at the back of his head, and he will seem to be looking off into space.

Take a lot of footage of secondary subjects like hands or gas gauges or people's feet or traffic going by or a minor character shaking his head. Go beyond your screenplay or shot list this way. You can often improve the continuity of an edited sequence by cutting away to subjects like these.

Consider long takes rather than short takes. Long has a better chance to produce better continuity.

Plan chases carefully. Stay consistently on one side of the action. Make sure that if, for example, the chasee is moving from left to right, so is the chaser. If you don't pay attention to this, you could end up with an edited sequence that seems like they are running away from each other or toward each other.

Directional continuity from *Super Runabout* by Kathy Verzosa and Sean Quentin. Both the chasee and the chaser are running in the same direction. If they aren't, it won't seem like a chase.

Continuity for Documentaries

As much as you can, try to apply these principles to your documentary. But again, it depends on how much control you have. If you can direct your subject like making a theatrical film, then the tips I just gave should serve you well. If you have little or no control, then . . .

Cutaway from *In Case of Earthquake*, a super 8 documentary about the demolition of a venerated college science building. The cutaway reminds us that the film isn't just about bricks and battering rams. It's about people's feelings, too.

Strive to edit in your mind as you shoot. What shot sequences do you see unfolding? Each time you come to a new subject, work out an edited sequence in your mind. Previsualize the sequence. Go for "classic" coverage: long shots, medium shots, close-ups of the same action or event. (Flip ahead to page 135 for information about editing the so-called classic sequence.)

Strive also to stay on one side of the action. That way you won't run into directional problems when you edit.

Shoot lots of cutaways of secondary action or subjects. Nothing solves a continuity problem better than slipping in a cutaway when the editing gets tough.

Avoid back panning—that is, don't pan from left to right, then back from right to left. Shots with random panning are very hard to edit. As a matter of fact. . .

Take mainly stationary camera shots; don't pan or zoom at all. Stationary camera shots, even handheld stationary shots, are the easiest of all to edit.

TRY THIS

Make a little film in which you pay extra attention to continuity. It doesn't have to tell a story or be an all-out serious film. Base it on something simple, maybe on one of the scenarios I described in the last chapter. Get people to move. Mix it up. Film a lot.

ANGLES

Angle should figure very early in your planning and shooting. Actually, you should work out your filming angle as you work out coverage and frame. I am doing this in v e r y s l o w m o t i o n. Experienced filmmakers consider all these matters—coverage, continuity, frame, angle—in a flash, all at the same time. Soon you will, too.

Many Possible Angles

There are many angles on subjects in both the worlds of still photography and motion picture photography. I'll just name all the ones I can think of:

Eye-level	Low, high	Side
Over-the-shoulder	Head in	Reverse
Front	Tail away	
Crazy	Overhead	

Eye-Level Angle

Ninety-five percent of still photography and cinematography worldwide is at eye-level. In other words, the photographer just picks up the camera and shoots at the same level or height, more or less, as the people he is photographing. Eye to eye. Eye-level photography carries no particular meaning. It's mainly neutral, and most of the time you want your angle to be neutral.

Low Angle

Low-angle shots, in which the camera is lower than the face of the subject, always jazz up the subject in some way. He comes off superior, menacing, in charge, macho, certain, willful, assertive, hurtful, and so forth.

From Byron Watkins' badass film about a high-stakes poker game. The guy on the left has been caught cheating. You know he's in big trouble, partly because of the low angle on the guy with the eye patch.

To take a low-angle shot, you get down on one knee, or you set the camera on the ground and point it up (see photo at right) or you lay on your back and shoot up, using the camera's flip-out LCD screen to frame. Or you rip up the floor and get down in the crawl space and shoot at floor level—which is what Orson Welles did in his *Citizen Kane* and Alejandro Gonzales Inarritu did in *Amores Perros*.

A very subtle effect results from shooting certain subjects that you want to glorify or enhance from about waist high—your waist. This only slightly low angle does not attract too much attention, but it lends a subtle dignity or superiority to the subject. View and frame your subject with the camera's LCD screen.

High Angle

High-angle shots have the opposite effect as that of low-angle shots. They make people look inferior, intimidated, subordinate, wimpy, uncertain, timid, or scared shitless.

Humor from angles.

Normally, you would take high-angle shots of characters who are sitting or on the ground or somehow plausibly positioned below eye level. You shoot down on them, as if the camera were taking a social position and looking down its nose at the characters.

A film called *Valentine's Day Blues* by Aaron Patton has one of the funniest high-angle shots I've ever seen. A guy shows up for a date at the doorstep of a girl he contacted through a personal ad. He doesn't know much about her. He knocks, the door opens, but he doesn't see anybody. Then he looks down. Cut to high-angle shot of a little girl about nine. Not what he expected.

Working with his high school students, Scott Donaghe shot part of this *Matrix*-style fight straight down from a balcony to lend the conflict visual interest.

Overhead Angle

This is straight down. You wouldn't want to use many of these, because they really do call attention to themselves. Now and then, though, they add spice to a sequence of shots.

Consider this: Bring a six-foot free-standing ladder along on your shoots. I used to do this. Every so often I'd climb up on the ladder and shoot something going on straight down. Once I shot two guys shaking hands straight down from the ladder. I framed just their arms and hands. Below their hands was the thing they were agreeing to, a box containing money.

Front, Side, and Rear Angles

As I've said, most filmmakers and photographers just shoot people frontally. But sometimes a side-angle or profile shot of an actor or person in a documentary could be just what you need.

> The side angle is good if the subject moves and you want to pan with him. Have the subject move in an arc so he'll always be the same distance from the camera. (More about camera movement later in the chapter.)

> Rear-angle shots are good for showing where a person is going. We see the destination. Really good actors love to act with their back to the camera. They act

with posture and small movements of shoulders, legs, or hips. Walk with the subject or stand still.

➤ Side-angle shots may provide a kind of psychological distance, which a character may need.

Over-the-Shoulder Angle

This is a medium shot of two people made different because, instead of filming them frontally or face to face, you get behind one of them and frame just the back of the shoulder and neck and maybe part of the back of the head of the person along the bottom of the frame and up one side while the other person is seen facing the camera in the rest of the frame. So the person facing the camera gets the emphasis, while the other person, over whose shoulder you are shooting, is relegated to a secondary role for this angle. But (and this is a big but) the secondary person is still in the frame. You don't want one person to be out of the frame. You want the sense of two people together in the frame.

After you take an over-the-shoulder shot of one character, you may want to reverse the angle and take an over-the-shoulder shot of the other character. You criss-cross when you edit. The editing has symmetry this way.

This side-angle shot from Sarah Hagey's *Salvation* involves us without being as intrusive as a frontal shot. The hair helps, too. Sometimes you don't want to show too much. If you wanted to make the woman even more obscure, you'd keep turning the camera toward the back of her head so that only a crescent of her face would be seen.

Over-the-shoulder angle in *Make Ups to Break Ups* by Onesta Francis. Drug dealer recruits an ambitious kid. Actually, for a classic over-the-shoulder frame, the camera should have moved behind the dealer so we don't see his face and the kid gets more attention.

Head-In, Tail-Away Angles

This is a two-shot sequence. First, you film someone moving toward the camera and out of the frame—walking, running, on a motorcycle. Then you reverse the angle and film him coming into the frame and on toward the destination. You have to keep the camera on one side of the action to maintain a sense of continuity.

In the first part, the head-in, we see where the person is coming from; in the second, the tail-away, we see where he is going. You cut the shots one after the other. You'd shoot this way if you want the camera to linger on something in the background as the person rushes out of the frame. Otherwise, just pan.

Head-in angle. Hitchhiker runs toward camera. From Dave Bletz's *Lucky Guy*.

Tail-away angle. Hitchhiker runs away from camera.

Reverse Angle

A reverse-angle shot is when you shoot in one direction and then you swing around and shoot the same thing, or almost the same thing, in the opposite direction. Each angle has its own revealing background. Background is important. What you can't see in one shot, you see in the reverse-angle shot.

An Fg/Bg angle from my film *Photo Finish*.

Fg/Bg Angle

Fg/bg is a notation I have used for years. By it, I mean composing a shot with one subject in the foreground and a second in the background. Usually both are in focus if you shoot in wide angle. However, if you want one or the other out of focus, you take the shot in telephoto. (For more about range of focus, flip ahead to page 112.)

Crazy Angle

A crazy angle is totally unexpected. A student whose name I forget made a film about a guy driving along a lonely country road. It was spooky. The radio started to act up—it started to talk to the guy and laugh at him. The filmmaker rigged a piece of transparent plastic to look like an AM dial—from 500 to 1600. Then he shot the driver through the plastic as though from the point of view of the spooky radio. (He had to scrunch down on the floor of the truck and take the shot as if from behind the dashboard.) Crazy angle, good effect.

In *Project 454*, a film I described in chapter 4, the guy who makes love to his Volkswagen kisses the headlight in full passion. Cut to a shot from *inside* the headlight with the guy's lips all over the place. Of course, I didn't really get inside the headlight to take this shot. I just shot the lover through an ice tea pitcher with headlight-like glass.

TRY THIS

Find the right backdrop for your angle. Maybe something is in the background that you don't want, like a billboard. So you walk around the subject a little to crop out the billboard. Or you do want a particular thing in the background, like a parked car or a couple of kids skateboarding. Move a little to make sure you pick them up. Your subject has black hair, which does not stand out as well against that gray building as it does against the sky. So get down on one knee to film her framed against the sky.

Tale to Tell: Finding Meaningful Backdrops

A backdrop is just a slice of a location, like a stucco wall or a creek with tangled willows. A few feet left or right, the backdrop might completely change. You are always on the prowl for just the right backdrop. When I was filming *Photo Finish,* the film about the girl who wants to commit suicide in a junkyard, I wanted just the right backdrop for one of her close-ups. I found it in the branches of a dead tree. I got down on one knee and filmed her framed against the dead tree.

Lesson: You arrive at a location, and you never know which way you will point your camera. All things being equal, you point it at something meaningful in the background. At the end of the day, you feel good having worked loose like this. In contrast, at the end of a ten- or twelve-hour Hollywood shoot, everyone ends up hating everyone else and goes home bone tired. No one feels appreciated. It has been just a lot of yelling at each other and ego-tripping.

Tale to Tell: Kurosawa's Backdrops

This is about the great Japanese filmmaker Akira Kurosawa. A critic once told him how he liked the backdrops in Kurosawa's *The Seven Samurai.* They seemed so appropriately medieval, with wooden fences and primitive huts. Kurosawa told the critic that it was all a matter of framing the right backdrops. Had he moved his camera a few inches to the left, he would have picked up power lines; a few inches right, tall buildings in a nearby city.

TRY THIS

MOVES

The way you move your camera has a lot to do with how you frame your subject and what angle you decide to use—which brings us to the big, ongoing, never-ending debate between handheld and tripod-mounted cinematography. How should you move the camera—by holding it and walking, swaying, bending, or extending your arms? Or do you pan or tilt with the camera on a tripod head? Or do you execute movement by means of some kind of dolly or wheeled device such as a wheelchair? There are pluses and minuses for all of these options, but I am going to come out in favor of handheld, moving-camera work.

Camera Moves

Movies, after all, should move. Here are some ways you can get your camera moving, for good reasons.

Handheld, Moving-Camera Shooting

To me, there is something nearly sacred about filming a subject as you walk in wide angle. If you can control the subject and get her to move, all the better. Shooting in wide angle— that is, in the fully zoomed-out lens setting—eliminates most camera jerkiness. Moreover, if your digital camera has an image stabilizer, which it probably does, the little unsteadiness that might be produced by your walking is pretty much smoothed out. Even if your camera doesn't have this feature, you will get fairly steady walking footage if you set your lens to wide angle. Just go into the camera's menu and make sure the stabilizer function is turned on.

Pun Tallee walks with a small, palmable DV camera.

I say walking in wide angle is sacred because it catches up the essence of minimalist short film-making: You work with a small DV camera you can cradle lovingly in your hands. You enhance the subject through body movement, as though you—your arms, hands, legs, feet, trunk—are a part of the technical-artistic process. You are the human tripod, the human dolly.

Also, you can move in several directions. You can walk and then crouch; you can walk and raise the camera over your head. You can walk and bend and turn and even lay down on your back as the action changes and ends directly over you. No tripod lets you do this. All this produces acceptably smooth footage.

You don't have to move far—I like slowly moving the camera with my arms from side to side as I stand in one place or straighten my legs from a crouched to a standing position.

Pun crouches for a low-angle shot, using the camera's flip-out LCD screen to frame.

Now Pun holds the camera high, again framing with the LCD screen.

Moving the camera a short distance laterally often lends interest to an otherwise static shot.

Walking in Telephoto

Handheld walking shots in telephoto always produce shaky, fuzzy, disorienting footage. Subjects at close range are not very clear. But this may be the very effect you are after.

TRY THIS

Walk with your camera with tape running in wide angle and assess the results. After this, walk with the camera in telephoto and see what that looks like. Or try some focal lengths (zoom settings) between the extremes.

SCHOOL YOURSELF

Watch *The Constant Gardener*, a classy British film directed by Fernando Meirelles, starring Ralph Fiennes and Rachel Weisz. The remarkable feature of this film is that 75 percent of it was shot with a handheld camera. I asked my uncinematic friend who saw the film and loved it, "Did the handheld shooting bother you?" He didn't know what I was talking about.

Sarah Hagey's Intriguing Camera Moves

It's the ever-changing frames and angles in Sarah Hagey's *Salvation* that are so appealing in this film about people initially separated physically and spiritually, then coming together and rescuing each other. In one shot, Sarah filmed an actor in frontal wide angle, then walked up to the person and around to reframe him in a tight, side-angle profile. In another shot, Sarah followed a girl walking down a mall and past the camera, then panned away to a scary-looking man who seems to want to do harm to the girl. After this, her camera followed the man as he got up and followed her, reframing so that Sarah shot over the shoulder of the man with the girl in the background—all in one take, all handheld.

Start of circling shot.

Closer.

Around the corner.

Finally stopping just inches from the eye. All one take.

From a walking shot Sarah Hagey took for *Salvation*. The camera moves in a wide arc from a front angle of the subject to a side-angle ECU of his eye.

Again

In this moving camera shot, Sarah follows a businessman on a busy mall. She completely circles the man with her camera running.

Sarah walks with her camera (in wide angle) to film the businessman from behind carrying his briefcase.

Sarah quickly scoots to the side of the businessman, camera still running.

Sarah now walks backward as she films the man straight on.

And on to the other side. The footage is remarkably smooth, thanks to the camera's digital steadiness feature and Sarah's shooting in wide angle, which also minimizes unsteadiness.

Don't Do This Alone

Get someone to help you take a shot like these two by Sarah Hagey. Exclamation point! You could run into someone or fall and damage the camera (not to mention sustaining injury to yourself). The helper guides you by placing hands on your shoulder or keeping fingers inside your belt from behind—while you constantly reframe by looking through the finder or LCD display.

Shooting from a Tripod

Films shot from tripods look rock steady, to be sure, but to me they seem inert, too—lifeless. Filmmakers get hooked on the super-steady look of tripod-shot footage, or want to ape Hollywood's obsessively steady look, and then are loath to get the camera off the three-legged thing and just shoot with their hands. Or they value the wrong thing—steadiness—to the exclusion of other values and other rewards—namely, the fluid look of moving, handheld shooting. Remember: You are not reinventing Hollywood. Hollywood's been done. Tripods and dollies are for Hollywood. You are making short films. They are not Hollywood. Cupped hands, smoothly moving arms and legs, supple trunk—these are for you.

On the other hand, steadiness, inertia, a dead-weight feeling may be the exact feel sought. If this is what you want, then use a tripod. I can't recall whether Marshall Chambers' fine film about a hitchhiker out in the middle of nowhere who declines to take a chance with a woman who stops for him was shot from a tripod or not, but it might justifiably have been done so. If the visual style is meant to be static and grim, stationary camera shots are perfectly appropriate. And tripod-mounted shots are even better.

Actor or Subject Moves

Actors or subjects in films may move in countless ways in relation to the camera. For example, here are some ways actors might move:

- Head-in, tail-away.
- Panning shot of subject running—camera in a fixed position by side of road
- Lateral tracking shot of subject running—usually taken from a car window.
- Rear-angle shot of subject running—also from a car window.
- Front-angle shot of subject running—usually taken from the back of a truck.

One option is best—for showing the action, for showing the background, for connecting with other shots. Your job is to have a good reason for deciding on a strategy.

In *Nocturne*, the nightmare-based film by Marcelo Moriega, the dreamer is constantly in motion. He paces in a small space like a caged animal, he throws a temper tantrum by flinging his body down in an old building and pounding the floor, he walks up stairs to a landing with a window from dark to light. Each movement has meaning.

When a character in an already highly symbolic film climbs toward the light, you know you have to pay attention.

Small Moves

Subjects do not have to move in large, gross ways to communicate states of mind. Often, it's the small moves that are effective. In the language of film, when a character's head is stationary but her eyes shift left and right, she is usually being evasive. A slight turning of the head away from another person "says" the same thing. When someone looks at his watch, he wants to get out. When a person taps on a table with his fingers, he's impatient. The culture has a large library of small moves like these for communicating states of mind, and you know all of them. Use them.

The Dance

Think of this interaction of moving camera with moving subject as a dance with graceful lines, elegant pauses, lovely arcs, reverse leads, abrupt stops, faster, slower, resting momentarily, starting up again—played out against a meaningful backdrop. Only thirty-one people on Earth understand how camera and subject dance. You are number thirty-two. (Flip ahead to page 93 for films based on moving cameras.)

TRY THIS

Make a little film with lots of neat camera moves. It doesn't have to be a film, but just an exercise. Walk around Little League players sitting on a bench, then pan to spectators behind the backstop, then reverse pan out to the infield, then pan back to the batter and catcher. Stuff like this. Walk with the camera set to wide angle. Turn, twist, stoop, rise, lean left, lean right, lift the camera overhead—all while the camera is running. Set the camera to SteadiShot, if it has that feature. Also walk with the camera in telephoto, just to see what that is like.

Or, make your camera moves from a tripod or wheeled device like a wheelchair. Here are some subjects: hitchhiker, purse snatcher, homeless man, homeless woman, prowler, stalker, female stalker, drug connection, drug bust, sporting event (or just one aspect of a sporting event, like throwing a runner out at second base or kicking a field goal).

6

Deeper into Shooting, Two

$\mathcal{S}$hooting is complex, so I need another chapter.

THE LONG TAKE

I invite my students to try what I call *long-take* or *single-take* films, which amount to a long continuous running of the camera, combined with various moves of the body and a moving subject, just to get the hang of the possible visual poetry that movement can create. Often, they have never contemplated the movement of camera and subject before as *art*. It is.

Turn Off

Turn Off is a long-take film about a guy who is awakened by the sound of a particularly grating alarm clock. He gets up, walks through the house to the garage, gets a hammer, returns to the bedroom, and smashes the clock, vanquishing disagreeable technology. Jared Dodds filmed this little story in one continuous take, which runs about two minutes. What I like, too, is the sound of the alarm—very loud at first, fainter as the guy goes out to the garage, then loud again as he reenters the bedroom. Then—*smash*—silence.

From *Turn Off* by Jared Dodds.
This film is on the DVD.

A successful long-take film tells a story or documents something. There is something lyrical or fluid about the story or the thing being documented. The long take doesn't end pointlessly. It builds to some kind of climax. As camera and subject move, the background changes constantly and meaningfully. This isn't easy. It's a game, a challenge—something you put together for knowing viewers.

Fluid, Another Long-Take Film

From *Fluid* by Sarah Morris.
This film is on the DVD.

Fluid, a three-minute, single-take art film by Sarah Morris, follows the life of a cigarette lighter as hands use it to start a gas stove, ignite pot, singe eyebrow liner, light candles for a group of people in meditation—things both mundane and sacred—all in the same dwelling, all in real time with the camera in constant motion. The angle is always on the lighter, not on people, though they are incidentally seen. Then the lighter gets taken outside on a date. The woman with the lighter lights a cigarette with it, but then drops it carelessly in the gutter. It's apparently lost forever. The film is sentimental and funny at the same time. It makes us think about the changing roles of a common object of living, and it's lovely to watch.

School Yourself

Watch *Lumiere and Company*, a remarkable film based on a concept by Frenchman Phillipe Poulet. The film appeared in 1995 and was produced on the occasion of the one-hundredth anniversary of the film medium. A hundred years earlier, two French filmmakers, Auguste and Louis Lumiere, had started making very short, single-take "documentaires," as they were called, in and around Paris. The Lumieres didn't work this way to be arty; they didn't know any better, and film editing was unknown at that time. In honor of the centenary and the Lumieres, Poulet arranged to have forty internationally renowned filmmakers—such as Spike Lee, Wim Wenders, and Zhang Yimou—work exactly as the Lumieres had by producing their own single-take films, all running less than a minute. The results are much like what I am trying to teach you: minimalist art derived from ingenuity. What is doubly fascinating is how Poulet restored the Lumieres' original camera and invited all the participating filmmakers to use it to make their filmlets. They loved the idea. It would be like contemporary writers having the chance to write with the original quills Shakespeare used. But I have to warn you: A lot of critics thought these one-minute films were silly, but by and large they knew nothing about minimalist film. You do.

One More Long-Take Film

Scott Donaghe, who teaches French in a Fresno high school, took four students outside and had them flirt with each other, in a cinematic sense. Two girls, two guys. At first the two pairs are on opposite sides of the courtyard. Gradually they notice each other. Then the boys approach the girls. Scott's nonstop camera work is pretty remarkable. First he is close enough to the girls to hear them talk (in French) about the guys. Then he walks across the courtyard with his camera running to the boys, close enough to

From this angle, Scott circled to the right to reach the girls, panning several times back to the boys, then to the girls. *This film is on the DVD.*

hear the guys talk about the girls (also in French). Then he follows the boys, camera running, as the boys walk up to the girls. Neat. Symmetrical, like *Turn Off*.

TRY THIS

You knew this was coming: Do a long-take film. Just one shot, one long-running, moving-camera, moving-subject shot that is an entire film in itself. Think in terms of a beginning, middle, and end, as in Jared and Sarah's long-take films. Think up a little story or a simple documentary you can do in one take with the camera constantly in motion. Shoot in wide angle.

SCHOOL YOURSELF

Watch these two films with numerous long takes.

First is *Y tu mamá tambien*, a coming-of-age film about two Mexican youths on a journey of discovery across Mexico. They meet a worldly woman who teaches them much about maturity. Note especially the long scene in the bar near the very end of the film. The woman and the two boy-men have a serious discussion about life.

Second is *Russian Ark*, a remarkable *tour de force* about the art housed in a famous Russian gallery called The Hermitage. Director Aleksandr Sokuro tells a story about the preservation of Russian art, how it was nearly destroyed several times during the turbulent Soviet era, and how it was saved. There are dozens of actors playing characters from history and many dancers as well. And here is the amazing thing: *This is all done in one continuous ninety-minute take* with a special DV camera recording on disc. It's a miracle.

Also, take in the famous long-take first shots of these films: *Touch of Evil, The Player, Snake Eyes,* and *Magnolia*. All of these opening shots run minutes and minutes as camera and subject move constantly. And take a look at the long take halfway through *Goodfellas* when Ray Liotta and Lorraine Bracco arrive at the back-alley entrance of a night spot, go through the kitchen, and are seated at a table near the stage where Henny Youngman gives his famous one-liners. These filmmakers—Orson Welles, Robert Altman, Bryan De Palma, Paul Thomas Anderson, and Martin Scorsese, respectively—did these long takes not for the masses but for the enlightened few. Consider yourself an enlightened insider if you bother to check out these marvels of rehearsal and logistics.

COMPOSITION

Composition has to do with how objects are placed in the film frame—what is foreground, what is background; what is high, what is low; what is left; what is right—and just as important, *why*. Most people have an innate sense of composition. If you have ever arranged objects on a shelf, moved stuff around on a desktop, or tidied up odds and ends in the trunk of a car to make everything fit, then you have dealt with composition, the art of arrangement.

Let's consider three kinds of film composition: *practical*, *formal*, and *symbolic*.

Practical Composition

When you compose practically, you make sure that everything that needs to be seen is seen. A certain shot depends on viewers seeing A, B, and C. Or they have to see D, which is behind E. They may have to see these all at once, or in sequence, as camera or subject moves. To ensure that important things are seen, you have to make modifications like the following:

> Arrange the things to be seen most advantageously
> Adjust your camera frame, by zooming in or out, to work everything in
>> Modify your camera moves
>> Make sure that the main thing is dominant in the frame

Practical Composition in *Little House*

To the left is a good example of a practically composed shot, from *Little House* by Annette Marin.

Sometimes you have to *fudge*, an old film term that means moving something just a little so that it, or something else behind it, can be seen better, even though the moving isn't quite realistic or faithful to previous takes.

Nothing fancy. We see all the people around the fire, with no wasted space.

Practical composition will probably figure in the majority of the shots you take—or should.

Formal Composition

This is harder to understand. When you compose formally, you really invade the territory of painters and still photographers who enjoy placing lines and shapes in their canvasses and photographs for their own sakes. It's art for the sake of art. You like the way a certain crooked-growing tree makes an arc with the top of a hill, itself an arc. A particular backdrop has a soft or lyrical texture—small, light-green leaves on plants. Light reflects beautifully off a river in late afternoon, and you know you just have to get the couple kissing against that backdrop. Or there are unrelenting parallel lines, perhaps created by redwood slats in a chain-link fence; perfect for that scene of violence you'll be filming.

Here are three examples of formally composed shots:

Formally composed shot from *The Silence Between Us* by Sarah Hagey and Katherine Jose. Curves produced by arms and shoulders blend appealingly.

This film is on the DVD.

Symmetrical composition from *Infinity* by David Bayouth and Craig Bolton. *Infinity* apparently is about a journey to death. It's a highly symbolic art film—but at first, you aren't sure what is going on. There are a lot of shots of a figure clothed in black moving through a kind of forest of young trees. Often the composition is symmetrical with the trees planted in neat columns, suggesting that what you see is not real. As you start to put two and two together, the idea of death might occur to you.

Sam Gill made a very formal version of *Macho Walk*, one of the scenarios I suggested you do in chapter 4. Sam turned the meeting of the two men into an Asian-style martial arts confrontation. The overarching tree evokes the Japanese art of bonsai while also providing an appealing triangular strategy of composition.

This film is on the DVD.

Symbolic Composition

Composition becomes symbolic when you include an element that has meaning beyond what it literally is. For example, in *Little Star*, a young woman is being driven to an abortion clinic. The driver is the father. The girl looks wistfully out the window, and the filmmaker—Kathy Verzosa, who plays the girl in the story—got a shot of herself with the cars and storefronts reflected in the window glass and slipping by in an endless, haunting stream. The shot was taken from another car. The reflection of constantly changing cars and storefronts is a symbol of the passing world, for reality catching up to the girl and her father. This feeling is accentuated by her look of lost innocence.

From *Little Star* by Kathy Verzosa.

This film is on the DVD.

In *Photo Finish*, a woman tries to find meaning in life by serious photography of junk cars. In one shot, she is seen completely enclosed by angular, twisted parts of a truck chassis. But this metal is not threatening or claustrophobic for her; instead, it's comforting. For the moment, she draws inspiration—and life—from the world of junk.

Nothing in a film is without meaning, not even scrapped cars.

Art films often engage in highly symbolic composition. For example, Lianne Neptune's art film *Americans' Stuff* is about how we Americans are addicted to spending, spending,

From *Americans' Stuff* by Lianne Neptune.

In this still from my *People Eating Silently*, I got lucky. I didn't realize at first that the huge, muted poster of the McDonald's hamburger hovering above these women had symbolic value.

spending. Lianne felt that we are blinded by the dollar. So she contrived a shot in which a guy literally wears dollar bills in front of his eyes. Why not? This is an art film. You couldn't get away with such a contrivance in a straight film.

Composing with Found Elements

By *found elements*, I mean the telephone poles, dead trees, billboards, and figurines that just happen to occur on the locations and sets where you film. Look around. Use these elements creatively in your composition strategies. Don't shoot until you've sized up the backdrop from different angles and found one that suits your film best.

Composing with found elements, in this case with junk cars and trucks. The camera has been tilted to increase the feel of unnatural things happening. This used to be called a dutch angle.

In *Photo Finish*, the junkyard setting provided numerous compositional opportunities.

Bring Key Elements with You

Bring along a poster, a book, a framed photograph—anything you can work into a shot to throw meaning on the main subject. Don't trust it to chance.

TRY THIS

Make a simple documentary with lots of thoughtful compositions. Strive for good practical composition, interesting formal composition, and, now and then, meaningful symbolic composition. Go someplace rich in varied subjects, like an outdoor mall or a Renaissance fair. Stuff going on all around you is the ticket.

LIGHT AND LIGHTING

Light—eventually, as you make more and more films, you will pay more attention to it, and you may seek to control it.

Shooting Heedless

Shooting heedless—a term I created—means not doing anything about lighting at all when you shoot. It means being heedless about the light—how much, what kind, what direction it comes from. To shoot heedless, you set your camera to auto-exposure and shoot, regardless of the light.

Occasionally, you'll get some shots that are interestingly composed or lighted. Though this may be accidental, it's still fun. In *To Go*, a film about a neurotic guy at a sandwich

It's fun to shoot where the light is varied. You work with the light you have and find the best place to shoot.

shop, Luke Freeman took a long shot with some interesting accidental lighting. The guy working behind the counter is normally exposed while the two customers are silhouetted.

Setting Exposure Manually

Most DV cameras set exposure (brightness/darkness) automatically. The camera measures the intensity of light coming through the lens and opens or closes the camera's iris (aperture) according to what it perceives the subject to be. Better cameras, however, let you adjust exposure manually. You can create a darker, moodier, or even suspenseful look by using the manual exposure dial to close the iris. For a brighter, washed-out look, or to avoid a silhouetted look, open the iris with the exposure dial. You can monitor all these changes in the camera's viewfinder.

Often, you can shoot heedless because of the remarkable ability of modern video cameras to record usable images in almost any kind of light short of total darkness. Of course, the results don't always look "professional." But you aren't professional. You make short films.

Even Old Hands Shoot Heedless

Speaking of professionals, some veteran filmmakers who have thought a lot about lighting actually prefer to shoot heedless. They just don't want to fool with a lot of brought-in photographic lights and a tangle of cords. They want to work fast. They want to make films the way a jazz performer improvises. Taking time for setting lights blunts their spontaneity. Maybe they *have to* shoot fast. Setting lights or constantly recomposing for maximum light would slow the pace.

School Yourself

Watch Traffic. Director Steven Soderbergh has revealed that he shot much of this great film himself, and often he shot semi-heedless, using a bare minimum of lights. This is highly unusual practice for a big-time Hollywood director. Soderbergh wanted to avoid the lead weight of dozens of lighting technicians and truckloads of cables and fixtures that the studio burdened him with during Erin Brockovich and Out of Sight. Of course, you have to keep in mind that Traffic, being a gritty, realistic film, probably benefited from minimalist lighting. Julia Roberts' agent probably wouldn't have liked it.

Though heedless shooting is associated with the films of beginners, these filmmakers aren't necessarily slapdash or disrespectful. Often, beginners make excellent films shooting heedless. And bringing in a bevy of lights is no guarantee of ending up with a good film. Some filmmakers who shoot heedless just don't know any better, and they usually get passably good exposures. So they don't think much about lighting. Most of the fine films I describe in this book were shot heedless. My advice: Shoot heedlessly only for a while, through two or three films. Then pay more attention to light and what you can do to get the most out of it.

Dealing with Backlight

Keep in mind that shooting heedless can be a crapshoot. If you aren't careful, you may not get exposures you like. One such situation is called *backlighting*. If you shoot a subject heedless toward a bright source of light, your subject is likely to turn out dark—so dark, in fact, that facial features cannot be seen. This happens all the time when you shoot heedless toward the sun or a big window from inside. What is happening is that the camera's auto-exposure system is reading the brighter backdrop and closing down the iris of the camera to avoid overexposure. The camera doesn't know that the object in the foreground is the real subject.

To avoid having just a silhouette of your subject, you have these two easy solutions: *Either* move the subject away from the light in the background. Your camera's auto exposure system will automatically brighten up the subject. *Or* set the camera's exposure to manual, and brighten up the subject by turning the camera's exposure dial.

Purposely Silhouetting

Actually, you may like the dark look you get shooting toward a bright light source, because your subject is rendered as a silhouette this way. Characters who are silhouetted sometimes seem sinister or mysterious. This might work for you.

Shooting toward the light renders an intriguing silhouette.

The Right Angle Alternative

Shooting at a right angle is an alternative to silhouetting. Instead of shooting directly at the bright light source, you shoot at right angles to it. Stay on auto exposure. You'll get a pleasing, softly illuminated, half-darkish look to, say, a face. The point is to consider working *with* the available lighting instead of *against* it. Go with the lights that are already in place, including the sun. Then use the opportunity to come up with something revealing or interesting.

Shooting Michelle, the fast-food lady, toward the bright window. She is rendered as a silhouette.

Shooting Michelle at a right angle to the window. Her face is now interestingly sidelit. No adjustments to exposure were made.

TRY THIS

Familiarize yourself with your camera's exposure system. Go to menu > manual exposure. Chances are there's a dial nearby that lets you brighten or darken the image. Strive to set exposure so that your main subject looks properly exposed, neither too dark nor too light. This may mean that the background will have to go light or dark.

Your camera may also have a backlight button. Experiment with it by shooting a subject strongly backlit. The subject is likely to be dark. Push the button as you shoot. The iris will open and the subject will brighten up.

You don't have to make an actual film to learn about exposure, although I hope you do. Shoot a subject toward a bright light. Note how the subject is silhouetted. Brighten the subject by going manual with exposure. Try the right angle remedy. Underexpose on purpose. Set up a shot so that the exposure fluxes unappealingly, then fix the problem with manual exposure.

Shoot the same subject from different angles and lighting. Note varying results. Link remedy or technique with visual result. Store results in the Rolodex of your mind.

Dealing with Low-Light Conditions

Say you are shooting in conditions of pretty dim light. Instinct tells you that you shouldn't shoot heedless. Here are some choices to sort through to increase light:

➤ Bounce more light onto the subject. This can be done with a large piece of white posterboard that someone holds during the take. The helper might even bend the posterboard a little to create a convex lens and focus the light.

- Bring in some extra lights—floor lamps, flashlights, shop utility clip-on lights— anything that produces light.
- Flip to a camera feature called *night shooting*, which produces smeary, greenish images with a kind of flashlight effect. You may not be able to use this, or you may not like the effect.
- Set your camera's shutter to slow or wide. This makes the shutter stay open longer so the lens can gulp more light. Access shutter speed from the camera's menu.
- Shoot heedless and live with the dark, colorless, grainy lighting.

Working with Movable Photographic Lights

You can do much to mold light with the purchase of a relatively inexpensive set of three lights with stands. Lighting kits include bowl reflectors for corralling light. Stands for the lights are adjustable.

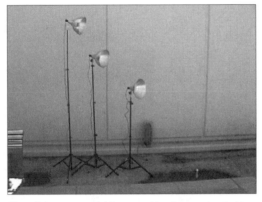

You don't have to spend a lot of money on pro-grade quartz lighting setups. Fixtures that take ordinary household bulbs are fine for DV shooting. Plus, you don't need superpowerful bulbs. One-hundred-watt bulbs are entirely adequate, unless you need to light a very large space.

A few of the setups described below are classic, but most are just improvised.

Three lights on stands. One stand has been extended to seven feet to create interesting down-light effects.

Two- and Three-Point Lighting

If you work with a trained lighting person, she will insist that you start your lighting education by learning so-called three-point lighting. The three lights are the key light, the fill light, and the backlight.

The key light is closest to the subject or has the brightest bulb and falls on the subject from about a three-quarter frontal angle. The fill light is used to make sure that the far or dark side of the subject does not go too dark. It's placed triangularly to the subject and key light and is either set back farther or uses a less

Imagine a triangulation of two lights on Leandra and Sterling. The right light has a bulb that is twice as bright as that on the left light. The result is a molding or modeling of the light from normal exposure to dark tones to black—much more interesting than frontal, flat lighting.

powerful bulb. The backlight is set behind the subject (at an angle so that the camera does not pick it up) and is used for defining the subject against a dark background.

I find that beginning filmmakers seldom employ the third light, mainly because they don't shoot in large interior spaces. The examples of lighting setups below make use of only two lights.

Additional Setups

1. Illuminate your subject with two lights of the same wattage and triangulate with the subject. Use the third light to throw light on a distant background, like a hallway, to brighten it up.

2. Place a light on one side of the subject and another light on the other side. In other words, the lights and the subject are more or less in a straight line, instead of triangulated. Experiment with having the subject move forward and backward (or move the lights forward and backward) until you hit on a pleasing combination of light and shadow.

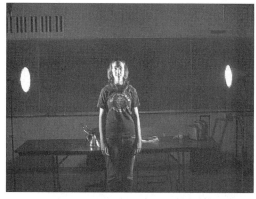
Lights for Leandra's cross-lighting were placed like this.

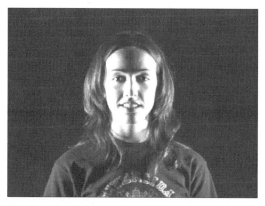
Note how the shadows on Leandra's face are symmetrical.

Leandra takes one step forward.

Darker still after two steps.

3. Use just one or two lights on one side of the subject, none on the other. The result is harsh "hatchet" lighting.

4. Rim-light the subject by shooting a strong backlight at an angle behind the subject. You want to go for a rim or crescent-moon effect. You may want a subtle front-fill light. I hate to say this, but the effect works better with blondes.

5. Suspend a light from overhead for downward illumination, which forms shadows under eye ridges and chin.

6. Can't come up with the several hundred bucks you will need for photographic lights and stands? Then pick up some clip-on utility lights from your local hardware store for something like $6 each. Clip them to the tops of doors, the backs of chairs, or to ladders.

Hatchet lighting.

This is Chrisie, rim-lighted. The light is just out of frame to the right, practically aimed at the camera. To pull off this effect, someone has to hold a piece of black posterboard over the light to eliminate flare

Sinister lighting.

Leandra holds the light over Sterling to show how the sinister effect of the last picture was achieved.

And here's a different look . . .

. . . brought off by having Leandra hold a light that shines up into her face.

Mark simply holds one of the clip-on lights. A second clip-on light has been clipped onto the back of a chair.

TRY THIS

Get your hands on a three-fixture lighting kit with stands. Buy the set or check one out from your filmmaking class. Get a couple of friends together and do steps 1 through 6 above. If possible, tell a little story that depends heavily on your lighting schemes for meaning or mood. You could get jokey about this, like changing the lighting incomprehensively with each shot.

SCHOOL YOURSELF

Read *Video Lighting*, by Des Lyner and Graham Swainson (Focal Press, 2000)—a short, readable primer on lighting. They are much better on three-point lighting than I am.

Also, study any feature film for lighting. What is the dominant strategy: soft, diffuse, modeled (molded), harsh, finessed and subtle, unidirectional, multidirectional? Try to figure out where the lights are placed beyond the frames. Here are some good recent films to study for lighting: *Bad Education*, *Napoleon Dynamite*, *Millions*, *Layer Cake*, *Shakespeare's Merchant of Venice*, *Batman Begins*, and *Sensitive Skin*.

And here are some classic films worth seeing for their lighting: *Gone With the Wind*, *The Wizard of Oz*, *The Sweet Smell of Success*, *The Graduate*, *The Godfather*, *Chinatown*, and *E.T.: The Extraterrestrial*.

Shooting Indoors with Super 8 Film

Practically speaking, there is only one "positive" or reversal super 8 stock extant, and that is Kodachrome 40, which needs tons of light to record an acceptable image indoors. You are practically obliged to acquire a three-fixture lighting set if you want to get good-looking interior footage. Plus, you will have to use something like 500-watt photographic bulbs available only from camera stores. (Watch out. Fixtures with these bulbs get very, very hot.) Shooting super 8 under lights requires that you:

From Byron Watkins' untitled poker film.

- ➤ Use so-called *type-A* bulbs or you will not get natural-seeming color rendition.
- ➤ Make sure your camera's built-in filter is set to the bulb setting and not to the sun setting, or else footage will come out orangish.
- ➤ Use only fixtures with porcelain bases for these 500-watt bulbs.

Working with Available Indoor Lighting

At one point in Byron Watkins' untitled poker film, the cheater goes off to stuff cards up his sleeve. Byron, the cheater, had someone shoot him doing this next to an ordinary table lamp—no other lights. The result is appealingly and appropriately darkish.

To illuminate his *I'm In the Jail House Now*, David purposely did not want to use anything like movable photographic lights. Instead, he employed several common household lights and positioned them in various ways to light the storyteller.

I'm in the Jail House Now

This three-minute film is by David Lennon, who shot it as an exercise in lighting. It's based on the song of the title. An older guy laments a life ill spent. As his narrative changes, so does the lighting.

The Intruder

Kevin Brunkhardt's reasons for making this film about a home invasion were similar to David Lennon's—namely, to experiment with available light and lighting. This shot shows the homeowner emerging from a well-lit room into a darkened room in which he thinks the intruder may be

So simple. The kitchen light provides strong backlighting.

hiding. Darkness, of course, cranks up the drama. Lighting? Nothing special. Kevin just left the dining room light on and turned off all the lights in the living room. Naturally, he shot at night.

Night Shooting with Available Outdoor Lighting

As I keep saying, it's just amazing how well modern video cameras perform in low-light conditions, including night shooting. You can get pretty good footage working under streetlights and by the light of storefronts. To be sure, the footage will be grainy and color values very weak, but minimalists just go with this. It feels more authentic.

November Apparition by John Neeley and Katherine Jose. The only illumination is a security light off-camera right.

But don't just set up and start shooting. Note where the streetlight is. If you have a choice of whether, say, a parked car can be a few feet forward or a few feet backward, or whether someone walking down the sidewalk could start walking a few feet forward or backward, then take the trouble to note how the streetlight shines down on the subject from different angles. If you set the subject back from the streetlight, she will be more or less fully illuminated. If you have the subject walk forward directly under the streetlight, she will be more darkly illuminated with deep shadows under her eyes and chin. The point: If you can't move the lights, move the subject to capture light most meaningfully.

Try This

Experiment with moving the subject forward and backward, side to side, under an overhead lighting fixture in a garage or under a streetlight. Take some test footage.

Pay attention to light and shadow when you shoot outdoors. I had a chance to get the right balance of sun and shade when I shot one of the characters in *Photo Finish* in an old shed with sunlight streaming through cracks. I spent some time positioning Bobbi a few inches backward and forward to get the look I wanted.

Daylight Shooting

As I have suggested elsewhere, you probably do not want to shoot toward the sun. Your subjects will go dark and, to repeat, may even turn into silhouettes. You may be tempted to constantly set exposure manually to brighten up dark subjects because it produces a look you like.

On the other hand, if look is not especially important to you, then plan your outdoor shoots so that the sun is *behind* the camera or maybe at something like a right angle to the camera and subject. The more the subject is fully front-illuminated by the sun, the more your exposure will be bright and clean with no shadows.

TRY THIS

Go outside and find a place to shoot that is rich in sun and shadow. Get a buddy to do something in front of the camera. Film her in various degrees of light—nearly all shadow, partly shadow, mainly sunlight. Consider waiting until the end of the day when shadows get long. Long shadows are always more interesting than the short shadows you get around noon. This little film doesn't have to be long or fancy. Shoot some shots two ways: toward the sun and with the sun at your back. Get the hang of working with and against the sun. Try manual exposure when shooting toward the sun. I almost forgot: Bring a white posterboard with you. Get a helper to use it to reflect light onto the subject. Do the white posterboard-reflected light thing for subjects who stand or sit in the shade while the backdrop is sunny.

Lucky you if you are reading all this in the winter or the early spring or late fall when shadows are long. As I said, the longer the shadows, the more interesting the lighting possibilities.

Daylight Shooting with Super 8

Kodachrome is really meant for shooting outdoors when the light is pretty good. It will look gorgeous in full sunshine. But it also comes across appealingly moody under overcast skies and positively enchanting in fog or mist. *Just make sure that the filter switch is set to the sun symbol (even when shooting under cloudy conditions or in the shade) instead of the bulb symbol.* If you don't, your footage will come out bluish. But then that may be just the look you are after.

TRY THIS

Now plan an all-out, serious film. By this, I mean that you are serious about lighting. Do as many things with light and shadow that I've discussed as you can. If you wish, let one of these prompts inspire you: fear, big knife, serenity, new baby, domestic quarrel, good dream, bad dream, romance, assertiveness, hope, despair, suicide, mom, dad.

OPTICS

Optics has to do with how lenses process the world they look out on. *Process* refers to two main optical qualities: *perspective* and *focus*.

Perspective

You know about *psychological* perspective. You plead with your friend who is all broken up because the loser she was dating dumped her. You murmur, "Hey, the guy was a jerk. Let him go. Get some perspective."

Then there is *optical* perspective. Your eyes are optical. They see far off things or close things in a certain fixed way. But camera lenses, also optical, often see things differently. They make some things seem farther off than what your eyes tell you or closer than what your eyes tell you, and this quality of changing perspective may be just what you want.

Distance in Wide Angle and Telephoto

Subjects appear much farther off when viewed in *wide-angle* zoom lens setting than when viewed in *telephoto* zoom lens setting. Wide angle means zoomed *out* all the way; telephoto means zoomed *in* all the way. "Normal perspective," if that's what you want, is achieved by setting the zoom ring somewhere between the extremes of wide angle and telephoto. If you need to be perfectly accurate and realistic, do this: Sight your subject with just one eye. Then, while looking through the camera with your other eye, zoom in and out until the subject is the same size as seen by your unaided eye. This lens setting becomes "normal."

SCHOOL YOURSELF

Investigate perspective by taping subjects with your camera in wide angle and telephoto. Here's how: Take two people out to a baseball diamond in a park. Or if you can't get people to go with you, take a couple of folding chairs. Have one person (or chair) stand on second base and the second person (or chair) way out in center field. You stand behind home plate with your camera and line up the two people (or the two chairs) in the viewfinder of your camera by getting them to move a little to the left or right. Zoom in all the way and note the size of each person relative to the viewfinder and relative to each other. Next, zoom out. Everything will seem farther off.

Walk up to the person on second base to make him the same size as you viewed him before in telephoto. Before, in telephoto, you were fifty or sixty feet back; in wide angle, you'll be within a few feet of the guy on second. Now look through the camera and note the apparent distance between your two stooges. In wide angle, the guy way out in center field will appear really far away, like he's standing in the world's largest ballpark. After this, view the same subjects with your unaided eye. So you see, perspective is relative.

Two shots of a fire hydrant and a parked car. The car seems farther off in the first shot in wide angle. For the second shot, I wanted to keep the fire hydrant framed the same size, so I set the camera twelve times as far back and shot in telephoto— twelve times because the camera's zoom is 12:1. So while the fire hydrant is the same size in both shots, the car seems much closer in telephoto. Telephoto compresses space.

Two shots at a mall, the first in wide angle, the second in telephoto. The first shot renders mall walkers less compacted than the second. As I've said, telephoto compresses space, while wide angle spreads it out.

Focus, Auto and Manual

The chances are good that your camera has a feature called *automatic focus* or *autofocus*, which means the lens automatically focuses on subjects by a kind of optical triangulation process. But the camera can be fooled. It doesn't know that you want subject A in focus; instead, it focuses on B, who, because of how you have framed, happens to be dominant in the field of view. If this happens, you have to flip off auto and go to manual, focusing on the subject by gradually turning the focusing ring on the end of the lens.

Beware of autofocus when you are taking a shot in which subjects rapidly change their range from each other and the camera. The camera won't know what to do. You might get some unwanted blurry footage for a second or two, until the focusing mechanism makes up its mind. Far better to focus manually, in which case *you* control who or what is in focus. In fact, the more you make films, and take shooting seriously, the more you will give up autofocus and focus manually.

Field of View

The camera's lens has a fan-shaped view of the world. The view in the finder fans out from narrow if the subject is close to wide when the subject is far away. You probably knew this just from taking snapshots. For a wide field of view, you have to get back, but the price you pay is that the people become proportionately "smaller"—not really smaller, of course, but optically smaller. What you might not have known is how field of view is much narrower for telephoto than for wide angle. How much narrower? If you have a 12:1 zoom lens, the field of view in telephoto will be only a twelfth as wide as in wide angle. Maybe this would be easier to understand if the term were "angle of view."

Depth of Focus (Depth of Field)

In general, subjects at different distances from the camera will be more likely to stay in focus in wide angle than in telephoto. In wide angle, you might be able to hold focus for both foreground and background subjects, but not in telephoto. In telephoto, you'll have to focus on one or the other but you can't get both in focus. You may have to flip from auto focus to manual to do this.

Another mall shot in telephoto with foreground subjects out of focus. In telephoto (zoomed-in) lens setting, you can keep foreground or background subjects in focus, but not both.

Often, to focus and frame a subject in telephoto, with its restricted field of view, you have to position them precisely and focus carefully. Again, this means going to manual focus.

The more you shoot in telephoto, the more these remarks pertain. As I have said, you have far fewer focusing problems in wide angle.

The technical term for *depth of focus* is *depth of field*.

Minimum Focusing Range

You want to be on intimate terms with your camera. One thing you want to know about it is how close in it will focus. So . . .

Determine how close you can focus with your camera. View a subject like a magazine cover at arm's length in wide angle with the camera set to focus automatically. Does the cover appear in focus? Is the printing sharp? Now gradually move the camera in closer and note how close you can get to the cover and still hold focus. You'll probably be able to get within inches of the cover and keep it in focus. Of course, the closer you move in, the more detail you pick up.

Do the same thing in telephoto, only you'll have to use a tripod because the image will jump around. And you'll have to get farther back, say four or five feet. Compare minimum in-focus width in wide angle and telephoto.

Watch face shot just inches from the camera's lens.

Steadiness in Wide Angle and Telephoto

I've said this before, but it bears repeating: You will get the steadiest, smoothest, handheld footage in wide angle. Meanwhile, subjects shot handheld in telephoto will jerk and jump around and will be hard on the eyes of many viewers. You may want exactly this, however.

I've also mentioned the image-stabilization feature of digital cameras before. It goes a long way toward smoothing out handheld footage and is a truly useful feature of digital cameras.

Zooming

Zooming is potent, so handle with care. There are two kinds of zooms:

Optical Zooming

This is accomplished by gradually moving elements of the camera's lens, which you initiate by pressing the zoom-lens rocker arm or button. Most modern DV cameras have zoom ratios of at least 10:1. This means that a subject viewed in telephoto is ten times larger than the same subject viewed in wide angle, though field of view decreases ten times, as I have said.

Also, with most cameras, you have some control over the rate of zooming. Press the zoom rocker lightly, the zoom is slow; press it harder, the zoom speeds up.

Digital Zooming

Zooming into a dome over a Starbucks in a Fresno shopping center. Optical wide angle.

Practically all DV cameras come with digital zooming. This means that the computer inside the camera takes over at the far end of the optical zoom and keeps magnifying the subject 50, 100, or even 450(!) times compared with viewing the subject in optical wide angle.

Digital zooming sounds intriguing, but it has two serious drawbacks. First, you need to be out in some very big space, like in the middle of the Mojave Desert, to make any use of it at all; and second, the subject is never in sharp focus.

Optical zoom in.

Digital zoom in. The letters, though really big, have gone fuzzy. But don't despair. Just don't zoom in so far.

When to Zoom and When Not to Zoom

So like I said, the zoom is a powerful technique. Don't overdo it. Zoom minimally. Films that zoom too much often seem pretentious and out of control. Consider *zooming in* when you want to:

- Go from a wide view to a tight view gradually, and not abruptly, as cutting does.
- Reveal a detail in the setting gradually—you make viewers wait a few seconds, the length of the zoom, before you reveal the detail.
- Suggest a gradual or growing awareness or importance of a character—zoom in on the subject's face.
- Reframe a subject without later cutting, as in a long take.

Consider *zooming out* when you:

- Want to place a subject in a larger setting gradually—instead of cutting from a tight shot to a wide shot.
- Have to reframe to show wider action.
- Want to integrate a tight action or setting with a wider action or setting.
- Need to reframe a subject without later cutting.

Most experienced filmmakers use their zoom lens for framing their subjects, not for actual zooming.

How Zooming Helps Documentary Filmmaking

Bob Warkentin happened to film a fight among some young people at an outdoor shopping mall. The stills below show how he put his zoom lens to good use—while standing back so as not to intrude.

First, a wide shot. Bob seems really far back from the girl, and he was.

Then a telephoto shot, which makes Bob look like he was practically standing in front of the girl. But he was in the same position he was for the first shot.

7

Deeper into Editing

*E*diting has a lot to do with temperament. You could learn a thing or two about what kind of artist you are by working through this chapter. Plus, this chapter provides you with some very practical advice for communicating through one of the most under-appreciated aspects of media, the *cut*.

SOME REAL BASIC THINGS

Here are a few fundamentals that every editor considers.

Trim, Trim, Trim

You edit a film by *subtracting, taking away, snipping, trimming*. The footage you took out there with all those good people and wonderful settings has much potential, but it has to be sculpted, the way a sculptor starts with a big granite block and chips away and chips away to produce something smaller and finer.

When you filmed, you were expansive—you took a lot of footage, and retook, and improvised, and followed your shot list, and deviated from it—and that was fine. That is exactly the way you should have filmed. But when you edit, you create by removing, getting down to less. This is true of all filmmaking, but especially of minimalist filmmaking.

From *The Job*. When Adam Klusener took this shot, he started it with the guy getting off the elevator, upper right. But how long do we have to see the guy walk to his car, lower left? Adam wisely cut many seconds from the head of the shot.

Trimming Heads and Tails

For starters, you trim the heads and tails (starts and ends) of shots. You sense when a shot is running too long. And you sense when a shot peaks, and should be cut at that moment, instead of letting it go on and on.

Splitting Shots

Next, it will occur to you to split shots and delete the portion you can't use. Or retain both parts and work them into different places in the film. Or you'll figure out that you can cut a shot into two, three, or more pieces and use the clips here and there. Then all these clips will probably need to have their heads and tails trimmed.

Dumping Adored Footage

Everyone takes shots they are totally in love with. Someone was backlit by the sun just right. That zoom in to the little girl turned out terrific because she broke out in a smile at just the right moment. But be careful. If the footage doesn't really work in the film, you shouldn't retain it. Love blinds you, just as in life. Getting real on adored footage is like getting real on babes and dudes you don't really need in your life. You have to ask yourself, *Do these shots really work in the film as a whole or are they just ornamental?* If the latter, dump them.

Rough Cut, Fine Cut

In the old days, before digital editing, editors thought in terms of a "rough cut," which merely brought together all usable shots in a right order but which inevitably ran very long, and a "fine cut," which approximated the finished film and was much shorter and tighter. But just as word processing killed the concept of the discrete "draft" among serious writers, so digital, nonlinear editing did the same to notions of discrete cuts. They now blend.

Still, you may want to work this way. So you get all your usable shots on your time-line, no matter how long they run, then start trimming and deleting to get the film as a whole down to the "right" length. Work from longer to shorter.

Right Length?

Now I get metaphysical. Every film has a right length, embedded in its soul. You must find it. *It* wants you to find it. Total running time depends on purpose, mood, action, event, story, and establishing the right balance between explicitly disclosing and discreetly suggesting. Flip ahead to pages 146–49 for a list of editing procedures you can carry out with both iMovie HD6 (for Macs) and Studio Media Suite Version 10 (for PCs), the two eminently useful editing programs I so heartily recommend.

REVIEW: A FEW BASIC CUTS

I bring these over from both chapter 4 ("The Starter Film") and chapter 5 ("Deeper into Shooting, One"). These basics occur in *all* films—Hollywood, foreign, indies:

The master shot. If you work from a master shot, keep in mind that you can cut it up in several pieces and use it in several places in the editing of a scene. You can go back and forth between wide (the master shot) and tight (follow-up shots).

Master shot from Joe Doyle's *The End*. The couple acted out four versions of the story.

As an exercise in editing, Joe Doyle actually cut his *The End* four different ways. Way one: She walks away. Way two: He walks away. Way three: Both walk away. Way four: They hug. Joe used just the one setup shown at right—a master shot of master shots—for nearly all the shots he needed for all four versions. Then he took tighter follow-up shots—close-ups and medium shots—and he had to get tape of the boy and the girl walking away.

The match cut. The match cut is two successive shots of the same subject matched for position and motion. (Flip back to page 55.)

From *The Matrix* by Scott Donaghe. Match-cut across two clips as Trinity throws guy to the ground. This means the poor guy had to be tossed around this way twice—once for one shot, again for the other, and maybe two or three more times during rehearsals.

Cross-cutting. This is alternating clips from at least two long-running shots that originally ran rather long. (Flip back to page 53.)

To illustrate most of these techniques, following are some stills from Kevin Brunkhardt's version of *Macho Walk*.

Cross-cutting, cut-in, cutaway: You have to imagine a lot of cutting back and forth among these shots with many more clips than I am showing here. Kevin-opponent-Kevin-opponent-girl-Keven-opponent-girl-Kevin-opponent, and so on. Cut-in to fist suggests determination, courage. Cutaway to girl tells its own story.

Poignant Point-of-View Sequence about Loss of Habitat

Mike Gomez went out to the edge of Fresno where a lot of new homes were going up, camera at the ready. He managed to work up some feeling for displaced gophers:

Mike calls his film *There's No Place Like Home*.

"What's going on?"   "Holy shit!"   "This used to be a good neighborhood!"

STYLE: MONTAGE VERSUS MISE-EN-SCÈNE

Shooting is about style. And so is editing. Soon you will develop your own style of editing. Editing style is detectable and makes a difference, just as all other areas of human endeavor have styles and make differences.

Montage and *mise-en-scène* are French words. Montage comes from the word *monter*, meaning *to mount* and mise-en-scène is a term handed down from the stage that roughly translates to *setting the scene*. *Editing* is primary for montage filmmakers; *shooting* and *set dressing* are primary for mise-en-scène filmmakers.

Working Montage

Montage filmmakers like to cut their footage on the elaborate side and end up with a lot of relatively short-running shots. Mise-en-scène directors edit only minimally. They prefer longer-running shots and aren't too keen about cutting into them. It's like virgin footage—sacred, highly respected.

The montage editor worships at the shrine of cut and paste. For him, editing is high art. Filming is okay, but it's only a means to the end of advancing to the editing bench or computer, where he shapes the *real* film. Often a resourceful montage editor is able to completely change the meaning of his film through editing. Or tweak it in one direction or another. Or maybe he went out and filmed with no clear sense of what his film would be about. He discovers his film through editing.

HO.R.S.E., a Montage Film

This film makes a joke of athletic competition, and it is done entirely through editing. It's about two guys who don't know each other very well. They play a game of one-on-one basketball in the driveway of a suburban home. One guy is big and tall and beats the shit out of the other guy. Then the little guy suggests they play "HORSE," which goes like this: One guy shoots, and if he makes the basket, the other guy has to make the same shot, or he gets a letter, "H." First player to get "HORSE" loses.

Overhanding a ball from behind a tree?

The little guy then makes five incredible shots. Here are three:

H: He goes way across the street, throws the basketball overhead like a baseball, and, incredibly, makes the shot. The big guy can't make it, so he gets an "H."

O: The little guy goes in the backyard, throws the ball over the roof of the garage, and, incredibly, makes the shot. Big guy can't follow suit, so he takes an "O."

R: The little guy gets in a car, drives down the street, and underhands the ball out the window toward the basket. Again, miraculously, the ball drops through the hoop. Hapless big guy takes the "R" hit.

No problem, thanks to editing.

And so on. Now of course you and I know that not even Michael Jordan could make all these shots in a row. So how was it done? It was all brought off in the editing.

So what may seem like one clip in the finished film is really two. The timing of the two clips has to be matched so that the two clips don't run any longer than one clip would. Of course, no one is fooled by this editing technique. It's just great fun for everyone—filmmaker, actors, audience. *H.O.R.S.E.* was made by Joel Dodds and Chris Urhle.

Working Mise-En-Scène

Mise-en-scène filmmakers work far differently. They know, absolutely, what kind of film they want to make from the moment they pick up their camera. They had it all planned out the night, or more likely, the week or month before. To them, their footage is fine just the way it came out of the camera. It won't need a lot of cutting up. Maybe some tightening, but nothing surgical. Instead of having filmed everything in sight, mise-en-scène filmmakers film only things they know bear on the *film in their mind*. There is only one possible film, the one they shot.

Or the mise-en-scène filmmaker invested a lot in particular shots—props, backdrops, time of day, expressive composition, or a long take involving lots of rehearsals. She'll be damned if she'll cut it all up. She wants viewers to see *the shot,* not cuts.

The Mise-en-scène Art Films of Anoush Ekparian

For Anoush, shooting is primal. She does edit, but only minimally—trimming heads and tails mainly. I described her *Above All Else* in chapter 1. Anoush had ten or twelve people say the same line in close-up: "Above all else, guard your heart, for it is the wellspring of life." It's *how* these people say this line and *how* they seem to relate to being taped that counts most, not any clever cutting. *This film is on the DVD.*

SCHOOL YOURSELF

Watch *Citizen Kane* and *Stranger Than Paradise*, two famous mise-en-scène films favoring long takes and minimal editing. The former film is, of course, a classic, a masterpiece; the latter, a highly respected art film.

Also, watch Alfred Hitchcock's *Rope*, a feature film made in 1948 consisting of only seven runs of the camera, each run consuming the entire reel of film loaded in the old Mitchell 35 mm cameras used in Hollywood at the time. This means that for this film, at least, Hitchcock was the champion mise-en-scène filmmaker, although, back then, no one made much of a fuss about it and they certainly didn't use French words to describe Hitchcock's technique. Still, it is fun to note how Hitchcock cut *within those sixteen-minute takes* by having people move and by recomposing with camera moves.

Working in the Middle

This is just all theory. I don't expect you to be so doctrinaire. Most filmmakers stick to the mid-range of style—working montage when that suits them, working mise-en-scène when appropriate. If they take a shot that feels fine as it is, without being cut into, they retain it. On the other hand, there are times when they feel like going montage. The only way to bring off a particular scene is to cut, cut, cut.

SCHOOL YOURSELF

Watch *Alien*, directed by Ridley Scott, then *Aliens* by James Cameron. The first film favors the long take with drama building within the shot and scary stuff going on (or imagined) off-camera. The action sequences of the second film are a blur of quick-cut shots. In fact, this film very well may have started the trend to super-fast cutting, which, while fresh in *Alien*, is getting old today.

After this, watch Scott's big hit *Gladiator*. The editing of the action is considerably quicker than in *Alien*, showing how Scott has been influenced by montage trends, maybe even against his own instincts. Note particularly when they try to behead Russell Crowe near the start of the film. How does he get out of it? He has the film's editing to thank. His wiggling loose is cut so fast that you can't understand it. You go, "Oh, well."

Also, watch any popular Hollywood action movie or thriller and study it for editing style. It will probably change with the drama. Action scenes will be shot and edited montage; calmer interludes, more mise-en-scène. A good film to study this way is *Batman Begins*.

CONTROLLING TIME

Film editors often affect viewers' sense of passing time, for the film as a whole or for any particular scene. True, film time is occasionally determined by shooting in slow or fast motion, and you can manipulate time with your computer by having the editing program convert shots to slow or fast motion.

However, controlling time by pure, old-fashioned editing technique is quite different and is felt throughout your film, not just at special moments. It doesn't call attention to itself nearly as much as slow or fast motion. In fact, much of the success of your film depends on how effectively you can control time with your editing. If you cut shots (and sequences) too long, viewers drift. Cut them too short, and viewers don't know what hit them.

Expanding Time

Film editors expand time by:

> - Letting heads and tails of shots run on the long side.
> - Overlapping action.
> - Including a lot of optional shots of secondary subjects.

The ever-fecund Byron Watkins expanded time as a visual joke in his *K.C. and Byron's Day of Fun*. K.C. and Byron are just fooling around one Saturday afternoon. They get some fast food, then go to a park. After this, a title sets us up for the "World's Longest Touchdown Pass." Byron goes out for a pass. K.C., twirling a football, frowns and waves Byron farther out. Cut to Byron, still running out. Cut back to K.C., waving Byron still farther out. Cut to Byron, still running. Cut to K.C., still waving. This gets to be funny, and the source of the humor is our old friend, cross-cutting—only cross-cutting way on the long side. Finally, K.C. throws the ball. It arcs up and arcs up. It hangs and hangs. Cut to Byron gawking over his shoulder, running like a madman. Cut back to ball, still hanging. Cut to Byron, still gawking and running, knowing he'll have to go *way out*. Cut to ball, finally beginning its descent. Cut to Byron's legs, churning like crazy. Then, finally, the ball arcs down into the frame, and Byron makes a spectacular catch. Viewers laugh. (Flip to the next page for frames of this sequence.)

Example: Expanding Time for an After-Sex Sequence

Suppose you want to create a languid, after-sex sequence. Excuse me: I guess it's okay to mention sex in a book like this. Sex and art are often great bed-partners. Anyway, a woman rises from her bed in the morning, a bed she shared last night with a guy. The way she looks, she doesn't want to leave this guy, probably her lover. The guy still sleeps. Now to the point: You shoot her getting out of bed three times, maybe with different frames or angles. Later, you cut the three shots so that they overlap in space and time, instead of match-cutting them to keep space and time unified and continuous, which is the usual way to do this. Maybe you dissolve them. Of course, this isn't realistic. It's formalistic—arty. But you aren't after realism. You want to create the languid feel of the morning-after, solely through editing. (Flip ahead to page 130 for more about dissolves and their uses.)

You have to imagine about a dozen clips interspersed among these five clips, which cross-cut K.C. and Byron *and* show the ball in a high arc in the sky, hanging, hanging.

K.C. waves Byron out.

Byron runs.

KC about to throw.

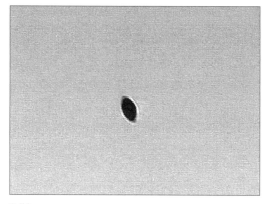

Ball hangs.

Byron snags the ball.

Compressing Time

Usually though in films time is compressed, not stretched out. In a typical Hollywood movie, time is compressed a dozen times for every instance it's expanded. For example, how much time *in real life* might it take a lover to rise from her partner, go into the bathroom, and get ready for work? Ten minutes? We might get it down to a half a minute by first filming ten or twenty seconds each of her doing all of this:

- rising
- walking into the bathroom
- showering
- drying off
- getting into panties and bra
- finishing her dressing
- leaning to a mirror and applying makeup
- doing her hair
- gathering up purse and laptop
- looking in on her still-sleeping lover one more time
- going out the door

After you pull all these shots together to make a sequence, you trim the hell out of them. You get each shot down to, say, two seconds—the peak or climax of each shot. Are two seconds too short? Not for cinematic communication. One second per shot would probably be enough. Thus what in *real time* took ten minutes takes only ten seconds or so in *reel time* or film time. Contemporary audiences see this kind of thing all the time and would understand.

Making a Pizza in Sixty Seconds

How long does it take to make a pizza *plus* sprinkle some crunched-up cockroach parts on it? Fifteen minutes? In her *Was a Good Boy, Was a Bad Pizza*, Annette Marin cuts the process down to twenty seconds with the following edited sequence (see next two pages).

Pizza guy looks at floor.

Sees cockroach.

Stomps!

Crunches.

Mixes cockroach parts in with olives, pepperoni, etc.

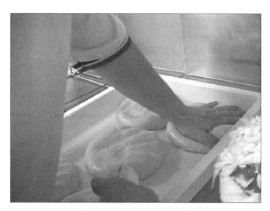

Presses out dough.

Into restroom.

Sprinkles scouring powder on pizza.

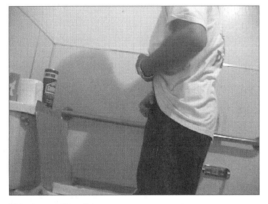

Urinates on the pizza.

Into the oven.

Then . . .

Out of the oven.

This is the unsuspecting customer who comes in to pick up the pizza. Did I mention that the pizza guy is her ex? He wants to get back at her.

Using a Cutaway To Compress Time

This is an old editing standby. Nearly all films use it. You are stuck with a long-running shot, like two guys trying to lug a dead body off the bed of a truck and drag it off to the weeds. You filmed all of it in one continuous single take, but it takes over a minute for the whole thing to play out. If you had a third person, say, an impatient woman, to cut away to, you could compress the main action considerably, like this:

1. Two guys tug body off truck bed (four seconds).
2. Cut away to woman looking on impatiently (two seconds).
3. Guys drag body to weeds (four seconds).
4. Cut away again to woman still looking, following (two seconds).
5. Guys stop dragging, far off the highway (two seconds).
6. Woman comes up to them (four seconds).

Total running time: eighteen seconds

Using Dissolves and Fades to Compress Time

An abortion obviously is a complicated clinical procedure that takes a considerable amount of time. Kathy Verzosa based her *Little Star* on an abortion that takes place in only twenty seconds of screen time by showing the father in the hall of the hospital

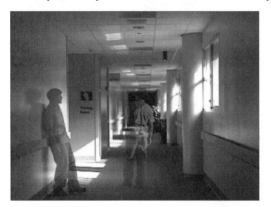

One shot dissolves into the next to suggest a passing of time.

during the operation waiting in several poses—leaning against the wall, pacing, and so on. The poses are connected with *dissolves*, which to most viewers suggest a passing of time. Kathy never shows the procedure. She filmed the father by mounting the camera on a tripod so that the background did not shift or change from take to take.

Fade-outs (to black) and fade-ins (from black) also suggest a passing of time. Dissolves and fades are part of our film heritage. We learned these things as children when our moms plopped us down in front of the TV to watch *Scooby-Doo* or whatever. Aren't you glad now she did that?

If you film in super 8 and do not use the services of a film lab, you have to create the fades and dissolves in your camera. Not all super 8 cameras do this, however. If you work in digital, it's possible to do fades in your camera (but not dissolves), but don't. Instead, make both fades and dissolves while editing. Both the iMovie and Studio support fades, dissolves, and about a dozen other transitions (Flip ahead to pages 248–49 for a longer discussion of computer-genreated transitions.)

Employing a Montage to Compress Time

The term *montage*, which I mentioned back on pages 122–23 to describe a certain style of filmmaking based on elaborate editing, has another meaning. It refers to a sequence of shots meant to compress hours, days, or even months or years into just a few moments of screen time. It's film's way of generalizing and covering time (and often also space) fast. Below is a montage from the screenplay *Bomb Ready to Explode*, which is found in chapter 9.

```
6. Montage. We see the couple in the kitchen. Close-ups of straw-
   berries and whipped cream. At the table, eating the dessert,
   appearing to talk. In the living room, with the TV on low, still
   talking. In the bedroom, in bed, the room darkened, Thomas still
   talking. Actually, Thomas does all of the talking. Vera listens.
   But when we see her, she isn't exactly looking sympathetic.
   She's more scared than sympathetic. During this sequence, Vera's
   facial expression changes from sympathy and understanding to a
   gradually backing away from Thomas and mounting fear. We hear
   Thomas's voiceover through all of this.

                            Thomas
                     (voiceover, to Vera)
            I can't seem to help myself. I did the
            time, too. I was away from children.
            I talked to the shrink in the joint.
            He was a nice guy and all, but you know,
            he never fixed me. I'd see pictures
            of kids in magazines, and want to be
            with them. So I get out, I start a new
            life. But I can't put the thing down.
            It's like some kind of addiction.
            Like I'm hooked on little children.
```

This scene would play in about a minute, yet it covers several hours of the couple's evening. It picks up only highlights. Viewers know that screen time isn't real time; it's been compressed to speed the story—actually, to show Vera's growing anxiety.

Watch *The Fugitive*, starring Harrison Ford, and watch how Ford's trial is edited—filmed and edited. It occurs about seven minutes into the film. As you know, movie trials usually take ten or fifteen minutes, but Ford's trial unfolds in about three. Study it closely as a primo example of the compression of time through editing.

Also, watch these films, notable for their treatment of time:

➤ *The Godfather*—Slow motion: Sonny gets gunned down at the tollbooth.

➤ *Bonnie and Clyde*—Slow motion: Bonnie and Clyde get gunned down in their car at the end of the film.

➤ *The Wild Bunch*—Slow motion again: The final shoot-out between The Bunch and elements of the Mexican army, near the end of the film.

➤ *Potemkin*—Time expanded through editing: The brutal Odessa steps sequence when Cossacks massacre civilians. Watch for the famous unattended baby carriage.

Without going into detail, here are a few more films famous for their treatment of time: *Citizen Kane*; *The Pawnbroker*; *The Godfather, Part II*; *Stranger Than Paradise*; *Back to the Future*; *Bringing Out the Dead*; *Pulp Fiction*; *Memento*.

Editing in Real Time

Actually, it's not often that filmmakers edit in *real time*, which means the scene, sequence, or entire film runs just as long on the screen as in real life.

One film I describe in this book that comes close to being edited in real time is *The Silence Between Us* by Katherine Jose and Sarah Hagey. (*This film is on the DVD.*) It's about a girl leaving a guy she probably still loves. She puts on makeup, gathers a few things, kisses her sleeping (ex)lover, and leaves with a suitcase. I guess in real life it would take ten minutes to do this. Katherine and Sarah's film runs close to that. (Flip ahead to page 176 for a thematic analysis of this film.)

Controlling Time When Cross-Cutting

When you cross-cut, or alternate clips of two long-running shots, you have three choices. You can edit to:

1. Keep time continuous and realistic

2. Expand time

3. Compress time

If you edit to keep time continuous and realistic, you, in effect, match-cut the two shots *in time,* so that what you cut out of shot A runs exactly the same length of time as the clip from shot B, and what you cut out of shot B runs exactly the same time as the clip from shot A. If you edit to expand time, you overlap the action of the two clips and expand the sense of passing time, so that overall the sequence runs longer than it would in real time. If you edit to compress time, you would cut the clips shorter and eliminate action to speed up the sequence.

PACING AND TEMPO

Pacing has to do with how slow or fast a film seems to unfold. This depends, of course, on the story, the action, and the mood—or if it's a documentary, on the amount of information you need to impart.

Chris Housepian and Dan Huffman's fine chase film, *Revenge,* is fast-paced, as we would expect a chase to be, whereas *The Silence Between Us* is slow-paced. It's meditative and private. The two films have about the same total running time.

Marshall Chambers' super 8 film *Lucky Guy* is slow-paced. Shots run long. It's a dream-like, existential film, set out in the middle of nowhere, and the hitchhiker has some kind of problem with people. Slow editing contributes to both the mood and the meaning. You have time to think.

On the other hand, *Ketchup* plays fast. It's a kind of hit film about a woman who has to pretend to kill her lover. The following frames from clips are a good example of cross-cutting, or cutting between two settings. First setting: Man alone in his room, fearing murder. Second setting: Woman entering building and ascending stairs. Back and forth. Room, stairs, room, stairs. Faster and faster. Until the woman enters the room—they embrace.

Scan the frames on the next page as you would look at a fast-cut scene in a movie.

SCHOOL YOURSELF

Study youth-targeted commercials to get the hang of fast pacing. You've probably already done this. A lot has to do with shot length, which is very short in TV commercials, not just to impart zippiness to the product, but because there isn't much actual time to make the pitch.

Also, study music videos on MTV and similar channels for quick cutting.

Seven clips from *Ketchup*. Fast pacing creates drama, especially when viewers don't know the man and woman are really lovers.

Woman enters building.

Man worried about being taken out.

Woman on stairs.

Man hears woman on stairs.

Woman enters apartment.

Man draws gun.

They are lovers.

Tempo is harder to explain. Think music. Think beat. Your film ought to have a rhythm to it. Not exactly a ta-ta-tum, ta-ta-tum, but a sense that all the shots are running the right length—not too fast, not too slow—and running the right length in relation to each other and to the film as a whole. You look at your film and think, *that shot runs too long* or *that shot runs way too short.* Many film editors have a good musical sense.

Film tempo is, in fact, a kind of music. Editors often cut their films as if they were composing music. A film *moves*, or as the old jazz guys used to say, *it swings.*

Editing Rhythmically

This means that all clips in a sequence run exactly the same length. This is easy—computer editing programs tell you how long each shot runs. When you *cut, cut, cut* like this, each shot running the same length, you are creating a certain kind of nonmusical music.

TRY THIS

Make a simple film in which the passing of time is important. Consider it an opportunity to editorially control time. Make time the main thing. Imitate (or emulate) cinematic ideas that you picked up in your viewing of the films I listed throughout this chapter.

CONTROLLING SPACE

The film editor is also deeply involved in the presentation of space. Story films don't make sense if viewers can't tell where they are. Nor do documentaries.

The Classic Sequence

The *classic sequence* refers to the establishment of setting by *first* showing a location in extreme wide angle, *then* cutting to a long or medium shot and some kind of action, *and finally* cutting to a close-up. So first viewers get oriented spatially, *then* the action unfolds. This practice assumes that viewers have short attention spans, because the editor cuts back to a snippet of the opening extreme wide-angle shot to *reestablish* space.

Actually, there is another reason for cutting to the extreme wide-angle, setting-dominated shot, and that is to *disengage* viewers and give them some "space" to think about what they have seen.

Establishing shot.

Closer shot.

Closer still.

Reestablishing shot.

The classic sequence in a film about one-on-one basketball by Chris Housepian and Dan Huffman. The film is called *White Men Can Jump*.

Variations on the Classic Sequence

Consider withholding the wide shot until near the end of the sequence. Start off with close-ups. Keep viewers in the dark as to where they are. You may have a good dramatic reason for doing this.

Tale to Tell: Working with Limited Footage of a Setting

Once a mountain resort hired me to make a promotional film that was supposed to feature summer activities. However, the weekend I shot fell on Halloween, and it was chilly in the mountains. The leaves of the oaks, poplars, and maples had already turned yellow. Also, most of the people at a dance—footage of which I just had to have—were in costume, which would make no sense if the setting were supposed to be summery. So as best I could, I shot around the stuff I couldn't use. I shot people at the dance who were out of costume. If I found a patch of meadow that was still green, I shot that. And I shot lots of stands of pines with their evergreen needles. I got a couple to take off their jackets so I could film them walking down the sidewalk past stores in their shirtsleeves, window shopping. I got a girl to go water-skiing and filmed her from the back of the boat. We all froze. "Smile," I directed her.

When I got to the editing, I really didn't have a whole lot to work with. I had wanted more summery-looking shots. The shots of the dance were severely cropped and tight to avoid picking up people in costume. The outdoor shots lacked panoramas so as not to pick up the red-leafed maples. To me, the editing was choppy and stilted, but I did what I'd been hired to do, which was nearly impossible—make a summer film in the mountains at the end of October. I premiered the film in the local beer hall for my employer, the staff, and some visitors—maybe fifty people in all. I got a big hand.

ESTABLISHING DIRECTIONAL CONTINUITY

Left and right are important, too. Like in a chase. If the chasee runs left in one shot, then the chaser had better run left, as well, in the next shot. I said this in chapter 5 but it's so fundamental that it bears repeating. If you don't keep track of what direction they are running in, your edited sequence will look like chaser and chasee are either (a) running away from each other or (b) running toward each other.

Say you have a scene where two people are talking, and you do it in close-ups of each. If one person is looking left and talking, the other had better look right—that is, apparently *at* the speaker. If the listener is also looking right, it will seem like her head is turned away, i.e., not interested. Even worse would be an edited sequence in which the speaker is looking left in one shot while the listener is facing right in the next shot. The sequence would come off as if they are talking with their backs to each other!

Two more clips from *The Matrix* by Scott Donaghe. If Trinity runs right-to-left, so must her pursuers.

Editing Moving-Camera Shots

Similar directional problems attend the editing of moving-camera shots. You could end up with a directional hodgepodge—that is, one shot going in this direction, the next in another direction, and the one after that in yet another direction. The result is a sequence of shots going every which way. Not graceful, unless you aim to be graceless. If you have a problem like this, maybe you can edit your way out of it. But if you can't, learn the lesson: pay attention to directional continuity during filming.

THE POETRY OF MOTION

The editing of a sequence of moving-camera shots is a kind of art form in its own right—*kinesthetic poetry*, I call it. It's the art of motion, based on smart craft. You do a cut, then look at it, *feel* it. It doesn't play right, so you recut it until the *flow* of shots satisfies you. (Thank goodness our computers let us undo!) You aren't satisfied with editing simply to tell a story or make things clear; you want to go beyond that to create a kind of dance with film, with things artfully blending into each other.

SANDING

Sanding is the term I use for final connecting and smoothing. It's like sanding a piece of wood, at first with rough sandpaper, then with fine sandpaper, until you have knocked off or smoothed out all rough places. As an editor, you look at your footage over and over to see where you can make shot-to-shot connections smoother. Usually, you want your film to play like silk, seamless and gleaming. You look at all of your outtakes, if you thought to save them. Maybe you retrieve a few snippets to insert here and there to improve continuity.

SHOCK AND VARIETY

On the other hand, your film might benefit from shock and variety in a few strategic places. Editorial shock is based on contrast or sudden, extreme clip changes. You can go, for example, from a slow-paced, serenely edited sequence to a fast-cut, in-your-face sequence. Or vice versa. An abrupt change of music—quiet to loud, classical to rap—or sound effects might accompany the cut to the new sequence and intensify the shock.

My *In Case of Earthquake*, a film about the demolition of an old building, cuts from a slow-paced scene of brick walls falling in slow motion, played to a wistful baroque *andante*, to a fast-cut, upbeat, vigorous montage of a new building under construction, played to toe-tapping rock. The first scene evokes nostalgia, loss, respect for the past; the second says, "Let's get on with life. We can't live in the past." Thus, the way you edit and pair music with your edited sequences is an important means of film communication.

The first shot is accompanied by gentle, mournful Bach; the second, by upbeat rock. Sudden change of image and music can be jarringly meaningful.

EDITORIAL METAPHORS

A metaphor, as you probably know, is a kind of comparison in which an everyday thing, like grass, becomes a grander thing like the hair of God, or light at the top of a stairway landing becomes truth. This last metaphor occurs in Marcelo Moriega's *Nocturne*. In this film, a figure is pacing back and forth in anguish in the old building that serves as the setting for his nightmare. Marcelo then cuts to a panther in a cage at Fresno's Chaffee Zoo. This cut deepens the first shot, by "saying" metaphorically that the dream figure is having a bad, claustrophobic time the way a caged-up animal feels claustrophobic.

Some people call this the "a + b = c" effect—that is, the whole is greater than the sum of the parts. The *a* means one thing, *b* another, but together, juxtaposed, they take on new meaning, *c*.

We can't help it. When one thing follows another, we automatically ponder what the two things in sequence mean.

TRY THIS

Rework some footage you have cut to include two shots in sequence that say something, that create a metaphor. Or splice a pair of shots that are more meaningful because they are juxtaposed.

EDITING DOCUMENTARIES

Many of the editorial choices I have explained for the story film apply equally to the documentary film.

Getting Clear on Purpose

However, before you can edit your documentary, you have to know your purpose for making it in the first place. Is it to give viewers a sense of what it feels like to do something or be in a certain place? Or do you want primarily to convey information? Both? What is your overall style—realistic, fanciful, interpretive, one-sided, multi-sided? Then select an editing style to suit your purpose.

Realistic or Something Else?

What kind of documentary are you doing? Is its approach matter-of-fact and realistic? Is it meant to persuade? Does it have a point of view, an axe to grind, a thesis? Or is its primary purpose to inform? If one of these, you probably want to adopt a no-frills editing style meant to be clear and discursive. You don't want to let your editing style overwhelm content. If, however, you are in the middle of a more personal documentary that is meant to convey how something *feels*, or what it was like to be present at an event, or to otherwise appeal to the heart while backing away from a hard message, then your editing might be more fanciful, including the manipulation of time and space, the use of dissolves and other appealing transitions, and the rendering of clips to turn them into slow-motion sequences or to alter their color or texture. Thus, the style of the editing is an analog to more ambiguous content.

Fudging

Documentary filmmakers often have to fudge some of their edited footage. Jeff Garcia did this in many sequences in *Riding High*, a documentary about kids shooting off model rockets. A rocket veers off and crashes. Cut to kids laughing and pointing at the hapless kid who owns the rocket. Cut to an adult shaking his head, apparently trying to communicate that it's not nice to make fun of someone whose rocket crashed. However, in real life, the adult had not shaken his head at the boys making fun of the kid who couldn't get his rocket to launch right. He'd shaken his head at two kids fighting over a rocket, which had happened twenty minutes before the crash. Editing makes it seem like one thing happens, and then another thing happens *because of the first thing*. It's not illegal or immoral. It's just the way you have to work sometimes.

Editing Documentaries to Control Time

As a film editor, you will have to control the viewer's sense of passing time, both for the film as a whole and for individual scenes or segments. You want some segments to play fast and others slow. You want to think about how all the segments play in relation to each other, how long they run, and how they are paced. You may want to "enhance" some segments by a rhythmic cutting of shots. Usually, the documentary filmmaker has an obligation to keep his film moving along and to avoid slack sequences.

Establishing Place

All documentary filmmakers have to establish setting or place, in one way or another. The person, event, or thing being documented must be or occur somewhere. All things being equal, that place is probably nearly as important as the person, event, or thing itself. It doesn't exist in a vacuum. Viewers want to know where the band is playing, where the artist lives, where the party is. You probably want to show this, or explain it in narration, sooner, rather than later in your documentary.

How to Control Figures

If you enjoyed much control during filming and took advantage of it, you probably have much useful footage to edit. On the other hand, if you were restricted while filming—you couldn't get up on the stage, you couldn't actually direct those children playing in the park—you couldn't get all the coverage you wanted. There were angles and frames you couldn't get. So you just shot all you could, went for variety, and hoped it would all come together for you at the editing bench.

Little House, a Moderately Controlled Documentary

Annette Marin made a documentary about a "party house," as she calls it, that falls somewhere in the midrange of control—that is, Annette enjoyed some control while shooting, but not complete control. The film is about a man and his party house—he likes to give parties, large parties on the weekends, small ones during the week. He just likes having people around him.

Interviews eventually anchor the film without dominating it. Annette interviewed the owner of the house at length and did a number of mini-interviews of the party people. She also took lots of footage of people talking, laughing, kissing, dancing, drinking, toking, playing guitars.

Cutting Little House for the Right Proportion

For Annette, the main editing challenge had to do with *proportion*—how much of her footage should she give over to each of the following subjects:

> Bill (the main guy and owner of the house)
> the interview of Bill
> other interviews
> dancers
> musicians

- people talking
- people kissing
- the backyard (darker, maybe more intimate)
- people at the bar

Annette decided to cut alternately to these subjects in a kind of roundabout—five seconds of Bill, five seconds of dancers, five seconds of a couple embracing in the backyard and smiling shyly at the camera, five seconds of this, five seconds of that, and so on. By cutting these shots mid-length—neither too short nor too long—Annette established a slow rhythm, matching the laid-back, relaxed style of the place. She then repeated the cycle and repeated a sense of numerous activities going on at the same time. It's like taking the viewer all around the house to be everywhere at once.

Annette fudged a lot, too. She had shots of a band, then cut to a couple apparently digging the band. I asked her about that because I was suspicious. She fessed up and said no, the couple wasn't actually digging the band, they were digging another couple dancing, and this happened a long time after the band played. Viewers are fine with this as long as the main point, i.e., people having fun, comes through.

Right Length

Annette's film runs under ten minutes. She didn't think it should be any longer. The tempo is in the middle range, but not draggy. She was an "equal opportunity" editor, which means no type of footage, no person, no activity dominates. All seem to get the same treatment.

EDITING SUPER 8 FILM "BY HAND"

To edit super 8 film, you have two options: by hand or in the computer. *By hand* means you work with pre-digital super 8 gear that flourished, if that is the word, in the 1970s and 1980s. Maybe I should have said *by fingers* because with this system you physically cut the film and splice it together with your fingers. Here is a list of the stuff you'll need if you work this way:

- a super 8 *editor-viewer*.
- a couple of spare 6-volt *bulbs*.
- a couple of 200- or 400-foot empty super 8 film *reels*.
- a *super 8 splicer* and *splicing tape*, preferably by Wurker, a German firm.
- a pad and pencil.
- a desk light.
- a pair of scissors.

- a makeshift *film bin* consisting merely of a strip of masking tape with half the width pressed lengthwise to the edge of the work surface and to which the heads of shots have been stuck.
- a small box lined with velvet for the tails of shots to fall into.

Super 8 editor-viewer and splicer.

Best Super 8 Web Sites

You can check out most of this equipment at pro8mm.com, probably the most comprehensive super 8 Web site. Also, check out the The Super 8 Film Format Metadirectory at lavender.fortunecity.com And of course, check eBay every now and then for used super 8 gear. Much useful super 8 gear can be found at swap meets, yard sales, and pawn shops.

The Shot Log

Look at your footage over and over again, and get to know it intimately. Make a *shot log* indicating which shots or takes are most useful and might end up in one of your cuts. Log by reels—reel 1, reel 2, and so forth. (Flip back to page 58 for more about shot logs.)

Pulling Shots

After making your shot log, you *pull* all the good shots from your reels of film—that is, you cut them out of your reels and stick them to that masking tape pressed to the front of your desk, which I mentioned earlier. Cut shots through sprocket holes, for reasons explained below. However, before you start this, scrunch in front of the masking tape and with a marking pen write numbers from 1 to 30 along the tape about three-quarters of an inch apart. This way, each shot you stick to the tape has a number. Enter this number in your shot log. Obviously, you do this so later you can find everything. Super 8 film is only a half-inch wide, and the frames are even smaller. You won't have much luck IDing the shots by sight. You really need that tape, those numbers on it, and your log.

Assembling the Rough Cut

After this, you assemble a *rough cut* by splicing the shots in your film bin (hanging from tape) tail to head, tail to head, tail to head in final order. Or after studying your notes, you establish a new sequence. If you want to save money on splicing tape, tape the rough cut together with quarter-inch masking tape. This is suitable *only for running through the viewer. Do not attempt to project this masking-taped cut through a projector.* The taped-together sequences will flow through the viewer together if you followed my advice above and used scissors to cut *through* sprocket holes, and between frames.

Proceeding to the Fine Cut

Now you have all your useful shots spliced together in something like final order. But you will need to trim them to run just the right length of time. Heed all the advice of trimming, controlling time, and controlling space I describe in this chapter. Toss out adored footage, no matter what price you had to pay for it. You may also need to *intercut* shots or *match-cut* them. This is the time to establish all your *POV sequences* and insert *cutaways*. Soon, working this way, going over the footage again and again, you arrive at your final cut.

EDITING SUPER 8 FILM DIGITALLY

To go digital, you have your super 8 footage transferred to digital tape, then edit it in a computer with an editing program. Again, visit *www.pro8mm.com* or The Super 8 Film Format Metadirectory for details.

EDITING DIGITAL VIDEO WITH COMPUTERS

Sooner or later, if you are serious about filmmaking, you will go digital. As I strongly advised in chapter 2, you will need to acquire a DV (digital video) camera (called a camcorder by marketing people) and a computer for editing, adding sound, and creating titles and other effects. To review a bit of chapter 2, I recommend the latest versions of two entry-level editing programs:

1. iMovie HD6 by the Apple Computer Company
2. Studio Media Suite Version 10, a PC program by Pinnacle Software Systems

iMovie comes pre-installed in new Mac computers—all new iMacs, eMacs, G4s, G5s, Powerbooks, and iBooks—and only Mac computers. Mac computers going back to 2001 also have it. iMovie is not available for PCs.

Studio is a "third-party" product, you and your PC computer being party one and party two. You buy Studio separately; places like CompUSA sell it, or you can get it online from *www.pinnaclesys.com* or *www.amazon.com*. It costs under $100. The latest version is 10.

For filmmakers who feel like venturing into more sophisticated editing programs, there is Final Cut, in three versions: Pro, Express, and Studio. Final Cut, by Apple, works only with Macs. For PC users, there is Premiere by Adobe and Liquid by Pinnacle. Prices for the "express" version of these advanced programs are about $500; full-tilt versions run about $1,000. This is not the book for detailed comparisons; nor am I your man for that.

School Yourself

Go to www.adobe.com and www.pinnaclesys.com for information about editing products, plus downloadable trial programs.

A GENERIC EDITING PROCESS FOR iMOVIE AND STUDIO

iMovie and Studio are not identical. Still, they are enough alike that I can describe a common process you go through to edit with either. This should give you a sufficient overview of how both programs work. But this is only an overview.

Both iMovie and Studio have excellent helps. iMovie's tutorial (accessed from the pull-down help menu) is plainly written and quite useful. So is Studio's. The latter program also comes with a manual you can actually make sense of.

School Yourself

Investigate *iMovie HD & iDVD 5: The Missing Manual* by David Pogue (Pogue Press, 2005). Extremely easy to read and full of tricks to make iMovie seem more flexible and professional than it is.

Setting Up

You will need to consult the help menus after scanning the list of steps below:

1. First, shoot. Shoot a lot. Tape is cheap. You have no reason to hold back. You will fix—trim, rearrange, pace—everything later during editing.

iMovie: Upper left: monitor for viewing shots; upper right: shelf where you park shots—something like a film bin; bottom: timeline for editing shots and sound tracks. Two soundtracks visible. The HD version supports wide screen and displays wave forms for ease in editing sound to picture.

Studio: Upper left, album, same as iMovie's shelf; upper right, monitor; lower, timeline. This deluxe version displays multiple sound and picture tracks.

2. Connect your DV camera to your computer (with either iMovie or Studio DV installed) by means of a *firewire* cable. Apple calls it firewire and owns the name. Pinnacle calls it an *iEEE cable*. Technically, it's the same cable. All new Macs come with firewire cables, and you get one of them free when you buy Studio. It is with this cable that your sounds and images will flow in real time from your original tape in your camera to the hard drive of your computer and from there to the editing program. You make an absolutely faithful *copy*, with no degradation of image or sound. Original sounds and images are still safe on your tape.

3. Next, turn on the computer and bring up the editing program. And after a few mouse clicks, you are ready to *import* your footage. The camera is now a slave to the computer. Before you, on both the iMovie and Studio screen, you have controls for play, fast-forward, stop, rewind, and pause.

4. *Importing*. As you import, a *thumbprint* of each shot is put on the screen. A thumbprint is the first frame of a shot. Apple calls the window where thumbprints go the *shelf*; Pinnacle calls it the *album*. Under each thumbprint, you'll find the running time of the shot in minutes and seconds. Each shot, too, is numbered. You can click on the number and give the shot a name, like "Joe CU 1."

5. To view shots in the bin, *select* a shot by clicking on it—the border of the frame will then change color—then click on the right arrow under the other big square on the screen, which I call the *monitor*. The shot will then play for you. You can stop it any time you want with the stop button.

6. *Editing shots.* You can dump bad shots by selecting the shot and dragging it to the trashcan or pressing Delete. For serious editing, you drag all the shots or all shots in the bin to the horizontal space at the bottom of the screen. This space toggles back and forth from a clip viewer to a timeline. The clip viewer retains the thumbprints of the shots you saw before in the bin. Some editing procedures are more easily performed in clip-viewer mode.

7. The timeline is a horizontal representation of each shot. Long-running shots take up a lot of left-right space, while short-running shots may be only slivers. You can still see the thumbprint, but it's very small. Some editing procedures are better accomplished in timeline mode. You edit in both modes by first playing the shot in the monitor and studying it to determine where you want to make a cut. Then you can split shots and delete portions you don't want. You can also cut up a long-running shot into several pieces and insert them at various places in your film.

8. You make actual cuts in at least two ways: 1) by clicking on Edit > Split Video Clip at Playhead or 2) by moving little handles left and right to mark the heads and tails of shots. The playhead is an arrow or vertical marker to show you the current frame—that is, where exactly you are in your film. Playheads occur in both clip-viewer and timeline modes. When you play a shot or sequence, the playhead travels from left to right, following the progress of the shot. When you pause or stop a shot, the playhead stops. You can drag or *scrub* the playhead quickly left or right by dragging the playhead.

9. In the clip-viewer and timeline modes, you can create dissolves, fades, and other transitional devices. In clip-viewer mode, you can also render your shots in a few different ways—you can turn color footage into black and white, you can lighten or darken shots, and you can create interesting pastel or high-contrast effects. (Flip ahead to page 233 for more about special effects.)

10. *Importing and editing sound. Live sound*—that is, sound that accompanies picture—is imported along with picture. When you play a shot, you also get to hear its sound. The screen has a volume control. Music and narration are imported separately in timeline mode. I guess you could say they are post-imported, meaning after picture and live sound are imported.

11. Both iMovie and Studio access music from CDs or from playlist generators like Mac's iTunes. You can also access music from MP3 players like iPod. Both iMovie and Studio provide two sound tracks, one for music, the other for narration, sound effects, or sound lifted from other shots. If you want your music to start at a certain point in the film, say when the babe in stiletto heels emerges from the limo, you slide the playhead to where the door of the limo

opens, then click on the music track you want in the on-screen CD menu—and the track is copied to one of the tracks at the playhead right when the door opens in one of the sound tracks.

12. You can import narration by simply clicking in Narration on the audio menu and speaking into either the computer's built-in microphone or an outboard mic plugged into the computer. Again, you cue the film to where you want the narration to start by scrubbing the playhead. Another way to get narration into your computer is to record it with either a digital tape recorder or a DV camera. If you use the latter, you import the shot as you would any shot, strip the sound from the shot, and drop it where you want it by clicking Cut and Paste.

13. Music tracks in the timeline have their own color. You can select them as you would select shots. When you click on music tracks, they turn a brighter color. Same for narration/sound effects tracks.

14. Depending on your editing program, you have much control over the volume of sound clips. Older versions of iMovie use a slide at the bottom of the timeline for adjusting sound level. Newer versions, and practically all other editing programs, work by grabbing a line running through your sound track and dragging the line up or down to adjust volume. To make any of these volume changes, you first have to select the track or the sound clip.

15. You can edit sound as you would picture: You can cut, trim, move, copy, and paste any sound. You can get sound to fade in or out or reduce its volume relative to, say, live sound. You can overlap or *mix* sound and adjust volume for each track.

16. Maybe I left you with the impression that early or lesser versions of iMovie and Studio have only two sound tracks. Actually, they have three: live sound, music, and narration/sound effects. Actually you can have more than three if you care to stack sound on sound. If you import a sound on top of a sound, the first sound doesn't go away. It only goes away if you select it and press Delete *before* you bring in the second sound. So more than one sound can occupy the same track. However, it's a bit tricky to build up a sound track by the sound-on-sound technique. Mixing levels is not easy. I don't recommend doing too much of it.

17. *Adding titles and credits*. Both iMovie and Studio offer dozens, maybe even an infinite number of choices for creating titles and credits. You have your choice of many fonts, sizes, and styles—rolling credits, MTV-style bottom-of-the-screen strips, credits on black, credits on red, credits on any color, or credits "superimposed" on actual clips.

18. *Saving.* Of course, you want to save often. If you don't and your computer crashes, you could lose all your editing. But you still have your original footage on tape. You can start all over, if the worst happens to you.

19. *Backing up.* It's a good idea to back up your edited work by simply clicking on Edit > Select All, then copying everything and saving it. If you lose your first version, you can always load your copy and resume your editing.

20. *Exporting.* When you are all through editing your film, you want to *share* it, as iMovie calls it, or *make a movie*, as Studio calls it. This means transferring the finished movie from inside your computer to a tape or DVD. You do this with the firewire cable running to the camera, or, if your computer allows it, directly to a DVD.

School Yourself

Investigate outboard DVD burners. You would do this if your computer does not have DVD burning capability and can't be upgraded. Outboard or external DVD burners cost about $200.

8

Deeper into Sound

*E*verybody knows that a film has to have sound, but audiences don't really pay much attention to it. If you ask them about the music of a film they just saw, they don't remember it. Don't bother to ask them about a particular sound mix or piece of sound editing. They will just look at you funny. I hope you are more attentive.

In this chapter, I aim to tune you in to good film sound and the art of making it. I concentrate on music, live sound, dialogue, narration, sound effects, sound mixes, plus what you must do to get good sound.

FILM MUSIC

My students—and I think many other young, beginning filmmakers—like lots of music in their films. They like more music in their films than I do. The film with the most music in this book is by far Byron Watkins' *K.C. and Byron's Day of Fun*, a zany, largely improvised film about two guys just bopping around town, eating fast food, playing a little football, discussing stuff, even getting into a fight. It's about friendship and male bonding. For most of the film, the pair doesn't really bond; they relate to third things— food, football, females. But near the end, they get down to each other with no third thing to distract them. They work things out after the fight. In this way, it's a great little film.

Musical Variety

All this is enhanced by varied music. Some of the music is European classical—for example, *Thus Spake Zarathustra*, the Richard Strauss number that's also in *2001: A Space Odyssey*. Byron uses a lot of oldie pop tunes, too, like "One Is the Loneliest Number." Also some rap, some rock, some very new stuff, some very old. He even throws in some tunes with Latin beats—like cha cha cha.

As scenes change, so do moods. Or the music changes, which changes the mood. Visuals cue music; music cues visuals. Sometimes, the music is "straight"—that is, meant to extend or complement the visuals: When Byron and K.C. have a fistfight and for a time sadly separate, we hear "One Is the Loneliest Number"—very appropriate. Other times, the mood is satiric as when K.C. throws the "World's Longest Touchdown Pass" to Byron—as we hear Vangelis computer music from the movie *Chariots of Fire*—overblown and poking fun.

I asked Byron where he got all this music. He said, "I have a big CD collection." (Flip back to page 125 for how "World's Longest Touchdown Pass" was edited. Flip ahead to page 189 for how this film works as a story.)

Tale to Tell: Finding the Right Music

But you have to do the music right. Lay down the wrong music and your whole film could flop. It happened to me. I made a story film with dissonant modern academic music. I thought I was being very clever. I "premiered" the film in one of my classes. The cast slipped in to watch. Then, for reasons I didn't at first understand, the cast started to exit one by one before the film had ended. My students didn't care much for the film either. I asked them why. "It was weird," they said. "Cold, harsh, no fun to watch." How could that be? I thought I had made a comedy. Then it occurred to me: The music was wrong. So I replaced the dissonant music with some bouncy, accessible guitar music. This time, I faired better with audiences. I later showed the film in Palo Alto, California—a high-class university town—and it was very well received. So keep listening. Play different music with your edited video to discover which works best.

At the same time, be true to yourself. I may have been too eager to please my audiences when I changed the music for the film I just described. If you feel that a particular piece of music really combines artfully and meaningfully with a sequence of visuals even though most viewers probably don't understand what you are up to, keep the music in anyway. To hell with them. You are the artist.

SCHOOL YOURSELF

Look into various kinds of music accessible to you, but go beyond your particular CDs or MP3 mixes. Some sources:

➤ Your local library has all kinds of classical music and modern near-dissonant music that you can check out. Much contemporary academic music makes good film music.

➤ Usually, in a town of any size, there is an alternative radio station that plays music more daring than the latest teenybopper slush. Often, it's the local college radio station. Start recording this music.

➤ Of course, there is lots of music on the Internet for all kinds of tastes, from classical (and pseudo-classical) to New Age to a category that is even called "film music." As you doubtless know, you can download this music and save it to the hard drive of your computer; better yet, burn a CD of it. I hope you pay for the music you download.

➤ Check out radio stations you can get online, like *www.radiotower.com*, one of many. This site lets you browse by station, country, and category.

➤ Go to the best music store in your town and find someone there with varied tastes in music. Tell her about your film. See what ideas for music she might come up with. Take her to lunch and show her your film on the LCD screen of your camera or better yet, on your laptop. Bring a headset for her. Buy a couple of CDs she recommends.

➤ If you are taking a filmmaking class, just ask the teacher whether you can stand up and make an announcement that you can't find the right music for your film, so could the class please watch my film and make recommendations for music that might work?

➤ Investigate local bands. I've engaged the services of local bands several times. They created songs just for my films, and none asked for money. They were honored that I would use their music in my films.

School Yourself

Locate Web sites from which you can buy uncopyrighted music, such as *www.royaltyfreemusic.com*. All *royalty-free* means is that you don't have to pay a copyright holder. But you do have to pay the Web site that makes the music available. The good thing, though, is that you only have to pay for the music one time, and you can use it as often as you like, and for many different projects. A license for copyrighted music would be much more restrictive and would usually pertain to the use of one piece of music for one project, and in one context only. Plus you will usually have to pay two fees—one for the music and one for the performer. As for royalty-free music, you acquire it in one of two ways, by downloading it or purchasing a CD of like music—all rap, all jazz, and so forth.

Here's a bit of good news: Most royalty-free music Web sites let filmmaking students use their music at no charge.

Try This

Make a little test film or experimental film in which you pair the same images with different music. Employ truly different kinds of music, such as jazz, classical, pop, etc. First, shoot some simple footage, like kids playing in a playground or cars streaming down the main street of your town—something like documentary footage you can go out and do on your own. Then find the music and play around, laying each down with the edited visuals. Note how each type of music makes the visuals feel different and even "says" something unique. Go for the unexpected: a Bach fugue played to footage of a baseball game; New Age music to footage of a parking garage; heavy metal to clips of headstones in a cemetery. If you have never paired music with visuals, prepare to be immensely entertained and inspired by this activity. Probably no filmmaking experience is as revelatory for a beginner as the playing of music to visuals. It's a unique aesthetic experience, and no matter how long you make films or how jaded you become, you will never get over it.

What about Copyrights?

First, flat out, you should not use copyrighted music in your film without obtaining permission to use the music *and* paying for that right. Having said that, allow me to get real. Go ahead and use copyrighted music provided that:

➤ The film will be shown only locally with zero chance that the copyright holder will ever find out; and

➤ The film isn't going to make any money at all, so nobody is going to care about permission. Permissions are all about someone making money.

Giving Credit

If you do this—use the music without permission or payment—you should, at the very least, give full credit, in your credits, to the band *and* to the composer *and* to the copyright holder.

The Exception: Exhibiting Online

However, if you plan to export your movie in something like Quicktime to the Internet, for the whole world to see, or if you send your film off to film festivals, then I strongly advise that you do not use copyrighted music. Either nab uncopyrighted music from music sites on the Web, or have a band compose and play music for you. You need to have the band sign a release or work out some kind of financial arrangement with its members—for example, you agree to pay the members of the band a couple of percentage points of any money the film makes. Put this in writing and get signatures.

OTHER APPROACHES TO FILM MUSIC

For $50 you can buy a useful collection of music loops and sound effects from *www.partnersinrhyme.com*. And that's it, no other charges. Also, Sony's Sound Series is a comprehensive collection of loops in every music genre you can think of, each on its own CD for about $50 per CD. For a time Sony offered a free CD with sample loops.

They might still. Check it out at *www.sony.com/freeloops*. Sony's stuff goes on both PC and Mac. If you are making films on a Mac computer, all versions of OS X operating systems come with a dandy program of music loops called GarageBand. If you buy one of the Final Cut programs—Express, Pro, or Studio—you'll also get Soundtrack, another useful music loops program.

Why loops? Loops are repetitive pieces of music ranging in length from four seconds to thirty seconds. Musical repetition is good for film music and in fact inhabits many of the best features you see. Film music usually should be background, a wash over the visuals, and for this reason loops, rather than up-front melodic or developmental music, work well. Actually you can vary the loops creatively. I have "composed" some pretty complex film music with, for example, the sixteen versions of what GarageBand calls "Chordal Synth[esizer] Pattern." I used only four versions. You would not guess that the music I made was "canned."

SCHOOL YOURSELF

Consider some unlikely film music:

➤ *A Knight's Tale*: This is a story of knights of old, jousting for the "World Championship" (going at each other on charging horses with lances). It has a lot of medieval-type music, but it also surprises you with the likes of "We Will Rock You" from time to time. The music saves the movie from becoming just another high-toned chivalry thing.

➤ *Crash*: For most of the film, the violence and cranking up of tension are not accompanied by the usual high-energy music. Instead, the music is often serene and contemplative, inviting you to rise above the conflict and think about its meaning.

EDITING MUSIC

It would be nice if you could hire a music composer who writes little segments of music to run just as long as the sequences they are meant to complement, with proper beginnings, middles, and ends. I am assuming that this option is not available to you. You will likely find that the music you want to lay down under an edited sequence is either too long or too short, or the sound you want to line up with a certain visual event doesn't want to cooperate. Accordingly, you need to learn a few things about editing music. Here, I am thinking of prerecorded commercial music. Some strategies:

➤ If the music is too long for the edited sequence, cut it down with audio fade-ins and fade-outs. Cut the music down to the right length, fade in the start of it, then fade out the end of it.

- If the music is too short for the edited sequence, import it twice (or more times), back to back. Drag the start of the second import to overlap the end of the first import by about a second. Or just copy and paste the music. Fiddle with segueing the two imports—that is, fade out the end of the first import as you also fade in the start of the second import. With some luck, you won't even hear the overlap, and even if you do, your viewers probably won't.

- To make a musical event synchronize with a video event, slide the sound forward and backward until the musical event—cymbals crashing, say—coincides with the visual event. You do this by selecting and dragging the music track or by repeatedly pressing the left or right arrow keys, which moves the sound one frame.

The traffic sounds seem to overwhelm the bicyclist. Through his use of sound, Michael is making a comment about people versus cars. Cars win.

MUSIC VERSUS LIVE SOUND

City Unplanning, by Michael Bradley, is a little documentary about urban traffic tangle, and it doesn't use any music at all. The only sound is that of passing traffic. As he filmed, Michael happened to pick up a threatened bicyclist peddling precariously down the street.

Who Supplies Meaning: You or the Music?

The significant thing about the lack of music in *City Unplanning* is its refusal to tell you how to react to the visuals. Music always swaddles visuals in some kind of emotion. It's a cinematic con game. Too often, the visuals aren't strong enough to stand on their own, so the filmmaker has to add music to hype up the footage. But *City Unplanning* doesn't do this. You have to supply the meaning that music would have added. This is a little work. Bit it's worth it since you supply meaning yourself.

It's a matter of taste. If you think it's okay, artistically speaking, to manipulate viewers' feelings with music, then go ahead and use music. But if you feel that you want to let viewers decide how to feel and react, without being strong-armed by the music, then consider using little or no music.

MANIPULATING SOUNDS

A film called *Crosswalk* by David Cutter feels like *City Unplanning*, only "worse." By worse I mean the sounds of traffic are even louder. The man in the frame on the following page is even more intimidated than is the bicyclist in *City Unplanning*. All he's trying to do is cross the street. David jacked up the sound by copying it and layering it on existing sound. He also extracted a honk and placed it on the sound track just after the man looks around nervously in the middle of the crosswalk. It's a perilous journey.

Live Sound in The Job

The Job feels a little like *Crosswalk* because it uses mainly live urban ambient sound. This time, the sounds seem cold and insensitive as we see a hit man going about his business, tracking down the mark, setting up. The sounds of the city make us think more about the psychology of the guy. We feel sorry for him, and what he has to do. He seems so alone. If the film had been wall-to-wall music, with no live sound, the sense of the city oppressing him would have been absent. Adam Klusener made this film.

From *Crosswalk* by David Cutter.

The building in the background acts as a sound reflector. The sound of traffic comes back to the camera louder.

SCHOOL YOURSELF

Watch as many of the following films as you can. All are about hard life in hard cities. Compare the mix-in of ambient city sounds: *Klute*; *Mean Streets*; *Taxi Driver*; *Fort Apache, the Bronx*; *Do the Right Thing*; *Last Exit to Brooklyn*; *Homicide*; *City of Hope*; *Menace II Society*; *Falling Down*; *Laws of Gravity*; *Fresh*; *The Interpreter*; and *Cinderella Man*.

Tale to Tell: Live Sound and Music in In Case of Earthquake

Why not have both? If you have set a film in a place where ambient sound is meaningful, consider cranking it up or muting the music in some scenes, while in other scenes subdue or drop altogether the live sound in favor of up-front music. This is what I did in a film I made about the demolition of a venerated college building. I fell in love with the sound of the bulldozer as it relentlessly demolished our beloved old science building. In some scenes, I really cranked up the crashing and bashing of the bulldozer. Meanwhile, for other scenes, which I considered more poetic or nostalgic, I dropped the live sound altogether for some sweetly sentimental baroque music. Back and forth. (Flip ahead to page 209 for more about *In Case of Earthquake*.)

SOUND MIXES

Mixing sound has just as much creative potential as scripting, acting, filming, or editing. You can use both live sound and music at the same time, and you can drop the level of either sound in relation to the other. You can bring in third or fourth sounds—narration, dialogue from other clips, sound effects, and have any or all come in, go out, come in again, come in louder or softer—and each technical decision has its own creative payoff.

From Steve Haines' *Priceless*.

This film is on the DVD.

The Dominant Sound

Almost always, one sound in a mix is dominant. For example, Steve Haines' *Priceless* effectively mixes music and narration. The film, only fifty seconds long, is a send-up to the "priceless" TV commercials by MasterCard. But instead of Dad and the kid fishing in the creek and bonding, Steve's film is set in a grungy 7-Eleven and features three-day-old chile-and-cheese chips and babes on the covers of biker magazines. It ends with the clerk outside the store nervously smoking in the dark. Steve satirically mixes tinkly, dumb-ass commercial music with this voice-over narration: "Surviving the graveyard shift without getting stabbed in the neck by a broken beer bottle: Priceless." It's a nice mix, with the music in the aural background and Steve's narration clear and up front.

MUSIC, LIVE SOUND, AND REALITY

Consider the interconnection among music, live sound, and reality:

> ➤ Live sound only: Most real, most immediate, least reflective and manipulative.
> ➤ Live sound and music: Real but less so, the music manipulates but, at its best, induces reflectiveness, so the sequence feels less immediate.
> ➤ Music only: Least real, most manipulative, most reflective.

You'd want to use the first option if you want to make a realistic film in which you do not wish to manipulate viewers' reactions with music. You want to keep your film like real life. Real life does not come with music. We go through life, making our own judgments and drawing our own conclusions without music. You want your film to be like that. You'd do the third option if you don't care to be especially realistic. In fact, you want to remove your film from the real and the here and now. You want viewers to think and interpret all the time, but not on their own. You want music to do the interpreting for them. You want that kind of control. That's what artists do, you say, they manipulate. You'd do the middle option if you are a moderate in these matters. You want to keep your film real, with live sound, but you also want the freedom to manipulate, with music. Most films, if they use music at all, take the second road.

School Yourself

Start paying attention to how directors use music. Accordingly:

> Jean Pierre and Luc Dardenne, Belgians, use no scored music at all in their films. *La Promesse*, *Rosetta*, and *Son* are totally lacking in scored music, and are great examples of the first live sound/music option above. The only sounds in the films are dialogue and ambient sound. This lack of music engenders great respect from sensitive viewers. You think, "Thanks for letting me react the way *I* want to. Thanks for making films that are clear and gripping without having scores." In general, foreign films use far less music than do Hollywood films.

> *The Ballad of Jack and Rose* is a pretty good American indie about a man who has isolated himself and his daughter from the world, which he finds largely crass, commercial, and soulless. At one point in the film, Rose joins a commune in New England. The scenes of the commune are played with only music, no ambient sound. You don't need ambient sound. Instead, you want to think. The music assists you.

DIALOGUE

Yes, sometimes you need dialogue, but if you find yourself using too much of it, you could end up with a stilted film that perhaps should have been a play. It should go without saying, too, that you need top-notch actors to bring the dialogue off. Beginners seldom have access to good actors. For these reasons, throughout these pages, I have always urged that you find *cinematic* ways to communicate—through your shots, through your editing, through your nonverbal sound—rather than have people just talk and talk.

At the same time, some matters of the human heart, and of the society it invariably is locked up in, are extremely difficult, awkward, or impossible to communicate by visuals alone. In *Sasha's Passion*, a story film describe on page 174, a guy comes into a deli, looks at a menu on a sign, and points to the sandwich he wants. Sasha, working behind the counter, nods vigorously. This is a great little film about males who don't get it, but when I show it, I sometimes make the joke that it's a deli for deaf people. It would have been so easy to have the guy simply say, "I'll have the pastrami" and get around the awkward pointing and nodding.

A Little Dialogue in Gals and Goons

Michael De La Cerda and Joel Mathis made *Gals and Goons*, a film about tough guys torturing a hit man about why he didn't take out a certain hit woman—woman, not man. The film has a little dialogue at the beginning and a little at the end. In between, it's all visual. In the torturing scene that opens the film, the tough guy says to the torturee: "All right, let's go over this one more time. We pay the money. You kill the girl. But for some reason, the girl's still alive. Why is the girl still alive, Jason?" Short and to the point, these few spoken words set up the whole film. No other spoken words were necessary—except at the very end when the guy who was tortured and the hit woman fall in love. The man asks the woman, "Why did you save me?" And she replies, "Well, I figure since you didn't kill me, I owed you one."

Dialogue starts and ends *Gals and Goons*, by Michael De La Cerda and Joel Mathis. In between is wordless, but perfectly understandable, martial arts.

TRY THIS

Do a film with a little dialogue in it. Make sure that the dialogue conveys matters that your visuals and soundtrack absolutely can't. The minute you start to get wordy, stop and figure out a visual or aural way to communicate the same thing. Improvise the dialogue you need, instead of writing it. Go ahead and write the dialogue yourself at first, and get that wordy Charlie Kaufman thing out of your system. Then get your cast together and have them just improvise lines. Tell them where to start and where to end, in terms of content, emotion, and so forth. Then let them have at it. Do it over and over again. Or maybe your actors have chemistry and smarts and will improvise effectively for you with the greatest of ease.

Tale to Tell: When Improvised Dialogue Proved Better than Written

I did a film about how hard it is to make relationships work in this day and age. At first, I wrote lines for my cast of two. But when they ran them, it sounded awful. So I suggested that they just make their lines up. They did and the results were terrific—smart, knowing, natural. This pair is in their fifties. They were word-smart and world-smart.

NARRATION

This is also often called *voice over*. It's an explanation added by someone—the filmmaker herself, a key person in the documentary, a character in the story. It's usually "off camera," meaning we never see the narrator when she is narrating, though we may see her during other times in the film.

Don't Narrate the Obvious

Please, nothing is more boring than to hear narration that isn't needed. The narrator says, "Okay, here we are on the mall." Duh.

Polish Your Narration

Rehearse before recording narration on your film. Better yet, write out the narration, see how long it runs, and practice delivering it. Have a verbal person check it out. Avoid having narration sound like it was made up on the fly.

Meaningful Narration

For my money, narration becomes meaningful when it adds information that you can't glean from the visuals. This information might even run counter to the visuals. In her *On Duty*, Darby Cogburn narrates what her visuals can't possibly show. It's a film about life in the Marine Corps, not combat life or life out on bivouac, but life in the barracks where the guys flip towels at each other and talk macho. Darby's narration emphasizes being separated from her boyfriend, who is one of the marines in the film

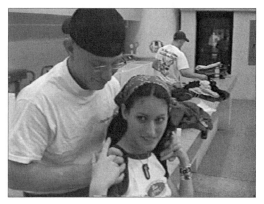

A sad shot from *On Duty*. She misses him much more than he misses her.

and how she misses him. She does this off-camera while we *see* the guys horsing around. These two lines of information, one visual, the other verbal, create meaning: The guy is having a better time than she is.

The potter is also the narrator. He doesn't try to explain every step. He makes narration an equal partner with visuals.

Raku is a documentary about an ancient and venerated Japanese method of making pots. The potter stays close to nature and trusts the final outcome to chance. The philosophy of raku is too complex to convey visually; thus, the filmmaker, Lori Woodruff, had the potter narrate. About half of this super 8 film is narrated, and the other half is accompanied by traditional Japanese string music.

Using Narration to Speed Matters Up

Written carefully and integrated with a screenplay that is also written carefully, narration can be a great way to speed plot or bridge scenes. For example, instead of setting up, rehearsing, and filming an entire scene having to do, with say, a drug pickup that's gone bad, you only have to film selected highlights of the scene and explain the overall situation through narration. What might take four or five minutes of screen time, if it were dramatized, takes only thirty seconds in narrated form.

SCHOOL YOURSELF

Watch the gangster films of Martin Scorsese in which narration is employed to speed complicated plots and provide background that would be boring to film. I particularly recommend *Mean Streets*, *Goodfellas*, and *Casino*.

TRY THIS

Familiarize yourself with the *audio extraction* feature on iMovie. I'm not sure what Studio's term is, but it allows it. This is stripping or extracting sound from a shot so that you can move it under another shot. This might be a more flexible way to create narration than simply recording it with your computer's microphone. For iMovie, click on Advanced >Audio Extract.

SOUND EFFECTS

You probably won't need to have specially imported sound effects in your film. Chances are that your live sound, which you recorded when you taped, provides all the sound effects you need. Now and then, though, the place where you did your filming may not offer the sound you want. You need to lay in a sound from another source.

John Neeley effectively dropped a sound effect, a siren, into the end of his *Blood Money*. This is a film about a guy who robs a woman at an ATM, shoots her, and takes off for the countryside. Close-ups of his face reveal regret and fear. He seems to be thinking: *Why did I do this dumb thing?* Then in the last few seconds of the film, wonderfully minimalistic, the sound of a distant siren creeps into the sound track and gets louder and louder. The robber looks relieved.

The rearview mirror works nicely here as the driver seems to look back on his life.

John just didn't get lucky and happen to pick up the sound of a real, live siren as he filmed the robber looking glum. He imported the sound from a film made by a classmate. Good craft, good art.

Sources of Sound Effects

Both iMovie and Studio have libraries of sound effects, but the list is short and the effects are jokey, home-movie stuff, like applause. You can also download sound effects from the Internet, at a small price. Go to *www.partnersinrhyme.com*, for example. Or simply type "sound effects" into any search engine.

You can also buy numerous CDs of sound effects at any music store. You then drop them into your film as you would a piece of music from a CD.

TRY THIS

Manufacture or find your own sounds. For example, slapping a folded newspaper on a hard surface is not a bad stand-in for a gunshot. Look around your place to find things that could make interesting sounds you can drop into your film, things like pots and pans, a toilet, a music box, or cedar shakes on which you scrape your fingernails. Record the sound with your DV camera, import the shot, strip the sound from the shot, and drop it into your film at the playhead.

GATHERING SOUND

Here are some aspects of recording live sound, or locating prerecorded sound, that might interest you.

Recording Dialogue

Buy a good microphone. Sure, your video camera's little microphone is of remarkable quality and records dialogue with good clarity, but it can't do everything. It works best when the person giving lines or talking is close to the camera, say, about arm's length. If the person giving lines is any farther off, two things can happen:

- ➤ If you are shooting indoors and the people speaking words are too far off, the spoken words could reverberate (bounce off walls) or sound distant. Also, the volume will be low and the sound muffled.
- ➤ If you are shooting outside and your actors are delivering lines too far away from the camera, normal outdoor sounds will be too loud in relation to the dialogue. The farther the camera is placed from the people speaking, the fainter the dialogue will sound and the more the background sound will increase in volume.

The problem here is with the automatic leveling feature of your camera's sound system. It works great most of the time, lowering or raising the level of recording without your help. But there are times when it doesn't know what to record. It's analogous to automatic exposure, which works great 90 percent of the time and fouls up the other 10 percent. Autoleveling doesn't know whether you mean to record that dog barking down the street or that human being muttering something twenty yards away. If it locks on the dog, your actor won't be heard well.

One Solution: An Off-Camera Microphone

For these reasons, you may need an off-camera microphone with something like a twelve-foot cord so that the mic can always be positioned at about arm's length from the speakers. You'll also need a mic boom to hold the microphone over the heads of the speakers and a boom person who has to be very careful about holding the boom. She

Recording dialogue with an off-camera microphone suspended from a boom. The boom allows the microphone to be positioned within a few feet (out of frame) of the speaker. You can buy adjustable booms like this (called *wands*) at paint stores.

should get a comfortable grip and avoid regripping or repositioning her fingers during the actual take. If she mishandles the boom, she could transmit rumbling sounds to the recorded sound. You can pick up reasonably priced, quality microphones at Radio Shack.

Also, check out your town's sound store—the kind of place that sells microphones, speakers, amplifiers, and so forth to bands. In addition, purchase only a *uni*directional microphone and not an *omni*directional microphone. The uni mic has a narrower pick-up pattern than the omni and thus is more likely to exclude unwanted ambient noise. There is another kind of mic called a *shotgun mic*, which has an extremely narrow pickup pattern. It can be a little hard to use, because it must be aimed very carefully, like a sniper's rifle. People who make documentaries like this kind of mic, because it picks up sounds from subjects the camera can't get close to.

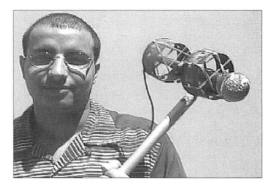

Mic boom fashioned from a shelf strip and two tuna fish cans with tops and bottoms removed. Three heavy-duty rubber bands are stretched around each can to provide a mic cradle.

Another way to go is with a radio microphone. This is something like a cordless phone. You tape a base to your camera, or hang it from your belt. The mic, which has no wires, has a little radio transmitter in it. It sends the signal through the air and to the base, thence into camera and onto tape. Slick. Not much money. But now we are getting a little consumer-crazy. Just keep it simple.

The simplest way of all is to record sound with only your camera's built-in microphone. Make this your default method of operation. It's the most minimalist, the easiest, and the fastest.

Getting Clean Dialogue Outdoors

If your film has a lot of dialogue that must be delivered outdoors, be prepared for some delays and frustration. You want to strive for "clean" sound—dialogue uncontaminated by intrusive sounds such as aircraft, trains, and the like. Actors ought to give lines only when the background sound is a gentle, constant, featureless hum, a mere audio wash. You'll want to cut the take when something extraordinary—someone shouting a few doors away or a dog barking—is picked up. You do all this to bring back clean footage for editing. Your editing will go better if you do not have to edit around such audio intrusions.

Wind Rumble

If you are taping outside on a windy day, or even just a breezy day, you will pick up a rumbling sound, the result of the wind striking the mic. You can prevent this by taping a piece of foam rubber over the microphone in your camera or enclosing your off-camera microphone in a *barney*, as the industry calls it. This is a zeppelin-shaped device that completely covers the mic. It's fashioned from a circular frame, screening material, and cloth. The job of the foam rubber and the barney is to break up the wind so that it doesn't impinge on the mic. You lose a little sound quality working this way.

If you still have rumble, you have to EQ (equalize) it out with a program like Final Cut. Basically, you have to lower the bass frequencies.

Recording Wild Sound

Before you *wrap* (pack up and go home) for a day of shooting outdoors, do this: Simply record two minutes of ambient sound. Picture doesn't matter—tape anything. Everyone has to be quiet while you tape the naturally occurring outdoor sound. This used to be called a *wild track*, for reasons I won't go into.

Why do this? As you edit, you'll doubtless discover vast differences in the sound from one clip to the next. The sound of an airplane is heard on one clip but not on the next. The result is a chopped-up ambient track that calls attention to itself. In iMovie and Studio, you have the option of turning off the original live or ambient sound that came with your shots and replacing it with your wild track. You strip away or extract the sound from the wild-sound footage and throw the video away. You lay the extracted sound down under the sequence of clips, which before had a choppy sound. You can also slide it left or right, relative to edited video sequences. The result is a smooth, continuous outdoor sound that flows glitch-free across numerous clips.

Laying in a wild track of ambient sound is exactly why advanced editing programs include more than two tracks. You lay in the wild track on, say, track four. If it's clean and featureless, you can copy it and paste it in as often as you like.

TRY THIS

Record sound in four varied exteriors—in a mall, in a parking lot, in a park, on the patio of an outdoor restaurant. The visuals don't matter. Go home and listen to the sound from these takes with a headset. In short, school yourself in the varying feels of outdoor sound.

Monitoring Sound

If you are shooting under difficult aural conditions—traffic, people talking in the background, wind—you will need to monitor the sound you are endeavoring to record with a better headset or earphones before you roll tape. You don't have to roll tape to monitor. Just set the camera to Record and Standby and listen with the headset. Try to exclude background sound with your cupped fingers. You will hear the traffic or people talking or wind much more objectively through the camera's sound system. Have the cast run lines. Can you hear them clearly over the background sound? If not, then try these remedies:

➤ Have speakers of dialogue move closer to the camera (or outboard mic).
➤ If you are using an outboard mic attached to a boom, get the mic in closer. This might mean taking tight close-ups or medium shots so that the mic is positioned either inches away from the speakers, just out of frame, from above or below.

- Move the speakers so that you are not pointing your camera at the traffic or other loud background sound.

- Get away from a wall, which might be bouncing sound back to your mic. Or film at an angle to the wall. This way, the sound does not bounce directly back to the mic.

- Always make sure speakers are facing the mic. For example, don't film speakers sitting in the front seat of a car if you are sitting in the backseat with the camera.

- Don't try to record live dialogue at all. Instead, take an extreme long shot of, say, the two people talking while walking down a sidewalk across the street. Get so far back that you can't see lips move. Then immediately after the take, have the people give their lines closer. Later, you'll strip the good sound from the second shot and import it under the extreme long shot. Viewers won't guess that two shots were actually involved.

TRY THIS

You can turn your DV video camera into an audio tape recorder by just going out and taping something that makes the noise you want, like a field full of crickets or birds or a passing train, and later extracting the sound from the video and laying it into your sound track under appropriate images.

RECORDING A BAND

In most cities, garage bands abound, each looking for its big break, and a few will actually be pretty good. Maybe you follow the local music scene and know which is which. The local bands I have worked with love to do film music.

Collaborate with a sound engineer. It's not easy to record a band live and get good fidelity. You really need to work with someone who knows what she is doing. As you probably know, nearly all bands have either a manager or a sound engineer—often the same person. If the band isn't famous yet, and is looking for ways to promote itself, you may find that the manager-engineer will be happy to make all the arrangements for recording the band. She will set the mics and do the mixing, and so on. They really do want to be in your film and are flattered that you asked them.

Or record the band yourself with just your digital camera. The recorded sound you can get with a DV camera is pretty good, often much better than with an analog camera or analog tape recorder.

Read:

Film Music: A Neglected Art by Roy M. Pendergast (W.W. Norton & Company, 1992)

The Practical Art of Motion Picture Sound by David L. Yewdall (Focal Press, 2003)

Sound for Picture: The Art of Sound Design in Film and Television by Tom Kenny (MixBooks, 2000)

Sound for Film and Television, Second Edition by Tomlinson Holman (Focal Press, 2001)

SOUND FOR SUPER 8

Super 8 film used to come with two tracks of recordable iron oxide—a main track and a "balance" track. Working with a stereo sound projector, which amounted to an analog audio recorder built into a super 8 projector, you could record sound on both tracks for a two-track mix.

However, sound film is no longer available from Kodak, the only manufacturer of the format. But you can get around this by recording "wild" with a DV camera or an audio recorder. By "wild," I mean that there is no electronic or mechanical link between your super 8 camera and your DV camera. At this point, you have several technical choices. Here are two:

1. Have your film sound stripped and transfer your sound to the film by means of a projector. Edit with conventional super 8 editing equipment.
2. Have your super 8 footage transferred to a DV medium, such as miniDV. Import the footage into a computer editing program and import the sound you recorded with a DV camera, or, if you recorded sound with an analog sound recorder, digitize that sound and import it.

This is pretty complicated stuff. Super 8 sound projectors in good shape aren't easy to find. They are no longer being manufactured. To find used super 8 sound projectors, visit eBay. Also try *www.8mm16mmfilmscollectibles.com* and *www.super8sound.com*. Another good source for just about anything having to do with super 8 is The Super 8 Film Format Metadirectory (*www.lavender.fortunecity.com*). From there, you can go to outfits that sound-stripe super 8 film or do transfers or sell equipment.

Going Crystal Synch

Creating synchronous sound-image events with sound recorded wild is not easy, and when you do achieve synch, you will lose it in a few seconds. You have to recue and make another transfer. You may prefer to go another way, and that is *crystal synch*. Crystal synch works just like your digital watch, which is so accurate because of a quartz crystal inside and the way it vibrates with remarkable consistency. Firms that make super 8 sound crystal synch conversions install a vibrating crystal in your camera and another in your tape recorder. Since they both vibrate at the same frequency, they maintain perfect frame synchronization. All this is done cordless. When you transfer sound from recording tape to film, you will maintain synch for very long periods of time. Or if you import both super 8 image and your sound on tape into a computer editing program, both media will be in frame synch with each other. Visit the Web site of The Film Group for more information about crystal synch for super 8—*http://members.aol.com/fmgp/index.*

But you know my bias. Crystal synch, even if it uses no cords between camera and sound recorder, is cumbersome, not to mention expensive. I tried it for a time as a super 8 filmmaker. I went back to simple—dialogue transferred to film wild.

EDITING AUDIO WITH COMPUTERS

Here is a list of things you can do with sound in iMovie and Studio, my favorite entry-level editing programs:

- Retain live sound recorded with shots.
- Drop live sound.
- Extract live sound from shots you don't want and slide it under other shots.
- Import music from CDs or from the Internet.
- Add sound effects.
- Add narration—at the computer, which usually will have a built-in microphone.
- Edit any sound—trim, copy, move.
- Fade sound up or down.
- Adjust sound volume.
- Employ silence between sounds.
- Mix any combination of music, live sound, and narration.
- Pair sound with image in countless creative ways.
- Undo audio mistakes.
- Redo audio things.

Help and Aids

For iMovie:

- Work through the iMovie tutorial. It will show you how the program works much better than I can.

➤ Consult the iMovie help menu. It is much better written and more useful than typical helps.

➤ Buy and read *iMovie HD and iDVD 5* by David Pogue.

For Studio:

➤ Install the Version 10 upgrade, which adds some important options.

➤ Read the generous, detailed user's manual, which for once is written in plain English.

➤ Consult the excellent help menu.

PART III:

Deeper into Ideas

9

Deeper into the Story Film

You might find it useful to think about story films in two broad categories: those based on everyday life and those based on extraordinary life. There are advantages and disadvantages to going either way. Story films based on everyday life might sink into banality—that is, become boring and unremarkable. On the other hand, a story film based on everyday life has potential to really hook viewers. They go, "Yeah. I've been there. I've done that. I've felt that way."

Story films based on extraordinary characters, however, might tumble into being implausible. On the plus side, films about people living on the edge offer the possibility of originality. Maybe viewers are less likely to identify with them, but they might just enjoy the ride.

All stories, in fact, are pulled in these two directions, the mundane and the remarkable. Take the film *Eternal Sunshine of the Spotless Mind*. Here is the thumbnail summary by the Internet Movie Database (*www.imdb.com*):

> A couple (Jim Carrey and Kate Winslet) undergo a procedure to erase each other from their memories when their relationship turns sour, but it is only through the process of loss that they discover what they had to begin with.

It's an extraordinary premise, erasing memories, and it's a story about everyday life—love. So in the pages ahead, I suggest how to do all three: do a short film based on everyday life, a short film based on something extraordinary, and a short film based on both.

SHORT FILM STORIES BASED ON EVERYDAY LIFE
You go deeper into the film story by:

- Making your characters more lifelike.
- Emphasizing everyday events and people.
- Basing your story on some truth (with a small *t*) of society or human nature.
- Exploring cinematics that enhance character and truth.
- Avoiding old, worn-out Hollywood or MTV models.

Seeking Noncorporate Models

No one makes up a story film in a vacuum. We reach around for models, and what do we come up with? Hollywood or TV. Unfortunately, these are not good models for makers of short films. There is no way that, as a filmmaker of limited means and experience, you can come close to the technical perfection of even the lowliest made-for-TV flick. If you imitate Hollywood plots—gorgeous lovers, undercover agents, intrepid heroes—audiences will just patronize you and go, "Well, that was nice." But they will say this in the same way that someone admires a dancing dog. It's cute, but far short of the real thing.

Instead, swear off Big Media models. Go with the essence of short films, which is simplicity and authenticity. Short film stories are ideally suited for exploring everyday life. They look at slices of life. When you approach film this way, no one compares you with Hollywood and gives you the sonny-boy routine.

Here are two films that do that.

Sasha's Passion

From *Sasha's Passion* by Sarah Morris.

Sasha's Passion is a five-minute story film by Sarah Morris that explores some very human aspects of character. Sasha works at a deli making sandwiches. A guy, Jeremy, comes in. He's young, good-looking, but a bit innocent and really not too perceptive. All the same, Sasha seems to like Jeremy, maybe for these very qualities. She keeps smiling at him from behind the counter; it's a nice smile, a winning smile, which makes her very pretty. The quality of the smile is very important, because it goes beyond just being friendly to a customer. It's a little flirtatious. But something in it holds back, too.

Jeremy, however, doesn't pick up. He's out of touch. That's his character, and the source of humor. Audiences start to laugh at how Sasha's flirting is wasted on the guy. Sarah directed all this with great finesse, keeping Sasha somewhere in the midrange of coming on—eager, but not obvious. As things unfold, the guy orders a sandwich, which Sasha lovingly puts together.

Sasha also writes her phone number on the napkin she wraps around the sandwich. The guy takes his sandwich to a table, sits down, and starts eating. Sasha keeps casting glances at Jeremy, but she's guarded, too, secretive. She won't just come out and ask the guy for a date, or whatever. Jeremy never notices the phone number. He finishes the sandwich, nods appreciatively at Sasha, wads up the napkin with the phone number he never saw, and stuffs it in a trash can. Then he's out the door. The last shot shows Sasha sighing.

Possible Themes in Sasha's Passion

Theme has to do with that "truth" I wrote about earlier, that insight, meaning, or lesson that all honestly told stories exhibit. A possible theme of *Sasha's Passion* is "we often fail to get what we want from life by not being forthright enough." Or, if you see it from the guy's point of view, the theme is "food takes precedence over romance." Contrary to popular mythology, food is not the way to a man's heart.

There are other themes in *Sasha's Passion* having to do with natural male obtuseness. They just don't get it. So there is a distance between Sasha and the young man. There is a barrier. Sasha can't just come right out and say something like, "Hey, pay attention to me!" Why is that? Because she is a woman? Because she is a lowly food worker? Because the guy is dense? Is this a man's problem, a woman's burden?

The Silence Between Us

The Silence Between Us is another simple film based on everyday life that, like *Sasha's Passion*, isn't all that simple. It's about a girl leaving a guy. Apparently, they live together. The guy is sleeping on the sofa. It's daytime. She puts on makeup in the bathroom, but she does this as if mulling something over, as if trying to make up her mind about something. The bathroom is a good place for her to do this. She has to look at herself in the mirror, which is to say, she has to look at *her self*. Should she leave the guy or not? Makeup equals makeover, a change of faces, new beginnings. It's a good symbol.

The woman leaves the man she'd been living with. A somber moment.

This film is on the DVD.

The girl uses her lipstick to write on the mirror, "Leaving you." Then she goes out, beholds the guy asleep—suggesting that he wasn't active enough for her—goes to him, leans over and kisses him, then leaves the apartment with a suitcase, always a symbol of moving out and starting over in film. This film was made by Sarah Hagey and Katherine Jose.

Possible Themes in The Silence Between Us

The Silence Between Us is a great font of themes because, one, the situation again is so human, and two, Sarah and Katherine stay simple and minimalistic. A girl leaves a guy. He's not right for her. But she's humane about it. You can sense that the girl still cares about the guy. You can tell that by the way she leaves him, almost regretfully, almost feeling sorry for him. Also, she leaves in broad daylight while the guy naps, as if wanting to get "caught"—instead of at night when he might be gone or sound asleep. She doesn't just slam the door behind her. Her caring, her conflicted state of mind, is the whole film. The complexity of her character suggests a few themes—hesitation, thinking twice, leaving a life that maybe wasn't so bad, but not terrific either, wanting more. You pay attention. Details count. You read in, which is a common thing to do with minimalist films.

TRY THIS

Make some notes on a character on whom you might base an everyday film. By "everyday," I don't mean boring. I mean all too human. Your character seems real because he's doing something that a lot of people do naturally, every day. We can see ourselves in him. Audiences can identify with him. After this, figure out a story that he drives. Then go ahead and make a little film about the character.

Plot Is Less Important

When you plan a short film with a character based on everyday life, you are less preoccupied with plot—that sense of things always happening and mounting tension that leads up to a wham-bang climax. Instead, character drives the story. There is a story, to be sure, and a plot, but these elements are secondary. You engage viewers not by a constant barrage of what-will-happen-next but by who-is-this-character? And what will happen because of him?

Simple Cinematics

Cinematics refers to the visual and aural aspects of film, shooting, editing, and adding nonverbal sound. Both *Sasha's Passion* and *The Silence Between Us* benefit from thoughtful shooting and editing. Much of the effectiveness of *Sasha's Passion* comes near the end when Sarah films Jeremy in close-up as he eats and Sasha in close-up as she steals glances at him. Then Sarah cuts back and forth between the two close-ups, alternating snippets, employing a time-honored technique called cross-cutting by which two shots are cut into several pieces and alternated (by editing) in the finished film. The close-ups isolate each of the actors and invite us to contemplate their characters. We gaze at one, then the other, and soon come to understand Sasha's unexpressed passion and Jeremy's doltishness. It's the perfect frame and the perfect editing technique for going deeper into the story. (Flip back to page 53 for more about cross-cutting.)

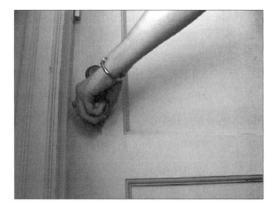

Often, beginning filmmakers neglect to take shots like this. They are interested mainly in wide and busy. Wide frames certainly have their place, but often the essence of character or theme resides in tight frames that show detail.

I just want to mention one shot from *The Silence Between Us*, and that is a close-up of the girl's hand lingering on the doorknob as she closes the door behind her and leaves. The shot runs two seconds longer than it probably should. Shot length alone, then, communicates as much about the girl's reluctance as anything else in the film. This is simple, minimalist cinematics—the best kind.

(Flip back to page 74 for more about film frames—long shots, medium shots, close-ups, and so on.)

SCHOOL YOURSELF

Check out these feature films, which are based on everyday people and events:

The Trip to Bountiful	Lovely and Amazing
Marty	Sweet Sixteen
The Graduate	Baby Boy
The Last Picture Show	The Good Girl
Ferris Bueller's Day Off	Thirteen
Fresh	Sideways
You Can Count on Me	

None of these films has thrills and spills in the usual Hollywood sense, though all have drama, everyday drama.

SCHOOL YOURSELF

Go to a video store and browse for films about everyday life. Take a chance on one or two. Let the slam-bang action films (which usually are devoid of common, everyday human qualities) just sit there on the shelves.

SHORT FILM STORIES BASED ON EXTRAORDINARY PEOPLE OR EVENTS

The other way of going deeper into the film story is to do just the opposite of making films about everyday characters and situations—that is, explore characters who are not so everyday. Instead, they are unique individuals, up against it, outsiders living on the edge. Their stories don't catch them doing everyday things, like leaving a guy, and yet they aren't like the usual run of cops, gangsters, or buff action heroes you see in Hollywood movies. They come from a different place, maybe the personal experience of the filmmaker.

Following are two negative-toned films. Both feature characters on the fringes of society.

Photo Finish

Photo Finish is a film I made about a world-weary young woman who wants to take her life by carbon-monoxide poisoning in her sealed-up VW bus. But she's interrupted by a

From *Photo Finish*. They strike a deal.

cynical photographer with designs to photograph the unhappy event for profit.

The setting is an abandoned junkyard strewn with rusted hulks of cars and trucks, but no people or dogs. The photographer saves her, but not because he's such a good guy; he saves her to interview her, then stage the suicide so he can sell the story and the photos to a tabloid newspaper. But she balks. She wants something out of the deal— namely, to take some pictures with his camera. Apparently, she's had some photographic experience. He reluctantly agrees.

The girl sees beauty in the junkyard. She finds interesting shapes and textures among the abandoned vehicles to photograph. The photographer has no sense for this and is impatient the whole time. Finally, she is finished; he can take the bogus suicide pictures. But his cynicism and selfishness anger the girl so much that she sends him away. Soon, she decides to go ahead with her real suicide. The photographer creeps back and takes photos of her dead in the bed of the bus.

Characterization in Photo Finish

I meant for the photographer to embody all the qualities of life the woman loathes and makes her want to check out even more. To the photographer, she is just a commodity. The woman changes for the better during the unfolding of the story. We want her to find renewal in the taking of pictures. We want her to tell the photographer to go away so that she can become a stronger and healthier person. The film could end with her in a pawn-shop buying a camera, starting a new life, bolstered by the art of photography. But it doesn't end like this. I had a darker vision.

Theme in Photo Finish

Much in this film is thematic—that is, meaningful—and this could be a fault of the film. The photographer represents all the negative forces against life. The girl, who represents sensitivity, just can't stand up to the photographer's negativism. The film "says" that sensitivity and artistic sensibility are fragile things, overwhelmed in the end by cynicism.

The Junkyard as Metaphor

In *Photo Finish*, the junkyard is the world. It also represents a second chance for the girl. Sure, the world sucks. It's strewn with bad accidents. It's ugly. But the trick is to see your own salvation or hope in it and turn its ugliness into beauty—and hope.

Cinematics in Photo Finish

I wanted the visuals of *Photo Finish* to make the viewers think. Much of the film rests on an elementary technique of shooting and editing called the point-of-view (POV) sequence. The sequence consists of three shots: 1) someone looking, usually in close-up; 2) a cut to what the person sees, as through her eyes; and 3) a shot that cuts back to the person to show her reaction to what she saw. *Photo Finish* has many POV sequences. As the woman photographs various things in the junkyard, she looks, we see what she sees, then she reacts—with interest, absorption, and delight. (Flip back to page 54 where nuts-and-bolts techniques like POV sequences are discussed.)

School Yourself

Check out these feature films, which are full of extraordinary characters—cut off and desperate. These are films, not movies.

Manon of the Spring	Edward Scissorhands
Easy Rider	Quills
One Flew Over the Cuckoo's Nest	O Brother, Where Art Thou?
Taxi Driver	Downfall
Wings of Desire	Tarnation
My Left Foot	

Bomb Ready to Explode

Although *Bomb Ready to Explode* is a fiction film, it's based on the true-life story of a registered sex offender whom a psychologist friend of mine treated for a time. My friend ultimately became discouraged, quit the profession, and went to work for Fresno City Schools. He made this film, which mirrors his frustration.

I don't have access to the original film, but with the filmmaker's permission, I have reconstructed *Bomb Ready to Explode* in the form of a screenplay, written in what is called "master scenes." The format of this screenplay is pretty close to the kind of screenplay that floats around the film industry. I thought you'd like to see it, not only to follow the story and the commentary that follows, but also because you may want to try your hand at this kind of scriptwriting yourself some day.

A SCREENPLAY FOR *BOMB READY TO EXPLODE*

1. A rural road. We see a sign by the side of the road that says "The New Rock Lompoc Federal Correctional Facility." A car speeds away from the facility, pulling the camera to the right, revealing a cluster of one-story buildings in the background surrounded by chain-link fence.

2. Cut to car. Woman drives. Man is buoyant, happy. He looks like a man who's just been given his freedom. She is Vera; he is Thomas. Vera pats him on the leg.

                    Vera
          Okay, Thomas. So all that's
          behind you now.

   Thomas nods. He wants to agree. He really does. But the slightest shadow of uncertainty clouds his face.

3. A parole office. Institutional, official, a little bleak. A parole officer and a psychologist interview, or rather lecture, Thomas. The parole officer is Philips, the psychologist Santini. Vera is present.

                    Philips
          You understand, Thomas, what we
          have here. One slip-up and
          back to Lompoc you go. I mean,
          you so much as look at a
          kid for over two seconds,

and I find out, I send
your ass back to the slammer.
You got that?

Thomas nods. But it's that same conflicted nod he gave in the car.

> Santini
> (to Philips)
> Hey, Dan, back off. It's going to be
> fine. I've arranged for Thomas to
> interview for a job. I mean, it's not
> a great job, but it's a job. Right, Thomas?

Thomas nods again, tries to smile.

> Santini
> (to Thomas)
> We're all on your side, Thomas.

Thomas smiles weakly at Santini.

Cut to Vera. She gives a subtle performance with her face, by turns hopeful, fearful, and confused. The scene cuts to her often. Each cut adds a layer of meaning.

4. Behind a McDonald's. Thomas is seen in a McDonald's uniform. He's sweeping in the parking lot. A car drives up, and a mother and her two children get out and walk toward the restaurant. Thomas stops his sweeping and watches the children. He watches and watches. He works up some real lust. He grips the broom tighter and tighter. The mother and the children go inside. Thomas looks like he's been through a lot. He resumes sweeping.

5. A modest apartment. It looks like night. The angle is an unfinished dinner on a table. Camera pans down to broken plates on the floor and food scattered around. It's like there was a fight and someone got up fast and sent the dishes flying. While we see this, we hear Vera and Thomas fighting, off-camera.

> Thomas
> I shouldn't have told you.
> I thought you'd understand.

                          Vera
              What's to understand? You see
              a couple of kids, you want to
              rape them. Damn you, Thomas,
              I don't know why I stay with you.

At this point, we see Vera's legs as she carries a broom to the
mess. She stoops to the mess and uses a dustpan to clean it up,
but the angle is three-quarters rear. We still don't see her
face. Thomas comes up. We see only his legs, and he stands
slightly menacingly over Vera, who now turns, shows her face—
she's frightened—looks up at Thomas, then rises to him.

                        Thomas
              I just want to talk. Talking helps.

Now, Vera rises and puts her arms around Thomas.

                          Vera
                    (affectionately)
              I'm sorry, baby. I'm scared,
              is all. Really scared. I do the
              time, too. I'm alone while you're
              inside. It's hard.

She maneuvers him into the kitchen.

                      Vera (con't)
              Come on, I got a little dessert.
              Strawberries with whipped cream.
              You can help me fix it.
              Then we'll talk.

6. Montage. We see the couple in the kitchen. Close-ups of straw-
   berries and whipped cream. At the table, eating the dessert,
   appearing to talk. In the living room, with the TV on low,
   still talking. In the bedroom, in bed, the room darkened,
   Thomas still talking. Actually, Thomas does all of the talking.
   Vera listens. But when we see her, she isn't exactly looking
   sympathetic. She's more scared than sympathetic. During this
   sequence, Vera's facial expression changes from sympathy and
   understanding to a gradually backing away from Thomas and
   mounting fear. We hear Thomas's voiceover through all of this.

                            Thomas
                    (voiceover, to Vera)
          I can't seem to help myself. I did
          the time, too. I was away from children.
          I talked to the shrink in the joint.
          He was a nice guy and all, but you know,
          he never fixed me. I'd see pictures of
          kids in magazines, and want to be with
          them. So I get out, I start a new life.
          But I can't put the thing down. It's like
          some kind of addiction. Like I'm hooked
          on little children.

     At the end of this montage, Vera turns away from Thomas. In the
     half-dark, she looks terrified. She says nothing.

7.   Day at the apartment. Vera comes in. Thomas isn't there. Vera
     goes to answering machine, presses a button.

                        Answering Machine
          Hi, this is Stan, manager at McDonald's.
          Look, we're short-handed today and
          really need Thomas. If he can still
          make it, we'd appreciate it.

     Vera is very worried. She looks around.

                            Vera
                           Thomas!

     No answer.
     Vera leaves, jingling car keys nervously.

8.   Near a school. Vera drives up and sees Thomas twenty or thirty
     yards away. He's sitting on a lawn, watching little kids get
     out of school. Cut to Thomas. He's not aware that Vera sees
     him. He watches and watches, dreamy-eyed, totally out of touch.
     Cut back to Vera. She is totally disgusted, at the end of her
     patience. She drives off. Thomas never sees her.

9.   At the apartment. Vera is frantically packing Thomas's things
     in a couple of cardboard boxes. It's like she wants to finish

the packing before Thomas gets back. She's weeping as she packs. She's in real agony. She stops briefly to sob. She pulls the boxes to just in front of the outside door. She writes a note, and tapes it to one of the boxes. She works fast, desperate, afraid. She gets her purse, goes out.

10. Outside. Continuous with scene 9. Vera pauses at the car door and puts a hand on her stomach. She gets in the car and drives off.

11. The apartment. Thomas arrives, enters, sees the boxes with his things, checks the things out, reads the note, lets it flutter to the floor. He stands like he isn't sure what has happened or doesn't know what to do. He is stunned, his reactions and feelings suppressed and blunted. He goes out.

12. Thomas walking down a sidewalk. He enters a park.

13. Thomas sitting at a picnic table in the park. A short distance away, kids play on playground equipment. A few parents are seen. Thomas sits and gazes at the kids. Cutaways tell us that he's especially interested in one pretty little girl. But his close-up changes. It starts off registering muted lust in his face, but his expression gradually turns to inner conflict and regret. He knows he is on the verge of doing a very bad thing, but he can't help himself.

Bomb Ready to Explode runs about twelve minutes.

Characterization in Bomb Ready to Explode

The most interesting character in the story is Vera, not Thomas. It's her story. It has to do with coping with an impossible situation. Vera changes. Characters who change usually interest us more than those who don't. Thomas doesn't really change. He did not get better in prison, and he goes back to doing bad things when he gets out.

Vera is a commendable character. At first, she apparently has faith in Thomas and wants to do right by him. But she runs out of patience. Or fear overtakes her. At one point in the story, Thomas wants to talk, but Vera ends up being very frightened. Now she has to face her situation straight on, and it scares her.

Vera packs up Thomas's belongings in a complete sweat. Her actions reveal her frame of mind. She's extremely fearful that Thomas will do something criminal, and she doesn't want to be around then.

Vera might also feel a little guilty, being partially responsible for putting Thomas back on the street. So, should she disconnect? Is that okay? Should she have stood by her man? Or is Thomas too much for her? Can we forgive her for putting Thomas out? This is really complex drama and complex characterization—for only twelve minutes.

We have to give some credit to Thomas. His confession of scenes 5 and 6 greatly extends his character. He isn't just some machine, being bad to children. He is trying. He wants to change. His monologue helps us understand him and feel for him. But his final close-up, when he changes from lust to inner turmoil, suggests that the bad side of him will take over.

School Yourself

Read a few screenplays, to get the hang of how they are formatted and how detailed they are. Here are three good ones:

Fargo, by Ethan Coen and Joel Coen (Faber and Faber, 1996)

Good Will Hunting, by Matt Damon and Ben Affleck (Miramax Hyperion, 1997)

Taxi Driver, by Paul Schrader (Faber and Faber, 1990)

You can buy screenplays at big bookstores and online.

Possible Themes in Bomb Ready to Explode

So what does all this add up to? Here are some possible truths—but with a small *t*—that cluster around *Bomb Ready to Explode*:

- Evil-seeming people aren't really evil. What, after all, is evil? These haunted souls struggle with dark forces within themselves. They have bad genes or bad chemistry or bad synapses in their brains or bad something. They can't help themselves. But they aren't just reincarnations of the devil.
- It's far more tragic to know you have a huge mental problem that could get you in very serious trouble than to just go ahead and do the bad thing without thinking about it or reflecting on it. Thomas is like this, and we feel sorry for him as a result. Monsters aren't aware. Thomas is.
- Women who stay with bad men may do so because they have faith that the men will come around and eventually adhere to a true, good course in life. (This could be turned around: Men who stay with bad women, etc.)

> Women (or men) who eventually have to leave their bad men (or women) are just being human. We should see matters through their eyes. They can be strong and supportive only so long. We don't condemn them for leaving.

> Specifically, there seems to be no cure for men (or women) who molest children.

Minimalist Cinematics in Bomb Ready to Explode

Here, I want to combine two aspects of the film: its filming and editing, and its minimalist strategies. The filming and editing are blunt, straightforward, and simple—nothing fancy. I remember the original film to have been a bit overproduced for my taste, with too many shots, too many close-ups, too many words, and too much editing. My conception opts for simpler and shorter.

However, one shot in the original film that I have retained is especially telling—and economical. It occurs when Thomas looks at the kids in the McDonald's parking lot. He holds a broom. He slides his curved fingers down the broom. Some viewers found this tasteless. To me, it was a minimalist suggestion of Thomas's problem. It should not be overdone. One second of it is all that is needed. It's the kind of effect every minimalist filmmaker should strive for.

Here are a few more minimalist aspects of *Bomb Ready to Explode*:

> The filmmaker didn't even attempt to film inside the McDonald's, where we might have seen Thomas behind the counter. That was just too hard to set up. And the filmmaker probably wouldn't be able to get permission to film inside, anyway. So he actually had someone make a McDonald's uniform for Thomas and filmed him in the parking lot behind the place. He had a friend walk through the shot with her children, though the children did not know what was going on. The filmmaker shot guerrilla behind the McDonald's. This means that you rehearse in a safe place, then go into the sensitive location and shoot as fast as you can, then get the hell out—all without asking permission.

> In the original film, soon after she packs up Thomas's things, Vera pauses to get her breath and puts her hand on her stomach. This suggests that Vera thinks that she could be pregnant.

> The end of the film—there is no actual, on-screen child molestation in the film. I hope you don't try to produce or film anything like this. You don't have to. Instead, you only suggest. I say this not only to protect the children in the film, but as a general precept of minimalist filmmaking, including scenes of violence and sex.

School Yourself

Drop by a bookstore or a library and browse through the film books. Locate books about the connection between literature and film. Buy or check out one or two. Because that's what you are doing when you make a film like *Photo Finish* or *Bomb Ready to Explode*, making cinematic literature. It would be good for you to know a few things about how literature works.

Or, take an introductory literature course. Consider some short films, maybe yours, a form of literature. Make a short film that works like literature.

Try This

Make a film about a person living on the edge. Possible character types: lovers; lovers and why they connect with each other; lovers just hopelessly in love to the exclusion of everything else; lovers just hopelessly in love to the exclusion of everything else and who get themselves in big trouble because of it; drug addicts; guy dumped, and how that feels; girl dumped, and how that feels; guy on verge of leaving woman with children he helped support; woman fed up with family life, wants to leave her man and children, start a new life alone, but feels guilty; someone suicidal, with good reasons for wanting to end it; a criminal or two; bored worker, really out to lunch, chafing, wants to be someone else, doesn't come back from lunch; a runaway; a crazy person; a homeless person; an assassin; man trapped in a woman's body; woman trapped in a man's body; gays in a town that hates gays; gays that hate straights; lesbian lovers; a spy; someone who abuses; someone who is abused.

Keep the film short. Use minimalist means. (Flip back to page 6 for the minimalist means for *Little Star*.)

LIGHTEN UP!

So much for heavy and dreary. Let's lighten up!

Pawn of Pawns

Pawn of Pawns is a film based on one of the most extraordinary characters in history, Jesus. Some people might think this film is blasphemous, but not me. To me, it has a major theme to get across: If Christ were crucified today, nobody would give a damn. Nobody would stop it. The public would just let him hang there and die. The film uses only two characters, a kind of soldier and a modern-day Christ

Pawn of Pawns is a super 8 film made years ago by Kirk Whitney.

who drags a pretty-big cross down a suburban street, through the parking lot of a shopping center, and up a hill of garbage at a junkyard stand-in for Calvary.

The cross is about six feet long and looks like it was made out of four-by-fours, but I think it was really fashioned from something like Styrofoam. The soldier brandishes a kind of spear and gives Christ a little poke with it every now and then. Christ's robe drags in the dirt. He looks at it, frowns, then gets the soldier to let him stop at a laundromat. He wants to be presentable for his big day. So he washes and fluffs his robe while the soldier reads *People* magazine. Then they get on the road again. Yes, this makes Christ vain, and I know that some viewers will object to this. It also makes him human right up to the end.

Crack Is Wack

Remember the old adage, "Step on a crack, break your mother's back"? This film, by Ian McAlleese, is that adage. It just goes to show: Anything is fair game for the maker of short films. Ian's film runs two minutes.

Ian plays the crack stepper. In this clip, he looks down to discover, to his horror, that he has stepped on a crack.

And here's what happened to poor Mom.
This film is on the DVD.

TRY THIS

Make a funny or spoofy film. You ask: "And just how do I do that?" For Kirk Whitney, the secret is irreverence—making Christ a vanity case who has to have a clean robe before he's crucified. Here are some other subjects we tend to worship, which you might treat satirically or irreverently:

Athletes	Pop icons	Social class
Cars	Schooling	Sports
Cellphones	Sex	TV
Education	Shopping	Work
Family		

Then you exaggerate. A teacher is totally, unbelievably pretentious or absentminded; work is mind-numbingly boring; family is oppressively possessive, demanding, or neglectful; shopping is obsessive, pathological; cars are transformed into lovers. (See my description of a film called *Project 454*, in chapter 4. It's about a guy who makes love to his VW bug.)

K.C. and Byron's Day of Fun

Okay, now back to the ordinary and everyday. *K.C. and Byron's Day of Fun* is about doing everyday stuff. It's amazing how Byron Watkins turns material like going through a fast-food drive-through or tossing a football around in a park into humor. Actually, this is one of the nuttiest films I have ever seen. If Jerry Lewis or Jim Carrey took my class, this is the kind of film they would make. I don't even know whether it should be called a story film. It could be a documentary; it could be an art film. Or maybe it's a home movie. It's actually not very deep, but it sure is different and fun to watch.

That's Byron on the left.

It's about Byron and his roommate, K.C., who get up one morning and decide to go out and mess around. It's about noon, so off they go for fast food. They drive through three or four places like Taco Bell and KFC, and later, in the editing, Byron tightens this up and seems to know just when to cut, like right after "I'll have a corn dog." Audiences always laugh at these cuts. It's like a comment on contemporary youth, driving around, eating bad food, communicating about profound matters like whether the chicken should be classic or extra crispy. Byron knows how to poke fun at the foibles of his generation. So maybe the film is deeper than I give it credit for.

TRY THIS

Improvise a film, as Byron did. Like I said, Byron does it all. He writes, acts, directs, cajoles, coaxes, and makes it up as he goes along. If you are something like this, kind of clownish and silly-ass, you may want to try your hand at an improvised film. Or maybe you know someone like this and want to base a film on his antics. The trick is to shoot a lot and shape the film into a story during editing. If you think you are after humor, don't be afraid to laugh at yourself. A list of some situations that provide focus and still leave lots of room for improvising follows. All have potential to be stories:

Camping trip	Driving to a big city	Hiking
Crazy guy preaching hellfire	Escaping	Hitchhiking
and damnation	Fishing trip	Panhandling
Decorating a Christmas tree		

MINIMALIST STORY FILMS

Byron's film required only himself, K.C., and a friend to run the camera. Here are a few more films like that—simple, minimalistic.

Chris set the camera on a tripod and filmed himself playing the addict.

Empty

Empty is a one-man film by Chris Garcia is about a love affair between a man and his cocaine. First, the addict scores with a crummy guy under a freeway. Then he goes off to an abandoned house and snorts up. End of film. Yes, it does seem too simple to be much of anything. But the slow pacing and the off-kilter visuals are accompanied by a seductive love song called "It's So Nice," which completes the sad, ironic tone of the film. It wouldn't be much of a film at all without the seductive, ironic song. Sometimes, the right music can make a film.

A Hero Will Rise

A Hero Will Rise is another one-man film about a man and his dog. It, too, is a love affair. Bryce Thurston, like Chris Garcia, set the camera on a tripod and filmed himself being with his dog, for whom he has total affection. Bryce lies on the sofa and looks dreamily

From *A Hero Will Rise* by Bryce Thurston.

at the dog, a few feet off. He beckons, the dog comes—and so on. Meanwhile, among three or four scenes of man-canine bonding, Bryce shows us a Batman headpiece on a kind of wig stand in the corner of the apartment where all this takes place. Then tragedy—the dog, while outside, is shot by someone. We don't see the actual shooting, but we hear the gun shot. Bryce carries the dog inside. He mourns and mourns. Then he snaps into action by donning the headpiece. The music swells. He means to avenge. At the same time, this is not a serious film. The first time you see Bryce in the headpiece, you laugh.

Even more, you marvel at Bryce's ingenuity in filming the dog being playful, showing affection, going in and out of the house, lying dead. The film is made entirely in the editing.

Planta's Suicide

Planta's Suicide is another spoofy "sad" story film about a plant—a flowering plant in a pot—that takes its own life. It's a film about an extraordinary plant, I guess. Planta, the plant, was brought home from the nursery by Hannah, her caregiver. At first, Hannah positively dotes on Planta, watering her, dancing round and round in the living room with her, even sitting with her on the sofa so the two can watch TV. But after a time, Hannah brings home another plant, and—sigh!—starts to neglect Planta, who then goes into decline. Her flowers droop, her leaves start to fall. Hannah notices this and does all she can to save her, finally deciding that she needs more sunlight. So she places Planta outside on a railing. But Planta does not want to carry on. She wills herself to topple off the railing and falls two stories to the sidewalk below. At this point, a title says "Planta had a quick funeral"—Hanna sweeps her up and deposits her in a trashcan. Hannah Rae made this engaging film, and she made it pretty much by herself.

It's just damn hard sometimes to get commitments from people to help you make a film. So forget them. Instead, whittle the film down to just you as the talent, a trustworthy friend behind the camera, a prop like a dog or a plant, and a good idea. These minimalist films are unique in the world. Hannah Rae is the talent here. She also wrote and filmed herself by placing the camera on a tripod and framing herself with the camera's LCD screen, which can be flipped around completed to face the action.

This film is on the DVD.

TRY THIS

Make a minimalist story film. Get a tripod and film yourself doing this and that in a simple story. Exploit a single prop like a potted plant, dog, or Batman costume. Or get one person to film you, or you film her.

SCHOOL YOURSELF

Spend some time with a good film critic to get the hang of film narrative values. It's hard to beat *For Keeps* by Pauline Kael. This is a thirty-year compilation of Kael's incomparable reviews for the *New Yorker* magazine.

School Yourself

SOUND IN STORY FILMS

Basically, you have these choices:

➤ Live sound: Ambient sounds or dialogue recorded on videotape as you film, or recorded on a separate tape recorder.

➤ Narration: Someone in the story, or not in the story, explains things, maybe background things, thereby considerably speeding up the film.

➤ Music: Maybe not much at all, as in *Bomb Ready to Explode*, which has just a little bit of dissonant string music at the start and end, or maybe a great deal of music as in *K.C. and Byron's Day of Fun*.

➤ Sound effects: Birds, explosions, cats meowing, applause, machine guns, horses' hooves, etc. All DV editing programs come with ten or twelve sound effects; you can download lots of sound effects from the Internet. You can also record these effects yourself, like next to a freeway or at a construction site or birds in a park.

➤ Silence: Perhaps underrated and too little used by beginners. Don't fear silence. Silence is expressive.

A little bit of dark dialogue from *Generations* by Irvin Benut. "Where is my dinner?" "I've been busy." "Yeah, and I've worked all day." Then he slugs her.

Developing Dialogue

As I have said, most of these narrative films do not include much dialogue. *Photo Finish* is the talkiest. Dialogue is short and to the point in *Bomb Ready to Explode*.

The best way to develop dialogue is to involve your cast: You write, they act out, they critique, you rewrite. Maybe two or three times.

TRY THIS

Do a film with a little dialogue in it. Make sure that the dialogue conveys matters that your visuals and sound track can't. To develop the dialogue, use both methods I suggest: 1) improvise and 2) write the dialogue down with the understanding that your cast and crew probably have good suggestions for revision.

10

Deeper into the Documentary Film

*M*aking a documentary film gives you more choices than you might think. And if you opt for a *short* documentary, you'll have even more choices. To get started, let's think of three kinds of documentaries:

- ➤ realist documentary
- ➤ formalist documentary
- ➤ *vérité* documentary

Now, if you were taking some courses in documentary filmmaking, your professors would not give you this particular breakout. They wouldn't understand "formalist" documentary, for example. And they might say that *vérité* documentary filmmaking is too limiting. But I am not a professor of documentary filmmaking, and this book is not film school. It's about making short films, don't forget. The form of the short film suggests different approaches to rendering reality. *Reality*—that is our anchor in this chapter.

REALIST DOCUMENTARY FILMMAKING

Realist documentaries are the kind you see most often—educational films, *Front Line* on PBS, TV news stories, segments from *60 Minutes,* feature films like *Enron: The Smartest Guys in the Room* and *Fahrenheit 9/11*. Even home movies may be considered "realist documentaries" in a sense. That is what they teach you to do in film school, make realist documentaries. Realist documentaries endeavor to present information and ideas about something "real" out there in the world with a minimum of distortion or cinematic rendering, although understand that due to the very nature of film, there is a lot of distortion going on.

Socially Conscious Documentaries

One of the deepest roots of realist documentary filmmaking has to do with calling attention to various social ills in a way that spurs viewers to action. After you see the documentary, you are then supposed to be on the side of one thing and opposed to the opposite thing. Often, the film is intimately related to politics of either the left or the right.

Save the Canal

The short film is ideally suited to local politics. *Save the Canal* is a socially conscious film that was part of a successful effort to ward off insensitive, county-level bureaucracy. The Metropolitan Flood Control District of Fresno County wanted to pave over a picturesque, dirt-bank canal—the last in Central California, in fact. But to the local residents, the canal was just fine, even if an old tire washed up on the bank now and then. It was a lovely, creeklike sliver of nature that supported aquatic plants, crayfish, frogs, trout, herons, and egrets—in the middle of Fresno, a city of half a million sitting in the middle of the semi-arid San Joaquin Valley.

When you make a documentary like *Save the Canal,* you have two choices. You can hang out at the canal all day, hoping people willing to be in your film will come along. Or you can arrange or "stage" things by having friends and family walk, fish, or ride bikes along the banks of the canal. Carol Piper and Stephanie Brown were filming some white egrets when this bicyclist happened by.

The locals fought back in several ways. Carol Piper and Stephanie Brown, avowedly pro-canal, made *Save the Canal.* They interviewed a variety of people: residents who walk their dogs along the banks of the canal, kids who fish in it, ecologists from the nearby university, schoolteachers. They got their film shown on local TV. The Fresno *Bee* did a couple of stories on their fight. The middle school, which flanks the canal, let the locals use its all-purpose room for various pro-canal activities. (This is in the film.) In time, the Flood Control District backed off. Ask Stephanie and Carol whether their film had anything to do with it. They will tell you it did.

The Cat House on the Kings

I got involved in this project, which I admit has a limited social purpose but a broader humane purpose, namely, to come to the rescue of 400 cats. That's right, 400 cats.

A very determined and caring woman by the name of Lynea Lattanzio lives on five acres out in the country south of Fresno on the King's River. What she does is rescue cats from people who abandon them and from the Humane Society, which wants to exterminate them. When I shot a home movie of Lynea and her place, she had 400 cats on her property. Feeding and cleaning up after these animals requires just about all of her time, and a lot of time of several cat-loving volunteers. It was easy to see that Lynea was nearly overwhelmed, a prisoner of her compassion.

Carol and I went out there, and I shot half an hour of footage with my old analog VHS camcorder, home-movie style—cats, Lynea, the house.

Then I did a more put-together film of the cat house, something beyond a home movie. I went back to the cat house and interviewed Lynea. Footage of cute cats would not be enough. I needed facts, and Lynea, a good interview, supplied me with lots of them. Later, when I converted my filmmaking class to digital and bought a DV camera myself (and an iMac to go with it), I made the film. I converted my analog footage to digital, then imported it into my iMac. I cut the footage down to five minutes, stripped most of Lynea's interview from her shots and paired it with footage of the cats, added some sweet dissolves, and put a languid, slinky Miles Davis ballad to it all. To finish, I exported the edited film to VHS tape—in fact, a half a dozen tapes, so Lynea could send them off to various funding agencies. This was several years before DVD went consumerist. Today I'd export to DVD.

Did I lose much in image and sound quality going from analog to digital and back to analog (VHS)? Surprisingly little. The film in its VHS version looks and sounds passably good. Digital is an amazing image preserver this way.

Poisoned Water, Poisoned Wells

Poisoned Water, Poisoned Wells is a thirty-one-minute super 8 documentary, and I guess the longest film in the book. It was made a number of years ago by David Frank, a chemist who was one of the first to call attention to the dangerous levels of the toxic compound DBCP, which is found in the water table of Fresno County. According to David, the application of DBCP by farmers has been the culprit. His film features footage of farmlands, interviews with both farmers and water experts, inserted slides and illustrations David had prepared for his classes on environmental chemistry—all narrated by Michael Loring. The film was controversial in its time—the issue itself was controversial. The farmers David interviewed were adamantly opposed to ceasing their use of DBCP, and felt the whole issue was overplayed. Water people and professors held the opposite view. It's a lively film this way.

Still, *Poisoned Water, Poisoned Wells* is professorial and fact-heavy. It lacks the Miles Davis cool of my cat film. It's not supposed to be cool. It's serious. Dave's film got shown several dozen times to large audiences in the Central California area. It's hard to say just what impact the film has had, but the entire agricultural community today is quite aware of the dangers of DBCP, so David feels vindicated, if not in some way responsible for the change of public outlook.

TRY THIS

Make a socially conscious documentary. Base it on some local issue, like the damage so-called city planners can do or the need for trees in the parking lots of your town. Interview city planners, people affected by city planning decisions, drivers who have to park in treeless parking lots in the middle of August, landscape architects, or shopping center managers. Read your local newspaper for stories that could turn into films.

Keep the issue very simple, like the need for crossing guards on a busy street near a school. That's pretty easy. Get shots of kids. Get shots of menacing cars zipping by. Interview a crossing guard, the principal, a few parents. Put it all together. Skip music. Keep the finished film very short—five minutes, tops.

Documentaries That Aren't Out to Save the World

Here are a few realist documentaries that aren't so political.

From *In Five* by Dave Bletz.

Mike probably needed a little more light to make this film. Dark is fine for many films, but in this film we should be able to see the piercing better. A helper with a clip-on light standing off-camera would have helped.

In Five

In Five by Dave Bletz goes behind the scenes to document the hustle and bustle of getting ready for a local TV newscast. The editing is brisk, and as the film comes down to actually going on the air, the tempo of the editing picks up, capturing visually the tension the crew and talent must feel. Dave's film runs four minutes and is in real time—that is, real time and screen time are the same. You have a lot of respect for the high level of professionalism the newspeople bring to their jobs and for the many details that have to be seen to leading up to a typical telecast.

Inksanity

Inksanity is a documentary about body piercing by Mike Gomez. It runs about seven minutes, and if you have never had your body pierced, it's pretty hard to watch. (Maybe it's hard to watch even if you *have* had your body pierced.) Mike goes through all the steps leading up to the insertion of a ring or a stud in a nipple, navel, and eyelid. The audiences I have shown this film to always go, "Ugh!" and "Yuck!"— yet they are transfixed, too. They can't look away.

What makes Mike's film work so well is its interviews with the owner of the body-piercing shop and a few of his clients. The interviewer speaks in a clear and confident voice and asks excellent questions. He brings out crucial facts. He gets people to talk about their reactions and feelings. The result is a balanced documentary, mixing powerful images with verbal information.

This film stands in contrast to so many insipid realist documentaries that beginners often make—documentaries about swap meets, model airplane flying, kindergarten teachers—that lack energy and daring, as well as talented interviewers.

Chris's Song

Chris Friesen has a lot of sound recording equipment in the basement of his house in Fresno, and he made this personal documentary about how a song is made—the recording of separate instruments on separate tracks, the singing of the song, the adjusting of bass and treble. It's a nice film that's out for clarity, not high art. You get a good sense of how a tune is recorded and mixed with this film.

This film shows how Chris Friesen makes songs—writing, singing, recording, mixing, cutting a CD. He goes through this process four or five times for different songs, but each time the editing of the steps gets shorter and shorter. This is a common editing strategy to speed the documentary. Joe Moffitt edited this film.

Historic Downtown Fresno, the Compilation Documentary

Compilation means that you base your film on movie clips and still photographs available to you. Many of the documentaries you see on PBS are made this way. Ninety percent of Ken Burns' stupendous documentary *The Civil War* was made from still photographs taken during the Civil War. In David Lennon's documentary *Historic Downtown Fresno,* he went to libraries and checked out coffee-table books with a lot of photos of early Fresno. David brings the film up to the present with photos of the transformation of Fulton Street into Fulton Mall in 1964—one of the first such urban transformations in the country. He sprinkles the film with shots of

The big advantage of making a compilation film is that you do it all alone—just you, your camera and tripod, and a pile of picture books.

important sculptures the city commissioned for the mall, and finally, shows Fresno's new downtown AAA baseball stadium going up. All this is played to suitable nostalgic music.

TRY THIS

Make a realist documentary about a visually appealing event like a garage band rehearsing a tune or a couple of skateboarders practicing some complicated moves. Get interviews. Make sure viewers get enough facts, visually or verbally, to learn what is going on.

Or, make a compilation film with pictures or art available to you, like old 33⅓ album covers or snapshots from family photo albums.

SCHOOL YOURSELF

Making Documentary Films and Reality Videos (Henry Holt, 1997) by Barry Hampe is "a practical guide" and a good one.

INTERVIEWING AND NARRATING

In a sense, interviews and narration are pure cinema's failure rectified. It would be nice if images alone communicated clearly, but often they don't. Important facts that must be a part of the film are seldom transmitted only by pictures. Even the silent-era masterpieces needed titles—words inserted between clips—so audiences could follow.

Documentary filmmakers insert words in their films in two ways, with interviews and with narration.

Interviewing

Some choices to consider during the interviewing process:

1. On- or off-camera.
   A. On-camera with both interviewer and interviewee seen—talk-show style.
   B. Off-camera, with only the interviewee on-camera.
2. With or without questions.
   A. The finished film retains questions.
   B. All questions for the interviewee are edited out of the finished film. Only answers are retained.

Some observations:

➤ 1A is the slowest, friendliest approach. But the interviewer, if he has much of a personality, might distract from the real subject, the interviewee. Also, 1A tends to run long and burdens the film.

- ➤ 1B is the way most documentarians go.
- ➤ 2A also slows the film, but is the most spontaneous.
- ➤ 2B is often employed by documentarians. The interviewee may need some rehearsing before you roll tape. For example, if you say, "Tell us about your childhood," and she says, "Well, it was magical," audiences won't know what "it" means. She has to be coached to say, "Well, my childhood was magical," so her remarks can be inserted anywhere in the film and stand alone. But too much coaching and directing are likely to render the interviewee self-conscious. She'll feel inhibited and may not cooperate. It's up to you to make her feel relaxed and to encourage her to talk loose and free.

Filming and Interviewing at the Same Time

Don't film and interview at the same time. Interviews really require three people: a camera operator, the interviewer, and the interviewee. You don't want to try to run the camera and interview simultaneously. You'll get distracted and lose your concentration, and the interviewee will feel that you are more interested in camera controls than with what she has to say.

Coaching the People You Interview

There are good interviews and bad interviews. Some interviewees catch on quickly, as the following Q & A shows:

Q. How do you feel about these animals being all caged up like this?
A. I feel sorry for them.
Q. Do you feel they are allowed to be "natural"?
A. Not really.
Q. Look, I need you to talk longer. Could you just push your thoughts out a little so I can drop them in my film later?
A. Well, I'll try. You know, /as a kid, I used to like zoos. My parents took me to this one, and the one in Los Angeles and San Diego, and it was fun and stuff. But now, I don't know. These animals don't look like they are having very much fun. I feel like one of those people at a freak show, looking at an oddity. I feel selfish, like they caged up all these animals so we can have an afternoon of observing animals we don't normally see. But what about the animals? Do they have any rights at all?/

This is good stuff. For the finished film, the material enclosed in slashes would be retained. The rest is unusable.

Narrating

Narration is a potent, sometimes indispensable, cinematic tool. It's easy to lay down next to your edited picture track. The main purpose of narration is to add important information, which visuals alone can't impart.

David Frank's *Poisoned Water, Poisoned Wells* would be incomprehensible without narration by Michael Loring.

What I like about *Raku* is blending the springtime setting and the Japanese technique of staying close to nature.

Effective Use of Narration in Raku

Raku is a short super 8 documentary about the making of raku pots, an ancient Japanese artform based on very specific techniques. The potter featured in this eight-minute film, Joe Broc, lives in the foothills near Fresno. Lori Woodruff, who made the film, filmed him making a pot in the spring of the year when the hills were green and wildflowers abounded.

Joe duplicates the Japanese pottery-making procedures in the film. He uses fire, water, leaves, and a homemade kiln to make his pots; the surfaces have a lovely random quality about them. Potters can't control the final look of their handiwork, and apparently both the Japanese and Joe find great meaning and satisfaction in this fact.

How do I know this? Joe tells us. He wrote everything down, all the steps of making a raku pot, plus much of the aesthetic and philosophical underpinnings. He narrates this, explaining certain visual sequences with background and description.

FORMALIST DOCUMENTARY FILMMAKING

Formalist does not mean that people wear ties and say "thank you" all the time. The emphasis is on form or technique. Like realist documentaries, formalist documentaries are about things in the real world and have points of view to get across, but they do this through a kind of "film poetry." Formalist documentaries are far less pretentious. Realist filmmakers club you over the head with their versions of "the truth." Formalist documentarians work with more subtlety.

Pushing and Extending

Think of formalist documentaries as art films. They push one or more aspects of cinematics—shooting, editing, or sound—beyond the expected and ordinary. They extend, process, render. Technique is primary. Meaning isn't secondary, but it's embedded in technique. In fact, that is the only reason for using a special effect or technique at all. It's to find meaning. If you don't push or extend for the purpose of conveying meaning, you probably should not push or extend at all.

When the technique is so extended, the subject of the documentary gets unusual treatment. It's a delicate dance between subject and technique, and ultimately, when the film seems to work, both partners are worth contemplating.

Tale to Tell: The Making of Blue Midway, a Film Poem

I happened to stumble on a method of working that resulted in a pretty good formalist documentary film, and the telling of it works here. It started when I took four rolls of super 8 film out to the midway of the Fresno District Fair one fine Saturday in the fall with the intention of just shooting up the stuff, home-movie style. I had fun and liked what I did. I found myself drawn to people having fun—young people, old people, children. But I also shot a lot of faces of what seemed to me lonely and unhappy people. In fact, I had to shoot unhappy faces because, curiously, I just couldn't find many happy faces. This really puzzled me. Here were all these people at the midway of a large district fair—with the Ferris wheel, the house of mirrors, the cotton candy, the ring tosses—where fun and frivolity were supposed to prevail, and yet they appeared sad, cutoff, even desperate. I went back out to the midway the

A busy frame from *Blue Midway*.

next weekend and, on a whim, brought some blue acetate to tape over the camera's lens and render footage coolish blue. I found myself filming not-having-fun faces in blue. Also, I filmed people moving in slow motion, often grim and robotic. I did this because I could feel the film pulling me in a certain direction, and I gave in to it. The film-in-the-making dictated that I would take two kinds of footage— first, of people seemingly enjoying themselves and oblivious to pain and suffering in the world, and second, of those who knew better: They knew that the midway was no balm. It was not real. They could not set aside the burdens of their real world. They could not truly enjoy themselves.

In time, as I worked on the film, I perceived the midway as a poet might have, not the real thing as itself, but a symbolic thing, a giant diversion, a hoax, like the Roman games, concocted to keep our minds off our wretched states so we won't rebel.

Feeling Your Way

I spend this much space on *Blue Midway* not because the film is so terrific, but because I think you might usefully adopt the method, the process, the approach—namely, following your intuitions.

To work this way, you start off not thinking so much about what you are doing, but instead feeling your way. First, find an event or a place to shoot. You like it. You feel that there is a film here. But it won't be a straight film. The soul of the thing needs to be revealed through technique, but just which techniques, you aren't yet sure. Never mind. Just plunge ahead. Follow your instincts. Start off with hunches, impulses, half-baked ideas. Shoot everything in sight.

Avoiding Formlessness

There will come a time when you ought to start shaping the film, and let your head take over from your heart. If you don't do this, you will wind up with a film full of cool things without meaning or purpose. Instead, you need to think, not just feel. You need to note what ideas are floating up from the material. What little truths do you glimpse in the interstices? Go after them. Don't worry too much about being explicit or even understandable. Do, however, start to guide your special effects or processed footage toward some purpose, goal, overall feeling, or maybe a theme. In this sense, you will have completed a wonderful journey from mere gut instinct to head control.

Getting Clear on Purpose

Another good way to avoid formalist foggery is to write out your purpose for filming—or for editing and finishing the film. Don't write it right away. Wait until you've gotten well into the shooting. Then try to shape a purpose. Examples:

SUBJECT	PURPOSE
A kite-flying contest	To capture the fluttering, fragile beauty of kites and the sweet, tender expressions of the people who get them up there.
The main drag of a big city	To show, first, how ugly it is, and second, how the human spirit has been leached out of it.
A Halloween party at a daycare center	To capture the faces of four- and five-year-olds as they see each other in costume, squealing and laughing.
A major zoo	To show the animals bored and crazy with confinement, confinement, confinement.

Restrain Yourself

Go easy. It's sooo easy to get behind a digital camera or sit at a computer and know you can render your footage in dozens of different ways. The effect of having so much expressive power at your fingertips is intoxicating. But stay minimal. Select only the two or three effects that have some purpose to them.

A Few Minimalist, Formalist Documentaries

The following formalist documentaries show commendable restraint:

Faces

Faces is a little film by Margaret Arroyo that started out as a home movie about a Halloween party at a daycare center in Alameda, California. The filmmaker shot everything— kids in costumes, parents, an apple-bobbing contest, lots of faces, kids running around, a table of food. It was memorably random, as is any home movie.

But the filmmaker wanted to work further with her material. She became enamored of those smiling, lovable, sometimes-uncertain,

Ironically, a film limited to just one subject, faces, probably has a better chance of succeeding, of making sense, than a film that records everything.

sometimes-cocky faces in close-up, and decided to throw everything else out. To avoid tipping the film all the way over into sentimentalism, the filmmaker selected a curious little piano solo by Claude Debussy to play with the faces.

SCHOOL YOURSELF

Watch these formalist theatrical films which, though not documentaries, capture the spirit of formalist filmmaking: *The Wizard of Oz*, *Lost Horizon*, *Batman*, *The Crow*, *Edward Scissorhands*, *What Dreams May Come*, *Final Fantasy*, *Tarnation*, *A Very Long Engagement*.

Children of the Sky

Children of the Sky is a super 8 film about hang gliding by Bob Riding. It doesn't offer much actual information, and it doesn't have a hard-silo point of view. It does have some spoken words, and a couple of short interviews, but they are casual, off-hand, and even obscene. For example, an older man speculates about guys in their

Flip back to page 73 to read about how Bob covered this film—that is, how he got all the footage he needed.

hang gliders masturbating up there in the sky as they glide around. It's a shocking comment that offends a few viewers, but makes most of them laugh.

What makes the film formalist is its lack of information—it doesn't tell you about wings and wires or updrafts and downdrafts. It's more about the life and feel of the sport.

TRY THIS

Make a simple formalist documentary. Don't use too many special effects—some color shifting, or maybe slow motion. Some everyday subjects you might transform into magic: birthday party, cars, clothes, cruising, Fourth of July, girl watching, inner-city squalor, old folks, skydiving, sporting event, swap meet, wildflowers.

This film doesn't have to be long. Shoot for ten minutes, edit down to five. Or three. Go for poetry.

THE PERSONAL DOCUMENTARY

This type of short documentary film takes as its subject a slice of the actual life of the filmmaker. It's what I call a *personal documentary*.

The Game

Dad puts the computer together for his son, Bryce, but the family doesn't feel very put together.

The Game, a documentary, is Bryce Thurston's personal take on family, or the lack of it, in his life. It is very subtle, very understated. The film is in two parts. The first half is like a home movie of a women's college basketball game. The girlfriend of Bryce's friend is on one of the teams, and she's pretty good. We also see the friend's brother and the friend's father. They whoop it up. It looks like a happy, close family. The second half of the film takes place in Bryce's apartment. His father has bought him a new computer. The dad sets up the computer for Bryce, but we never see him, at least not very well. We see only his backside as he leans to the computer to plug everything in. It's like Bryce was afraid to film him or was filming him on the sly. This communicates lack of closeness by what it does not show, or what the film professors call a *structuring absence*.

The contrast between the friend's close family and Bryce's fractured family—Mom is missing—is poignant. One half of the film throws meaning on the other.

Divorce

Divorce is probably the most static film in the book. The subject, David P., never moves. He films himself in the house he once shared with his wife, and all he does is sit and stare. He sits and stares in unlikely places, such as the hall of his house with his back to a bedroom door. He's obviously in a severe state of depression. The title explains it all. The camerawork is an analog to the filmmaker's state of mind. It's a self-referring formalist personal documentary, and for all of this, an art film.

Bonsoir My Love

Bonsoir My Love, a personal documentary, is self-satiric. Hannah Rae, who made the film, makes gentle fun of herself, getting fixed up and dressing just right to attract a man. She puts on her makeup nervously. She takes forever to find the right outfit to wear. The result is a kind of diary entry, one that is probably more truthful than straight entries.

Flip ahead to chapter 12 to find out how fast motion enhanced *Bonsoir My Love*.

This film is on the DVD.

THE MOCKUMENTARY

The mockumentary is a broad satire. It's not just one filmmaker lampooning herself; instead, the goal is to make fun of an entire genre of documentary film. It's not easy to make. You have to find a subject that is slightly ludicrous to start out with. When seen in a certain light and exaggerated, it's reduced to absurdity. Viewers laugh, as they are meant to do for all satire. You mock the subject, usually good-naturedly.

Free-Style Walking

Free-Style Walking is a spoof of the world of skateboarders. In that world, apparently there is a thing called *free-style skating*. It's wrapped in a lot of serious-ass huffing and puffing about self-expression and busting out of the confines of society, and about always being hassled by cops. David Bayouth and Craig Bolton, who made the film, have a lot of

I learned much about skateboarding culture by just tuning in to *Free-Style Walking* and the things it pokes fun at.

This film is on the DVD.

A remnant of a sign from an abandoned miniature golf course, very familiar to Fresnans. The film *7 Wonders* winkingly claims that the arrows point to an ancient landing site.

This film is on the DVD.

friends who went along with the gag by running and walking their way through a lot of moves normally done on skateboards. It looks pretty silly, and audiences always laugh. David and Craig film a mock-earnest interview about how a guy once was a skater but came over to walking because "I could be truer to myself," and so on. The film is sprinkled with trite slogans such as "walking is not a crime."

The 7 Wonders of Fresno

The 7 Wonders of Fresno is a satire of the sensationalistic chariots-of-the-Gods premise popularized in the 1970s by Erich Von Daniken. Von Daniken postulated that many otherwise inscrutable landmarks around the planet, like the monoliths of Easter Island or the miles-long parallel lines scratched in rock in Peru, were really signposts for aliens who visited Earth in the misty past and would return in the future. To contemporary viewers, *The 7 Wonders of Fresno* also sounds a lot like the overheated narration you hear in sensationalistic programs on A&E and the History Channel. David Hall made this film in super 8.

CONTROL

When you embark on a documentary film, any kind of documentary film, you have to assess how much control you will have over the subjects you shoot. The degree of control you have affects how and what you will shoot, which in turn determines the kind of film you will end up with. The locations you visit will vary in accessibility. You can get in here, you can't get in there, or you shouldn't get in over there. Or you have to shoot and run. Here are some perspectives on control.

Complete Control with Heavenly Light

Peter Chang, who made *Heavenly Light*, a documentary I described in chapter 4, enjoyed complete control. This documentary about the making of a stained-glass window was produced like a story film. Peter told me that he rehearsed the artist in performing this or that technique, often simplifying and "fudging" a process to speed it up for the camera. Documentary filmmakers seldom enjoy such total control.

No Control with Kites

Harry Cortez could control nothing when he made *Kites*, which is about a public kite-flying contest on a breezy Sunday morning in Fresno in the spring. The contest took place at a park with participants spaced about twenty feet apart by park officials who ran the contest. Harry could prowl with his camera in front of the participants, filming both them and their kites overhead. But that was all. He could not tell anyone to move or let out more string. If a certain lovely kite were right in front of the sun, spoiling the shot, he could not tell the owner of the kite to move, nor could he move the sun. He could move himself, and did, but not far enough to cancel the effect of the sun. He just had to do without footage of that particular kite. He filmed what was there, and what was happening.

Harry was smart. Like Margaret Arroyo, who made *Faces* (flip to page 205) he soon realized that the best subjects at hand were faces, not kites. So he filmed just a little bit of kites and hands letting out string, and a lot of faces—eager, tense, competitive, uncertain, confident faces—and based his film on those. So *Kites* ends up being a film about people who fly kites, less about kites.

Tale to Tell: Assertive Documentary Filmmaking

You can increase control by being a little nervy, as the following story illustrates. It's about a film I made called *In Case of Earthquake*. A venerated old building on my college campus was scheduled to be demolished over a period of about two months. I wanted to make a film about it. I kept running out to the site between classes to film what I could. At first, I didn't think I could control anything at all. Then I got to know the guy who ran the bulldozer with the big battering ram that did most of the demolishing. I got him to "save" the toppling of a tower of the building until after my three o'clock class. At four, I showed up with my camera. The bulldozer guy was in position. He waved to me. I yelled "action," ran my camera in slo-mo, and down the tower went.

From *In Case of Earthquake* by your author.

VÉRITÉ DOCUMENTARY FILMMAKING

Vérité ("ver-ee-tay") is the French word for *truth*. As a movement in filmmaking, it started in France after World War II, spread around the globe, and has transformed most serious documentary filmmaking. It has also had a big impact on theatrical filmmaking. Simply put, veritists loathe control. They manipulate their footage and their sound as little as possible. No fancy camera work, no flashy editing, no Debussy piano solos to influence viewers' reactions, no fudging by getting a bulldozer operator to postpone knocking a tower down. It's just straightforward, unadorned filmmaking, where, veritists maintain, truth resides.

Veritists as Ultrarealists

Veritists don't care to slant or fudge. They believe that their footage itself and whatever live sound happens to accompany it ought to be the only windows on "truth." They strive to film things as they really are, as if holding a flat mirror up to the world. They believe that the truth will leap out, if the subject is filmed directly and honestly, and if tricks, of either filming or editing, are scrupulously avoided.

Thus, *cinema vérité*, as the French call it, is not much to look at if you are used to seeing more consciously wrought films. Or you may find its plainness very elegant. You may discover great truths in such honest footage and begin to despise documentaries with a lot of manipulation. Shots in *vérité* films tend to run long. The camera covers a lot of territory. The editing is functional, nothing tricky, relegated to the job of merely splicing together long takes in sequence. The editing displays nothing like rhythm or purposeful pacing you find described in chapter 6. You don't see artful juxtaposing of images. Live sound dominates the sound track; interviews tend to run unedited, on the long side. You never, never hear the questions of the interviewer. In fact, straight interviews are avoided in favor of just getting the subject to talk naturally, as he might talk to anyone. The veritist prefers to capture natural, unrehearsed conversations of two or more persons rather than tape a sit-down interview. Explanatory "off-camera" narrations are absolutely banned, because they would inevitably spin the film toward one point of view or another. Never, ever music.

Unobtrusive Filmmaking

The rise of *vérité* after World War II coincided with the development of small, lightweight filmmaking equipment and low-light film stocks that made packing in heavy gear and extra movie lights increasingly unnecessary. The less equipment filmmakers needed, the faster they could work and the more at ease their subjects. The new cameras ran 16 mm film instead of bulkier 35 mm film. Later, the launching of the super 8 film format allowed a further reduction in the size and intrusiveness of cameras. You can't believe what a revolution in documentary filmmaking this downsizing and down-lighting brought. By 1965, filmmakers could film and scarcely be noticed at all. One, or at the most, two people, could go in and film and document everyday life as it really was without affecting the subjects being filmed very much.

All this is based on an important principle: *The filming should not affect the subject.* The goal of all good science applies: You should never let your observations of a subject affect the subject.

Digital carries this kind of filmmaking still further. The cameras are smaller and quieter, the tape much cheaper than film, and the sensitivity to light even greater. Digital is a natural for *vérité* filmmaking.

SCHOOL YOURSELF

These theatrical films either influenced *vérité* or were influenced by it:

The Bicycle Thief	*A Woman Under the Influence*	*A Time for Drunken Horses*
Pather Panchali	*La Promesse*	*City of God*
The Last Picture Show	*My Name is Joe*	*Turtles Can Fly*

SCHOOL YOURSELF

A contemporary expression of *vérité* that started in Scandinavia and has spread worldwide is called Dogme 95. Some examples of it:

Breaking the Waves	*The Celebration*	*Nil by Mouth*
Dancer in the Dark	*The War Zone*	*Italian for Beginners*

Two Short Vérité Films

The following short films were made by my students.

Cindy

Cindy is about a homeless woman making her way around downtown Fresno. The student who made it knew nothing about *vérité* as a theory of filmmaking, but had, I think, a natural inclination to avoid shaping the material as much as she could. I don't have the film to look at now as I write. I'll describe just one scene—actually, it's a single shot that runs maybe two minutes. The woman goes to the back of a restaurant and pokes around in a garbage can. Then a food worker comes out, sees her, and seems to recognize her. He says, "Wait a minute, Cindy," goes inside, and then comes out with a big, white Styrofoam take-out box. He gives it to her with no expression. She takes it, starts to go, then stops and lifts the cover of the box, looks at the food, shows no emotion, hesitates, then walks away. The camera never pans back to the food worker.

I was very moved by this one shot, and now, thinking back on it, I realize that it contains many truths—that is, little personal *vérités* for me. Here are three:

1. The food worker is kind to the woman because he knows that, as a low-paid nobody, he is just two or three paychecks away from being on the street himself. Or maybe he once was homeless. I can't say how I knew this, but I did—something about the way the worker stood around and watched the woman as she looked into the box.

2. The woman is ashamed. She won't look at the worker or thank him. She isn't rude. What she *doesn't* do is as significant as what she does do. She hurries off from the worker. She is not comfortable living as she does. She does not like to have to accept food from people. She'd really rather dive for it in a garbage can, alone and unseen. The "better" the food—less sullied—the worse for her.

3. There is a long pause from the time the worker says, "Wait a minute" to the time he returns. This would be too much of a lull for a conventional filmmaker. She would tighten it up, probably by cutting away to something. But the filmmaker just let the camera run and run, aimed at the woman. She passes the time by sitting on a cement step and humming something tuneless, as if nervous, then glancing resentfully at the camera. It's a poignant fraction of a second, her looking at the camera. It says, "I don't want to be filmed. Why is this person doing this to me? Fuck off!" And yet the woman doesn't object or run away. She just puts up with the filmmaker. Meanwhile, you have to wonder about the filmmaker. Was she embarrassed? Was she exploiting the homeless woman? As for you, the viewer, you feel ashamed for looking. You start to dislike the filmmaker. You think that everybody should leave down-and-out people alone.

These truths suggest how you have to look at, *really* look at, *vérité* footage. Some of the truths are about *you*.

School, Video Games, and Work

School, Video Games, and Work is one of the plainest films I have ever seen. At first, I was very severe with the filmmaker, Eric Herrera, for not making much of a film at all. Then I began to realize how Eric had made a strict realist film with *vérité* underpinnings. I don't get many films like this. Eric knew nothing about film theory. He does now.

His film starts off with a long shot of a guy playing a video game. We never see his face, only his back, because he is seated at the computer. We see the monitor, and we hear the various sounds of the game. Then the phone rings. The guy gets up, says hello, pauses, then has a short dialogue about how he doesn't want to go to work right now, but, okay, if you really need me, I'll come in now. He hangs up. He gets his wallet and car keys, and leaves. We never see his face. The film cuts to outside. The guy gets in his car and drives off. End of film.

This film has no music and is essentially unedited. It exists as about third-generation analog video, so the quality of the image is very poor. It has glitches at two or three cuts. Crude as it is, *School, Video Games, and Work* is for me a very affecting film. It's about the melancholy of working-class people, torn between amusing themselves as best they can, but finally having to go in to some dumbshit job. The reason we don't see the guy's face is to keep him anonymous, a nobody, an unperson. The poor quality of the visuals is like the life the guy leads. Dreary life equals dreary technique. I told Eric all this. Maybe I shouldn't have.

In the next chapter, I talk about how filmmakers who make art films are always trying to get away with something. Did Eric get away with something?

TRY THIS

Make a *vérité* film. Pick a subject that lends itself to low-key, unobtrusive filmmaking, even secretive filmmaking, so that you can capture subjects unawares, as though neither you nor your camera is present at all. You are like a spy.

Pick people doing things as they really are. Strive to film the essence of who they are. Some subjects: children, skateboarders, athletes, bikers, gays or lesbians, workers in certain "visual" professions such as horse wranglers.

Avoid manipulation. Favor long takes and an active camera that picks up everything that might have anything to do at hand with capturing truth. Edit minimally. No music. No effects. Only live sound. All right, I will allow you a title and credits. Let the viewers figure out what is going on. Consider yourself both a reporter, reporting on a slice of life, and a poet, presenting surfaces requiring penetration. I dare you.

Or, make a setup story film (the way I perceive that *School, Video Games, and Work* could have been).

Also, read *The Documentary Tradition* by Lewis Jacobs (W.W. Norton & Co., 1971), a fine academic account of the subject.

BAD MODELS TO AVOID

I save this bit of advice for the end of the chapter. There are lots of dreadful documentaries being made, especially for TV. You find them on the History Channel and on A&E. You also find them on PBS, I am sorry to report. I hope you do not emulate them.

Bad documentaries, first, have bad music. The music is hyped-up and melodramatic. Drums roll. Deep bass chords sound. Weird, otherworldly caterwauling creeps out between the cuts like cockroaches scurrying from the light. Such music is cheap, sentimental, and sensationalistic. It's meant to supercharge the visuals, which often are setups—that is, not real but produced just like a theatrical film—while you are supposed to believe that what you are seeing was filmed documentary-style with people as they really are.

The visuals, too, are melodramatic: bloody sheets, wrecked cars, knives and guns, the facades of cheap motels. And the subjects of these bad docs are male-angled: war, violence, missing persons—too often an attractive Caucasian blonde female—child molesters, serial killers, and assorted losers. Strong senses of good and evil hang over these documentaries. Clear-cut, simplistic good and evil. Missing entirely is the charming ambiguity of *Cindy* and *School, Video Games, and Work*. No truths emerge from such cinematic manipulation, except one: the constant pressure TV execs feel for high ratings, which forces them to go for low-life American sensibility—i.e., bad taste. It's video tabloid.

Maybe I was too harsh on PBS (the Public Broadcasting System), since, in addition to its appalling, grizzly docs about decapitation—an entire hour of *Secrets of the Dead* was devoted to this very subject—it does offer *Nova, American Experience, American Masters*, and *Front Line*, which often buy independently produced documentaries of note. Almost none of the documentaries you see on these programs are very subtle, mainly because they include too much narration. Occasionally, though, they have thematic depth. Recently, *Great Performances* ran a moving British doc about ordinary people—carpenters and supermarket clerks—trying out for parts in England's most prestigious opera company. And you can usually count on *Independent Lens* to find and run truly offbeat, engaging docs. Two such: *Oakie Noodlers*, about brave rural folk who catch six-foot catfish with their bare hands, and *Double Dare*, about female "stuntmen." Both docs have depth, subtlety, and meaning far beyond what their filmmakers originally intended—because they were produced outside of corporate entities.

All the same, I find that there is often more subtlety in a five-minute formalistic documentary made by a minimalist filmmaker than in five minutes of anything you'd see on PBS. Again, brevity makes all the difference.

SCHOOL YOURSELF

Rent these commendable indie documentaries, all of which offer subtlety, smart craft, and art:

Rivers and Tides	*Spellbound*
To Be and to Have	*Mad Hot Ballroom*
Tracking the Friedmans	*Enron: The Smartest Guys in the Room*
The Wild Parrots of Telegraph Hill	*Super Size Me*

11

Deeper Still: Doing Art Films

A lot of filmmakers don't like the term *art film*. They feel it's pretentious or meaningless. They say, "All films are art films because they utilize art—the art of story-telling, the art of photography, the arts of editing picture and sound." I agree with them. But I have decided to use the term here, all the same, as a way of making a point: You can do things in short films that you can't do in features or in "straight" films, and when this sense of getting away with something tends to dominate, I believe that you need a new name for this kind of film, and art film is as good as any.

GETTING AWAY WITH SOMETHING

People who make what I call art films like to experiment. They are eager to explore new methods and maybe new content. The films they make call attention to themselves. Something about them is different, surprising, or "weird."

Artists are always trying to get away with things. They are like mischievous children. When Mark Twain wrote his famous *The Adventures of Huckleberry Finn* in the words of an illiterate, unsocialized boy, readers were scandalized. The book was banned in many libraries. What Twain had wrought was an art novel, utterly unlike any other novel written to that time. Since then, of course, the world has seen many novels written in vernaculars. Twain got away with bad grammar and uncouth expression. When his great novel about a slave and a boy floating down the Mississippi River gradually won acceptance, he pumped his arm and went *Yes!* When Igor Stravinsky premiered his now-famous *The Rite of Spring* in Paris in 1913, the audience rioted. Believe it. Love it. People on the side of Stravinsky's dissonant, driving, pagan musical evocation of the return of life to earth fought those who thought the Russian composer was mad or perverse. Now the piece is a symphonic staple, played hundreds of times around the world every year.

Christopher Nolan's *Memento,* starring Guy Pearce, goes *backward* in time, not forward—that is, it starts at the end and goes on to the beginning. By the time he premiered this feature film, viewers were not so critical of his audaciousness, and *Memento* got great reviews. I don't know whether any film critics called it an art film, but I sure do. Nolan got away with a whole lot.

Makers of short art films don't get banned in Boston, nor do their viewers start fist-fights among themselves, but the spirit of getting away with something prevails among them. However, the very term "getting away" raises a serious objection to art films: They place technique over content. I understand this criticism and respect it, but I also know that the worlds of painting and sculpture do this all the time. It's the technique, seldom the "content," that arrests us.

But you take a chance when you make an art film. Audiences may not know how to deal with it. Often, viewers are fine with a unique technique or original subject for three or four minutes, then the film starts to go flat, or monotonous, or pretentious. The longer your art film, the more likely viewers will grow impatient with it. The lesson: Keep your art film shorter rather than longer.

THREE SHORT ART FILMS

The following short films should suggest a range of approaches.

Discovery of the Senses

Discovery of the Senses is a super 8 film that feels like a visual poem, as do many short art films. It evolves gradually from featureless white to full, rich color. A woman in a white body suit and white-painted skin sits morosely in a shadowless white setting. Then she indulges her senses one by one—she rings a bell, bites into an apple, feels a piece of fur. Each time she experiences a sensation, the set takes on color and so does she. Her face glows in blues and yellows; her body suit changes to bright red; moving colored lights flash on the backdrop.

Buddy rendered the original color footage in black and white. Black-and-white footage can mean many things. Most people associate it with grim and realistic premises, and doubtless Buddy had this in mind. But black and white is also a kind of abstraction.

Parking Lot

Parking Lot is a minimalist art film about a guy who can't find his car in a parking lot outside a J.C. Penney's store. He comes out of the store, looks around, goes down the rows of cars, retraces his steps, looks worried, and finally just stops, completely bewildered. You have to view *Parking Lot* as both a metaphor and a heightened state of mind. The parking lot is the world. We often get lost in it. At the same time, we have often experienced the terror of believing, if only for a few seconds, that our car has been stolen. *Parking Lot* touches that nerve. This film is by Buddy Chou.

A Blind Man's Film

This untitled art film is 90 percent black—that is, for 90 percent of its running time all you see is black. It was made by a young man who is nearly blind and is meant to convey some of the terror sightless people experience. When the film is black, it's meant to simulate the "point of view," if that is the right term, of a blind man—in other words, he can't see anything. Occasionally, and briefly, the film cuts to objective shots of the man so that we see him tapping along a street flanked by business buildings and parking lots. We also see a railroad crossing sign. But we hear the sound of the train during the black footage and before the cut to the RR sign. This is terrifying. The man stops. The train loudly rushes by. We get flash frames of the train, flash frames of the blind man's face, and flash cutaways to his red and white cane. The train passes; the man crosses the tracks. End of film. It's just a little

This film is outrageous. How dare a blind man make a film at all? How dare he include so much black footage? Darrell Randal, who made this film, dared.

slice of fear from the life of a sightless person. Neither words nor still photos can convey this feeling or idea as well as film, and it takes a special artfulness—namely, so much black footage—to really hammer the point home. (Flip ahead to chapter 12, "Special Effects," where a number of art films are described. The connection between special effects and art films is strong and stretches back for decades.)

SCHOOL YOURSELF

Here are a few feature-length art films—because it's hard to find short art films in video stores:

➤ *Triumph of the Will* (1935). An art documentary (or what I called a formalist documentary in the last chapter) about a 1934 rally of the Nazi Party in Nuremberg, Germany. It's anything but dull. Imaginative photography, creative editing. Directed by Leni Riefenstahl.

➤ *Citizen Kane* (1940). Though its photography and editing still seem fresh, the manner of storytelling makes this masterpiece an art film. Five overlapping and contradictory versions of the life of a deceased newspaper magnate. Directed by Orson Welles.

➤ *Blue Velvet* (1986). Probably the most commercially successful art film of all time. About a pair of innocent teenagers who confront perversity and try to make sense of it. Written and directed by David Lynch. Many art films are written and directed by the same person. This often ensures a unity of vision.

➤ *Eraserhead* (1978). Lynch's first film. It's about a drab, nightmarish business firm that grinds up the heads of dead people and makes pencil erasers of the gunk. But this is only a small part of this weird story and the bleak world it creates. You gotta see this.

➤ *Stranger Than Paradise* (1984). A minimalist feature film—no close-ups, no cutting within scenes, no emotion, no interaction, no sex—but plenty of negative meaning. One of the most admired feature art films of the last twenty years. Written and directed by Jim Jarmusch.

➤ *Pi.* (1998) A high-contrast film—no grays, only black and white—about discovering the mathematical formula that explains the universe! By Aaron Aronofsky.

➤ *Requiem for a Dream* (2000). Another film by Aronofsky. An effective blending of subject (drug addiction) and numerous extensions of techniques.

➤ *Being John Malkovich* (1999). Absolutely original story about people who slide (literally) into the mind of the real John Malkovich and see things as he does. Somehow this story is connected to an office that is only four and a half feet high. Directed by Spike Jonze.

ART FROM THE EVERYDAY

Potential subjects for art films are at hand everywhere.

Just think about gutters. They are ribbons of waste, linear comments on our society. Maybe Larry had this in mind.

Blackstone

Blackstone is about a gutter. An ordinary, everyday gutter. It consists entirely of shots of the gutter of Fresno's main drag, Blackstone Avenue. The filmmaker, Larry Budrin, simply walked with his camera set to wide angle and filmed junk in the gutter. When he came to a car, he stepped up onto the sidewalk and walked around the car, and as he walked he filmed only the lower half of the car. In fact, this is a film about looking down, never up. Blackstone Avenue is many miles long. Larry didn't film every foot of its gutter but only highlights connected by dissolves. The gutter is cleaner than you might think, but every now and then you see empty drink cups, candy wrappers, ants crawling over a half-eaten sandwich, a pile of cigarette butts dumped from the ashtray of a car, and inscrutably, a sock and a shoe.

Blackstone runs eleven minutes. A lot of viewers can't take it, it's so monotonous. I tried to get Larry to cut it down, but no go. I think more people would like the film if it were shorter. They'd go, "Imagine that. A film about a gutter."

TRY THIS

Base an art film on a common, everyday subject—even subjects other people find ugly or disgusting. Do something different with the filming, editing, sound, or special effects in order to make us understand the commonplace better. Make art out of junk. Other common subjects: a dump—think of the comment about waste you could make with a film about a dump!—an alley, walls, traffic signals (don't film anything else, just traffic signals), an empty parking lot (or a full one), puddles, license plates, garbage cans, freeway traffic, telephone poles speeding by from a car, fences.

ABSTRACTION

Understanding abstraction is extremely important for understanding and making art films. Abstraction refers to two things.

First: abstraction means nonrepresentational. You don't see anything "real," or anything that looks like it came from the real world.

Second: abstraction has to do with removing attributes from a recognizable subject until you are down to a kind of essence of the thing. If I were teaching now instead of writing a book, I'd bring in a boom box and play Louis Armstrong's "West End Blues" for the class. It's based on a simple tune, which the musicians keep making simpler and simpler by dropping notes. Then Armstrong reduces the tune to a single note, which he plays for four long, wonderful bars. As Armstrong plays, you hear the full tune in your mind. It's magic. Armstrong distills the tune's essence.

To me, this frame is beautiful, in an abstract sense. It has logic, design, purpose. Only the fragment of car in the upper right-hand corner hints what it is about. But this is only one still frame from a ninety-second film that constantly moves and changes. The frame is beautiful to me in its own way, and the film is beautiful in its own way, too.

They All Swish By

They All Swish By is a ninety-second abstract film by Sandie Wong. Sandie started off with real subjects, cars whizzing by on a busy Fresno street at rush hour. She abstracted the whizzing by pointing her camera at right angles to the flow of traffic. She set her lens to telephoto and the focus to manual. She purposely made sure the passing cars were a blur to the camera. Swish, swish. Blur, blur. Ninety seconds.

An Abstract Music Video

Most artistic abstraction has its own internal logic. Here the bead-like lines penetrate the cloud mass, then exit.

Ideoteque, a film by Sarah Hagey, is mostly abstract—that is, you can't make out much that is recognizable in the rapid succession of images. But the images always seem to be trying to be recognizable. Sarah lets them go just so far before they morph into total abstraction. We see a face or a recognizable Fresno intersection or a CD cover, but only for a second or less before Sarah makes it go out of focus or cuts away. There are many lights in the film, strings of Christmas tree lights, or lights of Larry King's backdrop, but they soon go blurry and you can't always tell what they are. All this is interesting technique and sets up the film's main tension between the realistic and the abstract. The music is by Radiohead.

Fast Food Abstract

This guy looks awful. Is this what fast food does to people? Greg thinks so.

This film is on the DVD.

It's useful to discuss this film in two places in the book: here under abstraction and again in Chapter 12 (see page 243), which is about special effects. While Sarah Hagey's abstract music video was created entirely in the camera by shooting various lights and moving the camera, *Fast Food Abstract* was made in iMovie by increasing contrast and shifting colors. The result is Greg Piper's funky interpretation of what fast food looks like, I guess, from the inside. It's like a kinesthetic contemporary painting. If paint artists can get away with their various departures from literal reality, why not filmmakers?

Some Mornings I Smoke

Some Mornings I Smoke is a different kind of abstract film. I mentioned it back in chapter 3. All images are recognizable. Rachel Irvin, who made this film, abstracted life (as she saw it) down to a messy backyard, a robe, a textbook, a cup of coffee, a cigarette, and a tattoo. (Flip back to page 29.)

In other words, she did not have a happy life. It was dominated by things she did not want to do and responsibilities she hadn't attended to. The essence of her life was not sex or companionship or family or ambition. It was sitting outside in a robe looking out on a yard that needed tending to and trying to find the wherewithal to start studying. This is a brave film indeed.

TRY THIS

Do some thinking about your life. Abstract its essence. What images really reveal what it, your life, is about? Make a film based on that.

From *Some Mornings I Smoke* by Rachel Irvin. *This film is on the DVD.*

THE ART FILMS OF ANOUSH EKPARIAN

Anoush Ekparian makes short, naturalistic art films. She does things like take her DV camera out on a Saturday afternoon and shoot processions of ants along a rivulet of water. We hear a bubbling sound, but we don't see the source. Anoush walks with the camera running, to film the ants. Later, at the end of the shot, we see the source of the bubbling, which is just a pipe in the ground, gushing water. It's sort of disappointing. Just a pipe. You expected more.

I call this a *gallery film*. In life, such sightings mean nothing. But when a filmmaker bothers to film ants like this and frames the event with a title and credits, she monumentalizes it. She aestheticizes it. It's like placing a wrecked car in an art gallery. In the junkyard, no one regards the wreck as art or even looks at it very long. But in a gallery, with a name, against a painted backdrop, in the context of aesthetics, it means something. If nothing else, the lines of twisted metal start to look like art. Or you think about the place of automobiles in our society—taking us to the store one day, killing us the next.

Anoush's *The Train* is deceptively simple. In it, a boy of about seven stands close to the train tracks at a train station. He spots a train coming in and starts yelling and jumping up and down with excitement. The train, amid a great whooshing and clanging, reaches the station, stops, takes on passengers, then roars off again. Anoush quick-dissolves the

The trick is to see art-film material in everyday occurrences.

This film is on the DVD.

Again, I say: Look around you. Turn a piece of Wal-Mart into an art film.

train stopping and taking off, to speed the action and maintain the boy's excitement. The boy, his adrenalin still pumping, runs after it. He is fearless. Contemporary society seldom places children so close to palpable danger. The kid loves being just steps from death. As we grow up, we forget how exhilarating this can be.

Carnival Sadness is an atypical "produced" film by Anoush. She costumed four young women in prom-like dresses and put them on one of those diminutive kiddy merry-go-rounds you see outside Wal-Mart. She directed them to wear glum faces. Then she filmed them as the merry-go-round went round. The film runs as long as the coin-operated ride, maybe two minutes. I saw the merry-go-round as a metaphor for the dismal life of young women—getting all dressed up, riding ridiculous contraptions (i.e., doing stupid social things) being passive, having limited choices, feeling gloomy about it all. I think this film is a brilliant feminist statement. Anoush told me, "No, that's not what I meant at all." That's the thing about art films. We disagree. Ah, well.

ART FILMS AND SUBTEXT

Many art forms are capable of producing "text" that resides beneath the surface of the obvious "text." Text in this sense means message or content. "Subtext" is the term often given to the hidden text. Art films are especially rich in subtext. You don't have to dig out the subtext of an art film to appreciate it, but it may be satisfying if you do. Sometimes, it's the only way to understand it.

In the opening pages of this book, I described a film by Anoush called *Above All Else*. To make this film, Anoush recruited about a dozen people in San Francisco to say, one at a time, on camera, the line "Above all else, guard your heart, for it is the wellspring of life." On the surface, this little film feels like a corny public-service TV commercial. But to me, it has a deeper meaning, a subtext. I was interested in how the speakers gave their line—variously sincere, cynical, shy, bored, or confident. The subtext of the film, then, has to do with how people on the street react to being filmed in close-up and giving bromidic advice. They should have just said, "Are you kidding?" and walked off. But they were curiously willing to cooperate with Anoush. So *Above All Else* is a film about being caught largely off-guard and told to say something banal on camera. Art films are often about the film medium itself.

LIKE BEING IN AN ART GALLERY

Painters, sculptors, and poets have been elevating technique and abstraction to a position of high importance for a long time now, over a hundred years—ever since they discovered that the subjects of their art do not have to be rendered as literal representations. It's not so much the nude that counts, as how the nude is rendered. It's means for the sake of means. Or means as end. Novelists, by and large, still have to learn this and apply it, and so do nearly all feature filmmakers. Unfortunately, they are tethered to public expectations and money. Also, they work in long forms. It's harder to break out in a long form. It's much easier for makers of short films to break out.

School Yourself

Visit a gallery of modern or contemporary art in your town. Or drive to a big city to such a gallery. Note the role that technique, for its own sake, plays. As you stroll through the exhibits, imagine short art films inspired by or based on the works of art.

Try This

Make an art film that is abstract, based on a subtext, or maybe both. Or is dominated by arresting technique. Follow Sandie Wong's example where you film something "real," like traffic, but in such a way as to render the subject totally abstract. Nothing is recognizable. The footage is all lines or random shapes or jumbled patterns, found in such subjects as grass, weeds, concrete, floors, clouds, and puddles. Two good ways to film for abstraction: 1) Film in extreme close-up and 2) move the camera rapidly. Or wait until you get home, load the film into your editing program, and do you abstracting there.

MOOD FILMS

Mood films are art films based on a single mood. Here are three mood films, all lacking forward momentum, for their own reasons.

From *Virtually Lonesome* by Ryan Scarbery.
This film is on the DVD.

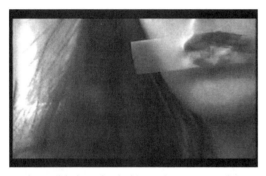

Maybe you've done dumb things when you convalesce, like apply lipstick and then stick transparent tape to your lips. Actually, Vanessa often experiments with altering image, not so much in the computer but during shooting, like shooting herself in a dirty mirror or making her lips look funny with tape.
This film is on the DVD.

From *Americans' Stuff* by Lianne Neptune.
This film is on the DVD.

Virtually Lonesome

This subject of *Virtually Lonesome* is depression. The film makes this state of mind visual and concrete. Everything you see in the film—all the details, all the close-ups and cutaways from the character—contributes to our understanding of the malaise which afflicts the young man in the film. We see the guy playing video games, surveying a junk-strewn patio, staring at a baseball mitt, and finally unable to punch up a number on his cellphone. He just gives up. He is inert under the weight of his funk. Ryan Scarbery made this minimalist film.

When My Feet Get Bored

When My Feet Get Bored is a film about when you have to stay in bed because you are sick but not that sick. Mainly, you are bored. *When My Feet Get Bored* captures that boredom. You want out. Vanessa Waring made this film and was the actor. She filmed herself with a camera on a tripod. She also held the camera and filmed her head and shoulders, and her toes sticking out from the covers. She films stuff around her—water pitcher, get-well cards, crossword puzzle magazines. Slow, moody music dominates. Unlike *Divorce* and *Virtually Lonesome*, which are about big subjects, *When My Feet Get Bored* is about a little subject, staying in bed. The only other art forms that render little subjects like this are poems and paintings.

Americans' Stuff

Americans' Stuff has two moods, fast and hectic, and serene. The fast and hectic part consists of fast-motion footage of Americans in malls frantically buying stuff, and the serene part shows an Asian person in a yard walking slowly to the camera. He holds something up; the camera slowly zooms in. It's a penny. A penny? I think the filmmaker, Lianne Neptune, wanted to contrast the mood of frantic, unfulfilling buying with the calm of an alternative frame of mind, something Eastern, as captured by the penny.

TRY THIS

Make an art film based on a single mood. Don't tell a story. Instead, pick a mood. Film things that seem to concretize the mood. Use two or three special techniques of filming or editing to enhance the mood. Add appropriate music. Possible moods: the blues, in love, fear, funk, anger, serenity, disgust, languor, paralysis, boredom, serenity, harmony, manic (as in manic-depressive), dissonance.

DREAM FILMS AND SURREALISM

Surrealism is a worldwide art movement, decades and decades old now, notable not so much for its minimalist techniques as for the dreamlike approach to content. It's very symbolic. Every element in the work of art is a symbol, leading us down to our unconscious mind where we enter the realm of dreams. Surrealism is based on the idea that dreams do have meaning. They are windows on our souls, our identities, our lifelong conflicts, yearnings, hopes, and fears. Some theorists hold that surrealism goes to deep-species memories known as "archetypes." Art films, and especially short art films, are ideal vehicles for traversing surreal landscapes.

Klaw

Klaw is an art film that yields to surrealist interpretation. It's about a scruffy-looking guy who walks, trancelike, through a tract house where everything happens backward: someone falls *up* stairs; a person drinks a glass of milk that gets *fuller*, not emptier; a swimmer dives *out* of, not into, a swimming pool; a dog seems to *expel* little morsels of food from his mouth back to the hand of the guy who "feeds" him. The walker is unaffected by all this.

You might interpret *Klaw* to be a dream of identity and confidence. The "straight world" (tract house) is negative (moving backward) and threatens to engulf the walker; but he resists and ignores (walking forward, never letting the backward events affect him).

This film was made by Chris Roberts and Kim Tamashiro. I'd like it better if the scruffy guy walked backward and everyone else moved in forward motion. That would make the walker the nonconformist, and the tract-house dwellers the straight people. (Flip ahead to page 244 for a discussion of this film based on the special effect of reversing the direction of the film.)

I Have to Go Now

I Have to Go Now is based on a dream of a woman I know. She is being pursued—or she thinks she is being pursued. She runs and runs, down malls, through stores, across parking lots, into parks, across streets. She stops, looks around, expects trouble, then takes off running again. She keeps looking back. She peeks around corners. But she never sees her pursuer. We never do see who is chasing her. Probably, no one is.

Like many short films, and especially many short art films, you can interpret *I Have to Go Now* two ways:

1. It's part of a larger realistic story, which explains why the woman must run. Perhaps a stalker is after her. Without the backstory, the film is incomplete and unsatisfying.
2. The film doesn't need a backstory because it's really a metaphor. You supply the metaphor. Something like, the woman's running is a metaphor for the way all of us keep running from things all of our lives. We keep looking back. Nothing is there. We are all a little paranoid this way.

The Film Chase as Nightmare

Many chase sequences in feature films are like nightmares. Accordingly:

SCHOOL YOURSELF

Watch *Enemy of the State*, which is a nightmare that is nearly start-to-finish chase.

Another film-long nightmare chase film is *The Terminator*. The former is about invasions of privacy; the latter is about machines out to get us.

An untitled dream film by Marshall Chambers.

Another Film Metaphor in the Middle of Nowhere

Marshall Chambers made a super 8 film about a hitchhiker on an empty stretch of country road. The film was suggested by the *Lucky Guy* film premise I put forth in chapter 4, but the hitchhiker in this film is not so lucky. Setting is everything. It is bleak, empty. Just wide-open, treeless space and a road to nowhere. No cars, no cars, no cars. The hitchhiker is seen in extreme long shot, making him appear small and insignificant against the emptiness. Then a car finally comes upon him and stops. The driver gets out; she's a pretty woman. He takes a step toward her, then stops. He takes a step backward. She takes a step backward. He turns around. She turns around. Finally, she gets in her car and drives away.

My students want to interpret this film realistically. They want to supply a backstory. They say, "The hitchhiker and the woman knew each other from before. They broke up. He just decided not to get the thing going again." Marshall says No. He did not work out any backstory. Instead, the film is more like a dream or film poem, which yields to dream symbol analysis. The woman isn't anybody specific or real. She is a dream figure standing for Opportunity Missed. Or the man is the figure who Missed Out, through fear, being a loner, or whatever.

School Yourself

If you are serious about making short art films, you must see the short films of Maya Deren, an early film artist. You might find a video of her work in your city's best-stocked video store. You especially want to see *Meshes of the Afternoon*, a surreal film that feels like a dream.

Also, check out the art films of Stan Brakhage and Jonas Mekas, contemporaries of Deren and early forces in the short art-film movement. Tapes of the works of these guys won't be easy to find. Again, try alternative videostores. Or contact Facets Multimedia of Chicago, which carries just about everything there is on video and DVD (1517 West Fullerton Avenue, Chicago, IL, 1-800-532-2387).

Out of Mind

V. Gonzales made this short art film called *Out of Mind*, heavily influenced by *Meshes of the Afternoon*, which I just mentioned. Both films are about young women, who, like the woman in *Discovery of the Senses*, seem depressed and imprisoned. Both films were shot in black and white, which contributes to the sense of abstraction. The woman in *Out of Mind* lives in a second-story apartment. She sits on a bare bed against a white wall and keeps looking to one side. She sees herself looking into rooms. She apparently is a writer. We get glimpses of her manuscript. We see "Chapter Two" and "out of place," "out of body," "out of mind." Then she sees a girl of about nine holding a large, lightly shaded, buoyant sphere like a beach ball over her head. The woman seems to envy the girl, who is happy doing what she is doing. Then a motorcycle pulls up outside. It's a biker guy, long-haired, leather-clad, maybe promising escape. The woman runs to the balcony, looks down with longing at the biker, but is helpless to follow him. Something holds her back. Then the large ball makes an escape, bounces down the stairs, out the door, and onto the feet of the biker, still sitting on his bike. The little girl runs out of the house to retrieve the ball. The biker takes off, and the little girl runs after him but can't catch him. Now the woman runs to the door and locks it, fearful of something. She goes to the ball, which somehow has been returned to the apartment, lifts it, peers into it, and then sees herself inside the ball, pressing against the round, inside surface, imprisoned and panicky. Gonzales does not deny that she wanted to make something like *Meshes of the Afternoon*. The film runs thirteen minutes.

I call this a "miscellany" film, which means that it amounts to miscellaneous images that don't at first seem connected, like a dream. Later, upon reflection, you achieve integration. You connect the images, as you might make sense of a dream.

SCHOOL YOURSELF

Watch some films by Luis Buñuel, the Spanish surrealist filmmaker. Buñuel made what is probably the most famous short surrealist film of all time. It's called *An Andalusian Dog* and features dreamlike images building up to the slitting of a dog's eye with a knife. You think that the dog is real and alive, and maybe it was. I am not saying that you should disfigure animals in your art films. It's the symbolic meaning of the dog's eye being slit that counts. Buñuel also made feature films, among them: *The Phantom of Liberty*, *The Discrete Charm of the Bourgeoisie*, and *Belle de Jour*—all with surreal elements.

TRY THIS

Think about those eerie, vivid, special dreams that live with you throughout the day and keep dogging you for interpretation. You believe that dreams have meaning. They aren't just arbitrary. They are your psyche or inner person trying to communicate with you. And since you want to know who you really are, through any means possible, you pay attention to your dreams. There are important schools of psychotherapy based on dream analysis. So take your dreams seriously. They could be the stuff of films.

THE ABSURDIST APPROACH

This approach is related to surrealism. Paradoxically, It elevates the absurd to a place of importance. It savages logic and predictability, as dreams do.

Absurdist filmmakers want to tweak you. They go, "ha ha" at you. Meanwhile, you don't know what is going on. You might even get angry. Surreal artists do this from time to time, but you never let go of the feeling that you can finally arrive at large meaning in their paintings or films if you just could figure out how the symbols work together. But absurdist films have no meaning. And that is their point.

Jimmy Walks Away

Eric Weinrib made *Jimmy Walks Away*, an absurdist film. He may never have heard of the term absurdist, but his film is laughably absurd all the same. It's about a dorky-looking man in his twenties who may have a mental problem. He goes around town making small trouble. He asks a gardener, "Do you mind if I ask a stupid question?" The gardener acts disgusted, as though he's been through this many times with Jimmy, and walks away. So this first episode defies the title. Jimmy doesn't do the walking away. We never find out what the question might have been.

Next Jimmy is on a golf course. He picks up an orange golf ball and holds it up to a nearby golfer. The golfer holds up his own orange ball, seeming to say, "Thanks, but I have my own orange ball." Now Jimmy walks away. (Thinking orange golf balls might be absurd, I asked a golfer friend about it and he said, yes, golfers do employ orange balls from time to time. So I can't go absurdist on that.) After this, we see Jimmy in bed, a large frozen face hovering above him. The face is sinister and threatening. Then the film cuts to wind machines set in tall grass. Jimmy asks, off camera, "Where do you bury your bone, little puppy?" Next, he's in a laundromat, shoveling dirt into a washer. A woman nearby reads a book. Jimmy asks her for soap, and she holds out a large box to him, never looking up from her book. Jimmy walks away, apparently without washing his dirt. Then Jimmy walks into a small diner where there is a sign that says, "Don't ask for substitutes." Jimmy then asks the waitress if he can substitute onion rings for french fries. "No problem, hon," says the waitress. The film ends at the parking lot of a supermarket. The camera lingers on a long row of nested shopping carts. Jimmy comes up to a woman loading bags of groceries in a car. He asks her whether she would rather have her head bashed in with a frisbee or with a lava lamp. He holds a frisbee in one hand and a lava lamp in the other. The last shot of the film shows the frisbee spinning in close-up on the asphalt. This film runs only a little longer than it takes to describe.

The meaning of *Jimmy Walks Away*? It's probably less important to find meaning in the film than to simply go along with the absurdities.

From *Buckshot* by Raphael Couret.
This film is on the DVD.

Buckshot

Buckshot is an outrageous film made by a student of mine. Nothing seems to go together. A young man has been to the doctor. The woman he apparently lives with asks him how that went. He says, okay. Then he is stabbing his arm in a sink. Blood flows. Then he has stitches. Then an adult has just finished reading a story to a guy in bed, as if he is a child. The adult says, "And that's why babies hate dynamite." The elements of this film couldn't be more different. I think the filmmaker, Raphael Couret, was just messing with viewers. Still, you can't always be sure. What to one viewer is being messed with is high art to another.

TRY THIS

Do an absurdist film. Summon all your powers of unthought to make sure nothing makes sense. Still, the film has to have some unity about it. This is what gives it creative tension: the need for absurdity and the need for order. Base it on a character, or on several characters at the same place. I mean, it can't be just random shots of things. Take the story along for a while, then insert something absurd, unpredictable, out of place. Keep doing this.

What do you do if in time you start to read meaning into your film, which you once thought to be absurd? Nothing.

UNDERGROUND FILMS: ART AS INSULT

The term *underground* has been around for a long time. We want to keep it separate from minimalist, surreal, and absurd. Differences:

- ➤ Minimalist filmmakers feel that most films are too bloated and explicit. Understatement and economy are their goals.
- ➤ Surreal filmmakers let their dreams, or sense of dreams, inspire them.
- ➤ Absurdist filmmakers feel that films are too serious, too meaningful. They want to shock you with bizarre situations and jettison meaning in favor of pure outlandishness. They want to end up with nothing.
- ➤ Underground filmmakers, on the other hand, feel that most feature films are too straight, too inhibited, too commercial, too long, too middle-class, too slick. They wage war on this kind of commercial filmmaking. They prefer films that are nutty, unbridled, rough-hewn, discommercial (that's my word), short, shocking, technique-heavy, outrageous, and above all, vulgar.

People who make underground films have a certain kind of tract-house-dwelling, nine-to-five, standard-issue bourgeois, SUV-driving moviegoer in mind, and strive to offend her. If she were to get up and walk out on your underground film, it would make your day.

Brouhaha

Brouhaha is a short underground film included in a recent collection of films shown at the New York Underground Film Festival. *Brouhaha* is a black and white film. It starts off with a listless figure, a man, in close-up, singing the ballad "It's Now or Never." Turns out, he's been drinking. He's in a funk or drunk. A woman enters the scene and takes the bottle away from him. She stands behind him and throws knives and forks at his back—they are in a kitchen. Several of the knives and forks stick loosely in his back. He keeps saying, "Helen, please." He picks up a knife, almost pokes her with it, then drops it, and kisses her. Six or seven knives and forks still stick out of his back. The photography, too, is weird—lots of wide-angle stuff with barrel distortion at the edges of the frame and extreme high-angle shots as if the apartment or house had no ceiling.

Then a party develops. A dozen or so people float in. They seem barely alive. One guy plays the devil. He has horns coming out of his skull. He gets the leg of the fork-throwing woman on his lap and tells her that her breath smells good. Meanwhile, the main guy, whom we saw in the first shot singing "It's Now or Never," remains in a stupor naked in a bathtub. The devil then beats the very woman whose breath smelled good to him. No one minds. Everyone is in a stupor. This is about a third of the way through Jay Beckman's twenty-minute film. Had enough? Then try . . .

Lick

Lick is no less strange. We are not going to escape strange in this section. *Lick* is all cartoonish set-building and set-decorating and strange costuming and heavy makeup and the adding of prosthetic big noses to actors to make them look weirder than they doubtless are in real life. It's blatant, blast-away color, too. The main guy goes around and licks things, including his own arm. From my notes: "GI Joe doll in swamp. Weird guy doing opera. Someone laughs at him for eating off the dump. Finds a painting and calls it beautiful. Girl with weird pilot. Weird costumes, woman sexy in weird way. Crazy crude mechanical contraptions. Cartoonlike houses in real-life setting. Keep waiting for sex, but none happens. Man with big hair tells woman she is good looking. Funny twanging sounds. Girl-woman skipping rope. Man still licks himself. Old guy with tubes coming out of his eyes. Cut to monster or robot. Mom looks at baby, which is the licker dressed as an infant. Older sister got a manatee for her sixteenth birthday—that sort of flabby walrus sea creature. Pretty girls determined to jump off cliff. So they do, one at a time. Man runs across the sexy woman again. She says she has never felt so curvaceous; he kisses her. Then man runs into rope jumpers, one falls and breaks her leg, which juts out at impossible angle. Really weird rock music. Mathew Sidle, 1994."

Okay, this could be surreal, this could be absurdist, this could be a dream. One thing is for sure: you ain't gonna see it at your local multiplex.

SCHOOL YOURSELF

Visit your town's best video rental store. Here's hoping it has a festival section where you are likely to find entire VHS tapes or DVDs of the kinds of alternative art films I've been describing. So rent, view, learn.

THE FINE LINE

There is a fine line between art and trash. The more a film risks, the more likely it will topple into trash. The odds of its ever being regarded as art are short, indeed. It's hard to make true art. Sometimes, I feel that you either have it or you don't. I really hate to tell you this. Good luck.

SCHOOL YOURSELF

Read about art films:

➤ *A Guide to New York's Fetish Underground*, by Claudia Verrin (Citadel Press Books, 2002)
➤ *To Free the Cinema: Jonas Mekas and the New York Underground*, by David E. James (Princeton University Press, 1992)

Also, read a few academic things about film. When you do an art film, you participate, or ought to participate, in a knowing tradition that takes the medium very seriously. Accordingly:

➤ *The Oxford Guide to Film Studies*, edited by John Hill and Pamela Church Gibson (Oxford University Press, 2000)
➤ *Velvet Underground Companion*, edited by Albin Zak (Music Sales Group, 2005)
➤ *The Cinema of Generation X*, by Peter Hanson (McFarland & Co, 2002)

12

Special Effects

Special effects, sometimes written or called "sfx" or "efx," has to do with processing an image to alter the way it looks. It used to be "normal" or "real"—more or less—but after *rendering*, it changes. The colors of a clip now tilt to the cool side, a sequence has been converted from color to black and white, or the contrast of an entire film has been increased or decreased. Contrast? What is that? you ask. When you get into efx, you may have to learn a new lingo. We will do this step by step. First, the oldest and most primitive types of special efx, those made in the camera.

IN-CAMERA EFX

Special effects are most often associated with digital filmmaking, which arrived in the mid-1990s, but efx occur in some very early films. For example, in *The Great Train Robbery*, a sixteen-minute film made in 1906, a robber appears to throw one of the train's crewmembers off the roof of one of the cars while the train is moving very fast. Actually, he just threw a dummy off the train. It's nearly convincing; naïve audiences of 1906 went *Ohh!* Director Edwin S. Porter achieved the effect by:

1. Having the thrower lay hands on the throwee, a real man.
2. Stopping the camera while the thrower froze and the throwee got out of the picture.
3. Substituting the dummy.
4. Having the thrower assume the same position he was in, the moment the camera stopped.
5. Starting the camera (which was not moved) and having the thrower complete the motion of heaving the dummy from the train.

So what was really two shots is seen as one continuous take, if you squint. Porter's technique is also called *editing in the camera*, meaning the effect is made while filming and not at the film lab or inside the editing computer. In Porter's time, there were no film labs, and there certainly weren't any computers.

F. W. Murnau, an important German filmmaker of the silent era, created an in-camera sequence in his famous feature *The Last Laugh*, which suggested the disorientation of a drunken man by shooting a scene of a riotous party, rewinding the film, then shooting a second party scene, then a third and fourth, each time rewinding the film to create layer upon layer of images. The result was one of the first attempts to capture a state of mind in cinema history.

Two In-Camera EFX in Blue Midway, a Super 8 Film

Serious super 8 filmmakers who can't afford lab-produced efx do their own in their cameras, often by rewinding the film and double-exposing, by taping colored gels to their lenses, or by screwing on special-purpose lenses like a fish-eye lens. To get the dismal look I wanted for my formalistic documentary *Blue Midway*, I taped a piece of blue acetate to the lens of my camera. I also filmed in slow motion, to create a zombielike, nightmarish effect. In the old days, footage was hand-cranked through motion picture cameras. If the operator "undercranked," the result was fast motion; if he "overcranked," it was slow motion. By 1980, when I made *Blue Midway*, all cameras ran on batteries, even super 8 cameras. All I had to do to get slo-mo was to set the camera's running speed to seventy-two frames per second.

Flip back to page 202 for more about formalistic documentaries, including *Blue Midway*.

This frame is on the DVD.
Look in "Frames & Clips-Chapter 12."

Discovery of the Senses

Discovery of the Senses is another super 8 film that would be meaningless without special effects—in this case, the effect of changing colors. Created by Joan Carter a number of years ago, *Discovery of the Senses* is a metaphor for how sensation can chase the blues. But it doesn't tell a story or explain anything psychological. Instead, we see a woman in a white bodysuit sitting morosely before a white, draped backdrop. A bell appears, she rings it, and suddenly her bodysuit and face take on the color red. After this, an apple materializes. She picks it up, takes a bite, and the white background magically changes to yellow. Next, she picks up a swatch of fur and rubs it; her hands turn red. She marvels at these changes and gradually comes out of her funk.

All these color changes were created by stopping the camera, changing the backdrop, the actor's costume, or coloring parts of her body, then resuming filming with the actor in the same position as before, just like Porter pulled off the throwing-a-body-off-a-train trick.

This black-and-white frame doesn't show how the bands on her eyes and below her nose are red and blue.

Two Nondigital In-Camera Effects in Kit Kat Kid, a DV Film

Andy Kith's DV film, *Kit Kat Kid*, is an elaborate, efx-laden version of *Snatch,* one of the off-the-shelf scenarios I suggested you try your hand at in chapter 4. Andy does all kinds of cool things to develop various comic, good-natured chases and fights involving a bully who steals a skateboard from a kid about ten. Andy got a hold of a fish-eye lens and screwed it to the end of his camera's fixed lens. Fish-eye lenses are ultra-wide angle, so extreme, in fact, that the world is rendered an orb. Horizons look like the inside of a barrel. The edges of the frame are not rectangular but circular. Also, extreme wide-angle lenses spread out space so that background and midground subjects seem much farther away than in real life. Meanwhile, subjects close to the camera are disproportionally enormous.

Andy also staged a *Matrix*-style freeze-frame effect by having the actors themselves freeze their punches as Andy, shooting in wide angle, circled the duo. Audiences pick up on the *Matrix* reference right away and laugh. They know they are not in a serious film, because the effect is not very successful and actually becomes a sly comment on amateur filmmaking.

Andy could have simply frozen this frame with his editing program, but he thought it would be funnier if he just had the two guys stand still—or try to.

This frame is on the DVD.
Look in "Frames & Clips-Chapter 12."

These are not digital effects. They were not made in the camera in the sense that they were processed by a computer chip. The effect using the wide-angle lens was an *optical effect,* the other a *production effect.*

Kit Kat Kid is not a serious film, as is *Discovery of the Senses.* The extent to which you may "get away" with this or that efx depends on how your audience relates to your film. Joan got her audience to accept her color changes because they know that the colors were metaphoric in nature. Andy pulled off his stunts because audiences know a jokey film should be granted license.

LABS TAKE OVER EFX

Back to a little film history: Courageous filmmakers made efx in their cameras for years and years before film labs provided efx services, among other services. Film labs flourished from the early 1920s until around 2000. These labs were for celluloid filmmakers. Labs did things like dissolves, fades, double-exposures, split screens, multiple images, and color correction, the last not usually considered a special effect. If you were a professional filmmaker or worked for a studio or production company, you were a prisoner of one lab or another. You relinquished your *camera negative* to a lab for striking a *work print*. You edited your film with the work print. After editing, you *conformed* your work print to your camera negative—made it match—and had more prints struck during which the lab did whatever special efx you needed. After this, you got an *answer print* from the lab. The answer print was like a proof. If you liked it, you then had the lab do *release prints*, from which multiple copies of your finished film would be struck.

If you were making a 16 mm film, your finished film could easily run $1,000 a minute, four times that for a 35 mm production.

Still, labs were great advances over trying to do efx in camera, for those who could afford them. It was much easier to start and stop the film in the film printer than in the camera during actual shooting. The printer, too, could mask footage for double- or triple-exposure much more precisely than could a camera operator.

I go into all this to give you just a glimpse of what filmmakers were up against before digital. Without question, filmmaking during the days of film labs was an elitist enterprise because it was so costly. You had two choices. You could make amateurish super 8 films, as I did, in which you did your effects in camera and edited as well as projected your camera original, or you sent your films to labs and paid a lot of money for all the work you needed done.

IN-CAMERA DIGITAL EFFECTS

All prosumer DV cameras come with an array of special effects produced by the camera's digital circuitry. All you have to do is press the Menu button on the camera, then select Effects, then select the effect you want. When you start recording, your footage is altered. My old hi 8 DV camera offers these effects: black and white, mosaic, negative, solarization, sepia, and stretch.

You know what black and white is. In the mosaic mode, the subject is transformed into little squares of varied colors and sizes. In negative, whites are made dark and darks white. Solarization creates a cartoon-like effect by obliterating the mid-range of colors. Sepia converts footage to brown tones, like old photographs. And stretch stretches the image, either up and down or side to side. I can't show these in-camera effects in a book like this. But I can on the DVD. Accordingly:

These effects can be seen on the DVD in color in "Frames & Clips-Chapter 12." Select the sub-menu title, "Six in-camera effects."

When would you use these effects? Not very often, I hope. Only when you can't get similar or identical effects inside your computer editing program. The big drawback of making in-camera digital effects is that they are irreversible. There is no "undo" button on your camera that you can press to make the effect go away. You may change your mind and wish you hadn't done those shots as efx. On the other hand, if you do the effect in your editing program, you can always undo it and change the film back to its virgin state.

In-Camera Digital Effect in Waking Life?

So, as I say, the best reason—actually, the only reason—to do an in-camera digital effect is because you are after a look, which your computer-editing program does not supply. But your camera does. So you do it in-camera. This is what Hannah Rae decided to do for

her *Waking Life?*, a seven-minute film that closely follows Richard Linklater's *A Waking Life*, a remarkable feature film based on a dream in which characters motormouth various philosophies of life at the bewildered dreamer. What is significant about Hannah's film is the *solarization* of the dream scenes—an effect that eliminates gradations of color and creates a cartoonlike look. Hannah left images "normal" before the dream starts. At the end, when the central character thinks that she is at last awake and says, "What a dream!" she is still solarized, so we know that she is still dreaming—a dream

From *Waking Life?* by Hannah Rae.
This frame is on the DVD.
Look in "Frames & Clips-Chapter 12."

within a dream. The point here is that the computer editing program Hannah used didn't let her solarize in quite the same cartoonish way that her camera did.

Woman

Woman is another film based on effects made in the camera. I described it in chapter 1. It starts out as shots of hills silhouetted by the setting sun. Then you begin to perceive that the black areas aren't hills at all, but the hills and valleys of a woman's figure,

From *Woman* by Travis Leeper.
This frame is on the DVD.
Look in "Frames & Clips-Chapter 12."

lying prone. Or maybe both. You can't tell when the sequence changes from real hills to feminine curves.

Travis Leepter, who made this film, also made the footage pastel, which makes colors very vivid. It turned the sky purplish. He did this in the camera. I asked him why he did this. "I wanted to glorify woman," he told me. (Not "women," but "woman.") "The pastel was so beautiful," he added. I asked him why he didn't wait until he got home and do the pastel in his computer. He said, "Hey, I was there with the woman on the side of the hill. We were alone.

She stripped down for the film. I did the pastel in the camera. I wanted her to see the results right away." Good reason.

TRY THIS

> Go out with your DV camera and run off ten or fifteen minutes of some kind of film done entirely with in-camera digital efx. Do all the efx of which your camera is capable. I know I just said that you shouldn't do much of this, but you need to know what your camera can do in case it does stuff your computer can't do, and vice versa.

IN-COMPUTER DIGITAL EFFECTS

I'd like to give you more examples of films that legitimately make use of in-camera digital efx, but I can't think of any, none that my students have made anyway, or that I have seen. Usually, these in-camera efx aren't for you or for any serious filmmaker. They are for dads who want to shoot cool home movies and get some laughs and who probably don't have a computer editing program, or if they do, don't appreciate its value. As for you, you want to shoot normal and save efx-izing until you get your film inside your computer. Even then, you want to go easy.

Some EFX Available in iMovie

Here are some ways you can change the look of a clip, sequence, or entire film with iMovie HD6, the latest version:

> ➤ Alter the colors of a clip.
> ➤ Make a clip darker or brighter.
> ➤ Convert color footage to black and white.

- Adjust contrast, higher or lower.
- Create a crystal look, which is like looking at something through a shower door.
- Insert a left-right mirror image of the subject or action.
- Convert color to sepia tone.
- Make a sequence of action run backward.
- Cause it to rain on a parade and on other events, too.
- Cause an earthquake—make things shake.
- Drop in bolts of lightning.
- Sprinkle a clip with fairy dust.

Lightning bolts? Fairy dust? Now we are getting pretty ridiculous. Effects like these let slip iMovie's home-movie kinship, like a relative from the sticks using bad grammar at the Thanksgiving dinner table. But you never know. What seems cornball for many filmmakers or in most films might work just fine in other films, if used in moderation. For example, an early version of iMovie had an effect called *ripple* that looked like waves lapping over the clip—not an effect I would want to use. But Courtney Fontes used it for a short clip to suggest that her hitchhiker was falling asleep by the side of the road. Not the whole film—just one clip. It was the visual equivalent of the old standby harp music to suggest nodding off. In fact, so many of my students have used this ripple effect for

From *Lucky Guy* by Courtney Fontes.
This frame is on the DVD.
Look in "Frames & Clips-Chapter 12."

dream transitions that it got to be a cliché in the class. That's the downside of efx. When you see an effect too many times, it seems worse than if the clip had not been rendered at all.

Slow and Fast Motion

Here is an effect you may find very useful: Making the action run faster or slower. There are many uses for this effect. Often, just a slight speeding up or slowing down of an action—not so much as to be really noticeable—lends your film the right feel. Here are two films that benefit from speed changes:

People Eating Silently

The subject of my film, *People Eating Silently*, is people in fast-food restaurants eating alone, self-engrossed, deep within themselves. I guess it could be called an "art documentary."

We go into fast-food joints but seldom notice people. We are too much into ourselves and the food we want, really fast. That really was the point of my film: To pay attention to subjects whom we usually ignore. With my camera's zoom lens, I could reach out and

From *People Eating Silently*.
A clip from this scene is on the DVD.
Look in "Frames & Clips-Chapter 12."

take big, full-screen close-ups of these solitary subjects. I didn't ask their permission. I just sat the camera on the table or in my lap and used the unobtrusive flip-out LCD screen to frame. If, after a time of filming them they discovered me and looked at the camera, I stopped recording and just smiled at them. I edited out the parts where they looked at me. I was a spy in McDonald's.

After editing—that is, figuring out an artistic and meaningful sequence for the faces—I selected the whole film and slowed it down by one click on the iMovie slo-mo slide in timeline mode. I think this efx reinforces the subjective feel of the film and sends out a stronger invitation to viewers to observe and ponder than would normal motion. It took about twenty minutes to render the slo-mo, which turned a four-minute film into a five-minute film.

Speed dressing in Hannah Rae's *Bonsoir My Love*.
A clip from this scene is on the DVD.
Look in "Frames & Clips-Chapter 12."

Bonsoir My Love

I first described *Bonsoir My Love* back in chapter 10 as a personal documentary. It's about what women have to go through to snag a man. Hannah Rae made it with a camera on a tripod set up to film herself in her apartment doing all sorts of things to look beautiful. First, she has to decide what to wear, but this is not easy. She tries on what must be every skirt and dress and blouse and outfit in her entire wardrobe, the camera, on its tripod, running, running, picking up all of this. It's not so much that she can't make up her mind; it's just that her inse-

curity makes her hesitate. Obviously this took a lot of time, and the camera recorded a lot of stuff Hannah didn't need in her film, such as walking back and forth from the closet. But she edited all this out. Then she strung together a sequence of her putting on and taking off about a dozen outfits, turning and posing in front of a mirror, trying to decide on the right thing to wear. After this, Hannah speeded up the sequence with that same motion slide I used in the iMovie timeline for *People Eating Silently*. Hannah selected the putting-on and taking-off sequence, then slid the speed marker all the way over to extremely fast. After about ten minutes of rendering—that is, converting the normal motion to fast motion—Hannah ended up with about a minute of super-accelerated clothes craziness, the exact right effect for capturing her particular frantic state of mind.

Color Shifts

Among iMovie's effects is a menu choice for shifting the color values, contrast, and brightness of clips. Contrast has to do with the range of light from light to dark in a clip. High-contrast subjects have very little range. Grays are eliminated. There is a sudden dropoff from black to white and white to black. Subjects in low contrast are just the opposite, with lots of grays and not much in the way of pure black or pure white. Subjects look "washed out." Colors, too, may be adjusted from the cool end of the spectrum to the hot. iMovie gives you three slides to fiddle with—hue, color, and lightness—thus providing a near-infinite range of possibilities. Here are three films that benefit from color shifts:

Soft Life and Man Research

From *Soft Life* by Andy Kith.
This frame is on the DVD.
Look in "Frames & Clips-Chapter 12."

Soft Life and *Man Research* are low contrast and brightened up, yet each has a different feel. *Soft Life*, another film by Andy Kith, is an art film featuring the leaves of a liquid amber maple. That's all—just leaves. Liquid ambers have large, interestingly cut leaves, and Andy shot about ten minutes of the leaves swaying in a breeze in telephoto. He then cut the footage down to two minutes and dropped in lots of dissolves between the clips. Finally, he adjusted the colors and the contrast to create a lovely— not beautiful—effect of leaves barely seen at all. It's one of the most understated art films I have ever seen. The screen is mostly white, then you perceive leaves in slow motion—not computer-generated slo-mo but slo-mo created by breezes. This film doesn't mean anything. It's just nice to look at.

Man Research is another one-man film. It features the buff body of the filmmaker, Marcelo Moriega. It's an exercise in egoism. Marcelo filmed himself with the camera on a tripod or simply held it out in front of him as he walked or turned. He struts, he flexes, he looks at his face—he's a handsome fellow—he walks in several settings, indoor and out. He never smiles or grimaces and affects any kind of facial expression. He is impassive, deadpan.

As you can see, Marcelo felt compelled to white-out and fuzz-out this clip of himself. In fact, most of the film is this way. But why? Did he consider the plain, unrendered shot of himself too obvious, lacking in mystery or meaning? Did he feel that he could understand himself better by hiding his face behind special effects? I can't say. Flip back to page 219 for a related discussion of abstraction in art films.

This film is on the DVD.

Marcelo really shaped the film in the computer with iMovie. He cut his twenty minutes of footage down to four, then rendered, and rendered, and rendered—slow motion, fast motion, reverse motion, and what I want to stress here, low contrast combined with a brightening up of some of the clips. After this, Marcelo did one more thing: He applied an effect that throws some of the clips or parts of clips out of focus. To Marcelo, each of the effects makes a comment on his identity.

Try This

Make a film like Marcelo's, which is a poem to yourself, about yourself. Two challenges: What kinds of visuals best capture you, in a symbolic sense? How might you render the edited footage to communicate, again through visual symbolism, even more about yourself? All very suggestive and low-key. Let viewers fill in the blanks.

Robin could not remember how exactly he produced this remarkable effect. "I just fiddled with the effects until I got it," he told me.

This frame is on the DVD.
Look in "Frames and Clips from Chapter 12."

Canal Banks

In terms of special effects, *Canal Banks* is remarkable because you think you are looking at a black and white film, then all of a sudden you see blue sky! This film, too, is a metaphor. A young man walks down one side of a canal, a young woman on the other. They walk toward each other. They are so obviously in cinematic black and white, but just as clearly the sky over them is blue. The filmmaker, Robin Stein, cuts back and forth between the pair. They draw closer and closer. You can't help but be romantic about this. They will notice each other, you hope, stop, look longingly at each other, and find a way to get together. But no. They just start walking past each other. The metaphor has to do with how people miss opportunities, even when they are physically close.

It would be nice if I could figure out some grand meaning based on the nearly all black-and-white look of the film and the blue sky, but I can't.

Run

Run is a remake of *I Have to Go Now*, a film I described in the last chapter. A woman runs and runs. We don't know why she runs or who or what she is running from. Is she crazy? Like so many films I describe in this chapter, this is an art film. Art films don't always make literal sense. The filmmaker—who doesn't want her name in this book—meant for the woman's running to stand for inexplicable running away from imaginary things.

High contrast makes the alley look dirtier and creepier than it really was.
This frame is on the DVD.
Look in "Frames & Clips-Chapter 12."

This film is rendered in very high contrast black and white. There are no grays. It was shot in the alleys of downtown Fresno. Because of its inner-city setting, it's a more unified, more together film than *I Have to Go Now*, which is all over the place. The high-contrast images of bricks, fences, steel doors, and filthy Dumpsters make the setting look especially bleak and menacing, the woman's plight all the more hopeless.

Fast Food Abstract

Fast Food Abstract shifts color and bumps contrast to such a degree that the result is abstraction, as described in Chapter 11. You can hardly tell what is going on. There's much black. You get only flashes of the "real" subject, the interiors of several fast-food restaurants.

Black and White for Flashback

Happy Endings is an extended version of a starter film scenario, *Macho Walk*, which I

From *Fast Food Abstract* by Greg Piper.
This film is on the DVD.

described in chapter 4. It concludes with a fistfight between a nerdish guy and a tough guy. This is the pair's second encounter. First time, the tough guy beat the shit out of the nerd. Then the nerd got some martial arts training from a master. He feels confident the second time around. Just before he gets into the fight, he flashes back on his training. You see the master looking very wise, and you see the nerd doing this and that with his fists and legs. This flashback, as it is called, is rendered in black and white, and runs about ten seconds. The rest of the film is in color. You know instantly, from the black and white, that the training sequence is a flashback. You don't have to be told this. You don't have to see a title like LAST YEAR. The technique of doing flashbacks in black and white is part of our collective film heritage, as much as when someone hears "will," she knows it means the future.

Andy Kith, who mainly made *Happy Endings*, selected the flashback and clicked on "Black And White" in iMovie's efx menu. In two minutes, the sequence was converted.

(By the way, the tough guy beats the shit out of the nerd again. Ha Ha!)

Old Film Look

One effect I didn't mention in the list of things in iMovie's efx menu is "Old Film Look." When you click on this menu item (after selecting a sequence), you get not only black and white but tram lines (scratches) and a jerky, missing-sprocket-hole look. Dave Larez wanted to do a film that looked like the old Charlie Chaplin comedies. His *Old Times* has that feel. After rendering the entire seven-minute film to old film look, the film appeared very authentic indeed. Finally—you have probably guessed this—Dave speeded up the film just a little, too. It is meant to simulate the accelerated look of many silent films we see today, a result of projecting at twenty-four frames per second when silent era films were originally shot at sixteen.

Backward-Running Footage

Klaw is based entirely on an efx I also described in the last chapter: running the film backward. Normally, beginning filmmakers and students don't use this effect very thoughtfully. They just render a clip to run backward because it looks cool. But Chris Roberts and Kim Tamashiro had a more serious purpose in mind when they made *Klaw* (did you notice the films title is "walk" spelled backward?). The main character walks forward while the other people in a conventional, straight suburban house walk, move, and perform backward. The film is a single long take—no cuts—running two minutes. A young man pulls up to the house, gets out, goes inside—and into a backward world: Someone falls *up* the stairs; a kid sips milk with a straw but the glass gets *fuller*; outside, someone dives *out* of a pool. Meanwhile, the visitor walks in forward motion. He walks through all of this and back out of the house, but he doesn't seem to notice a thing. It's as if he's in a trance or a dream. At the end, he drives off.

To my thinking, *Klaw* is a great example of using a special effect meaningfully. The visitor looks scraggy and scruffy. The world around him is straight, clean-cut, neat. It's the contrast between the way the forward-walking character looks and the stuff going on around him that speaks to me. The film is another expression of the classic fish-out-of-water story about the nonconformist, the person who is out of step and out of touch. But the visitor is true to himself. The backward-moving goings-on around him affect him not at all. He continues straight ahead.

Am I reading too much into *Klaw*? Yes and no. Maybe Chris and Kim had something like what I got out of the film in mind and maybe not. The fact is, sometimes artists aren't aware of what they have wrought. It takes a patron, a viewer, or maybe someone like me to penetrate to some kind of significance. In fact, I think the best art works like this. Artists work *intuitively*. This way, the art they make is capable of multiple interpretations. If artists were as rational as plumbers, their work would lack charm, broad meaning, and suggestiveness. It doesn't matter if I read too much into *Klaw*. It satisfies me.

(By the way, Chris and Kim achieved the backward-action effect by having the main guy walk backward as they filmed him while everyone else did their bits normally, forward. Then, when Chris and Kim selected the entire film and clicked on Reverse in iMovie's effects menu, they got the effect I describe.)

TRY THIS

Remake a film that you have already made but which before you considered just cool and not really meaningful. Be generous toward yourself. Experiment with effects that assist you in communicating, but don't be too rational about this. Follow your instincts, too.

Effects in Studio Media Suite Version 10

Studio Media Suite Version 10 (the latest) neatly categorizes its effects in five ways. Here are a few effects from each type:

Cleaning Effects

➤ *Color Balance* makes a shot that came out too warm or too cool look more "normal."
➤ *Brightness* makes a shot brighter or darker, same as iMovie.
➤ *Stabilize* smoothes out the jerkiness of a clip.

Time Effects

➤ *Strobe* creates frozen motion like the effect of a strobe light on a fistfight.

➤ *Speed* sets the speed of a clip from one-tenth normal speed to five times normal, also like iMovie's speed-change effect.

Color Effects

➤ *Black and White*, I've said enough about this.

➤ *Color Balance*, brightness and contrast.

➤ *Saturation*, muted color or vivid color.

Fun Effects

➤ *Lens flare*, for an arty, washed-out effect.

➤ *Water drop*, like a drop of water that ripples out from small to large.

Style Effects

➤ *Blur* makes the whole clip is blurred in iMovie. With Studio, you can blur just sections of the image, such as the background or one person in a clip of two people.

➤ *Emboss* simulates a painterly look, like on canvas or bas-relief.

Blur for a Ghost Film

Ken Johnson made a ghost film with Studio's selective-blur feature. All the characters were in focus except for the ghost. Cool, but no tremendous meaning involved here.

Super Runabout by Kathy Verzosa and Sean Quentin.

This frame is on the DVD.
Look in "Frames & Clips-Chapter 12."

Color Saturation for Heightened Drama

Another Studio film—I'm not sure which version—that makes good use of effects is *Super Runabout*, a basically simple but very competent chase film. Never mind why one guy is chasing the other. At one point, the chasee dashes into a street and nearly gets hit by a car. The filmmakers, Kathy Verzosa and Sean Quentin, took this two-second clip and rendered it high-contrast vivid color with a bright purple dominating. The purple element is a swatch of wall in the background, but it didn't start off as purple. It was probably some kind of brown. It ended up purple in Kathy and Sean's computer. The whole film isn't this way—this isn't an art film. The one dramatic clip is meant, of course, to heighten the drama.

SCHOOL YOURSELF

Watch the following feature films, which are notable for their color adjustments. Understand that nearly all big-time films today, not necessarily indies or low-budget films, are shot on 35 mm celluloid, digitized, and brought into a computer for editing and for the adding of efx. After this, they are transferred back to celluloid for distribution throughout the world:

➤ *Traffic* (2000)—This great film, directed by Steven Soderbergh, is about stopping the flow of illegal drugs into the United States. It takes place in Mexico and in Washington, D.C. Basically, all of the Mexican footage is rendered a dirty, high-contrast sepia. All the Washington footage is bathed in blue. Sepia equals passion, danger, risk. Blue equals inept officialdom.

➤ *25th Hour* (2002)—This is probably Spike Lee's best film. It's about a man, played by Edward Norton, and his last day as a free man. Tomorrow he will go to the slammer for dealing drugs. At the end of the film is a long sequence in which Norton spends time with his father, trying to patch things up, assessing what his father, Bryan Cox, can do to keep him out of prison. It is an optimistic scene. Cox is supportive. But the scene never happened. It's a fantasy. And we know this because the footage has been brightened up, its colors highly saturated. Nothing else in the film looks like this.

➤ *Man on Fire* (2004)—An alcoholic former assassin, played by Denzel Washington, struggles to redeem himself. For my money, this is the champion efx film of our time. Director Tony Scott no doubt learned a great deal from *Traffic*, and pushed efx about as far as he dared to go in this film. There is cool footage, warm footage, frozen footage, color-saturated footage, speeded-up footage, slowed-down footage. There are a lot of subtitles in the film—it takes place in Mexico—and Scott does wondrous things with breaking up the subtitles, animating them, enlarging them, and superimposing them on crucial images. You watch in awe. Sure, it's overdone and will probably be unwatchable in ten years. Still, for now, you learn a lot about the relation between efx and meaning.

➤ *Birth* (2004)—If you want to see a film with (practically) *no* efx, then see this one by Jonathan Glazer. It's a curiously compelling story of a widow (Nicole Kidman) whose once-dead husband returns to tell her, in the form of a ten-year-old boy, that he loves her. This is a quiet, well-mannered, competent film. People *do not* shoot at each other.

➤ *Millions* (2004)—An incredible film about kids for whom a fat bag of paper money falls off a train and into their laps. What to do with it? Directed by the fantastic Danny Boyle, who uses a number of efx—with restraint, sensibly.

➤ *Lords of Dogtown* (2005)—This is a film about the origins of skateboarding in L.A. Practically the whole film is color saturated—I guess, to suggest youth, vitality, innovation.

Transitions in iMovie and Studio

Transitions are specialized efx meant to join two successive shots. The "default" transition is no transition—that is, a *direct cut*. One shot ends and the next commences, abruptly. As contemporary film viewers, we have no problem with this. Film audiences of a century ago were not quite sure what to make of direct cuts, because most films of this era consisted of just one long, unedited take. Gradually, though, as editing became a necessity, films depended on the direct cut. One minute, audiences were inside a telegraph office at a train station, then—direct cut—they were outside watching bandits waiting at a water tower for a train to stop. Believe it or not, this was confusing. Finally, in a few years, viewers caught on and went, "Oh yeah, it's a story. First the robbers rob the telegraph office, *then* they go out and rob the train. Just like in a novel." The point is, as collective viewers, we had to *learn* to understand the direct cut. And so we did. You don't remember. You were just a toddler watching Saturday morning cartoons.

Very early in the history of cinema, filmmakers learned to do three classic transitions, and in doing so gave birth to alternatives to the direct cut. These are the *fade in/fade out*, the *dissolve* or lap dissolve, and the *iris*. They did these transitions in the camera. They did fades by gradually closing either the camera's shutter or aperture, and they did dissolves, as I suggested above, by fading out a shot, backwinding the film a few seconds, and fading in the next shot. And they also did *irises* by mounting a contraption on the lens with blades that closed gradually to create a circle that went smaller and smaller until it closed to black. They also did transitions called *wipes* by again backwinding the film, then sliding a black panel slowly over the start of the next shot. Later, labs did these things, and now we do them in computers.

Fades, dissolves, wipes, and irises were meant to suggest a passing of time, something like the ending of a chapter in a novel and the start of another, perhaps three days later. Dissolves can also be used to make a sequence of clips lyrical, cushioning the potential blam-blam effect of a series of direct cuts. This is what Andy Kith did in his *Soft Life*. You might also think of fades and dissolves, which occur infrequently, as delimiting a related sequence of direct cuts, like bookends.

Both iMovie and Studio let you fade and dissolve with the greatest of ease. The sound, too, fades or segues, though you can override this. In both programs, you just pull an icon from the transitions menu to the timeline between two shots, and wait a while for the transition to render. You can also control the length of the fade or dissolve, from, say, one second to four. And you can fade out and cut directly to the next shot. Or cut one shot and fade in the next shot. The computer actually reshoots, digitally speaking, the two shots for you, adding the fades or dissolves. Fades and dissolves are so classic, so common, that they probably shouldn't be called special effects at all. Special effects are what we are not used to. The fact that images projected on a screen could move at all—back in 1895 when movies began—was the first efx.

Plug-ins for iMovie and Studio

A plug-in is a little program that you install to piggyback on a bigger program and supposedly enhance it. You can buy plug-ins for both iMovie and Studio, which add dozens of effects besides the big four I just described. Most of them are Mickey Mouse. You get transitions like Warp, Twirl, Disintegration, and Heart. The latter is especially egregious. A clip ends with a tiny heart, which grows bigger and contains the start of the next clip. Heart is for babies or sweethearts and maybe for films that spoof home movies and romance.

Effects in Final Cut and Premiere

Final Cut, Premiere, and other top-end computer editing programs offer hundreds of transitions, filters, and effects. Some of them are identical to those in iMovie and Studio. For example, Final Cut includes both pond ripple and blur. In general, though, Final Cut and Premiere eschew cornball home-movieish transitions in favor of more functional transitions.

We are still in the stage of excessive special effects. We are always in one stage of excess or another. Twenty years from now, if someone retrieved a contemporary tape of, say, the *Fight for Iraq*, a recurring series on CNN, from a time capsule, and she saw all that multiple flipping and churning at the start, she would laugh at the lack of restraint. Many of these effects will date rapidly.

As I said in chapter 2, both programs give you dozens of picture tracks. So you can have picture on picture on picture. You can make one picture continue through any number of pictures that swim in and out of

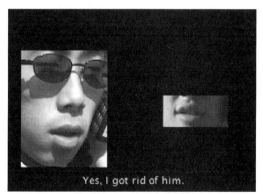

Yes, I got rid of him.

A restrained, good-taste approach to a phone conversation, made with Premiere by Tim Tsurda.

This frame is on the DVD.
Look in "Frames & Clips-Chapter 12."

the clip. And so on. This is called *compositing*. And each of these images can be separately efx-ized. One can be high contrast, one posterized, another pastel, another on bas-relief.

Both Final Cut and Premiere also offer a very useful way of processing sound. They come with a built-in equalizer, so you can adjust or override bass and treble. Why do this?

Nice credit made with Premiere. Distinctive but not over-cooked. From a film called *Vraginromono* by Tim Tsurda.

You can beef up rap-style music by boosting the bass; you can reduce wind rumble to practically nothing by turning it way down.

This business of excess has afflicted the motion picture industry and abused viewers throughout the history of cinema. With the introduction of sound in the late 1920s, characters ate celery instead of mashed potatoes so viewers could hear the crunch. When color came in, Hollywood saturated it like mad. Close-ups of Judy Garland and her slathered-on lipstick in *State Fair* made you go, whoa! And when wide screen debuted, we got a lot of costume epics, outdoor films with vast panoramas, and people speaking to each other at a distance of fifty feet. For about ten years, Hollywood cranked out many 3-D films, which, while technically great, were artistic disasters, victims of technological excess: Primitives were always chucking spears at the camera and making the audience duck. It was all so cheap.

At any rate, if you want to really goose your titles and credits, then get into one of the advanced programs. You will have zillions of choices.

SCHOOL YOURSELF

Watch a couple of Woody Allen films just for their credits, which always are simple white lettering on a black background and in a simple font like Times New Roman. When you really get into Allen, you look forward to reading his credits, anchors of simplicity and predictability in a turbulent sea of efx excess.

ANIMATION

Hannah Rae again—she schooled my class on how to animate with a bare-bones iMovie program. No plug-ins. No after factory. Just a plain-Jane iMovie. It wasn't supposed to be possible to do animation with a low-ball iMovie program, but Hannah did. She made a cute, short story film about a cookie who is used and abused but still comes out smiling—an actual cookie, like chocolate chip, with a smile. The name of the film is *One Tough Cookie*.

To make this film, Hannah drew dozens, maybe hundreds, of cells of a cookie with a face in various poses. She also drew cells for a rival cookie who torments her. But the good cookie gets back at the tormenting cookie by making a batch of cookies that get their crunch from little bits of cat food.

After this, Hannah filmed all these cells in sequence with a handheld(!) DV movie camera. She filmed each cell with a little squirt of the camera, perhaps a half second per cell. Then she imported her footage into iMovie and simply cut the shots down until she got clips of the right length to run at the right speed and fit her narration of the story.

Hannah drew the face of the cookie and everything else about the cells crudely, on purpose, emulating the artwork of a child. The fact that she handheld the shooting of the cells introduced unsteadiness, thus increasing the childlike sense.

Charming results from scant means. From Hannah Rae's *One Tough Cookie*.
This film is on the DVD.

Hannah produced a film in a style that was in keeping with the limitations of her program and equipment. Art from smart craft. *One Tough Cookie* runs about a minute and a half.

School Yourself

Investigate the numerous animation plug-ins for iMovie. Insert "iMovie animation" into any search engine. It makes animation smooth and easy compared to how Hannah worked, if that is what you want.

A Flash Film

Flash is an animation program that can be installed in Final Cut or Premiere. Joe Moffet made his *Abduction* in Flash. In the film, Joe is a harried film student with so much to do that he's nearly nuts. He takes a break from studying. He takes a nap. This part of the film is live action. During the nap, he has a dream, and now the animation comes in. Joe is camping in the mountains next to a stream. He pitches a tent. His car is nearby. All this is in a charmingly simplistic style,

From *Abduction* by Jim Moffet.
This film is on the DVD.

nothing like Disney, nor was it meant to be. Then the abduction. A spaceship flies into view. It first hovers over the camper's car, and with a funnel-shaped ray, sucks it up. Then the spaceship moves over the tent and sucks it up. Joe awakens. Now it's back to live action. He turns to a tablet and adds this note: "Make an animated film about a camper who gets abducted by aliens."

THE END

This book is based on a contradiction. It invites you to make short films because I believe you can say more with a short film than with a long film. The longer the film you make, the less potential it has to say anything worthwhile or involve viewers. So go short—and good luck.

PART IV:

About the DVD

13

About the DVD

The thirty short films on the DVD which comes with this book were chosen for their variety, their educational value, and their entertainment value. I've arranged them into these seven main-menu groups:

Starter films (chapter 4)
Story films (chapter 9)
Documentary films (chapter 10)
Art films (chapter 11)
Minimalist and long-take films (chapters 1 and 3)
Animated films (chapter 12)
Frames and clips from chapter 12, "Special Effects"

The copyrighted music used in nearly all of the films had to be replaced with royalty-free music because neither Allworth Press, my publisher, nor I could afford the royalties that copyright holders demanded. It's okay—in fact, perfectly legal—for a student to drop a Radiohead tune into the sound track of a film she made for a filmmaking class, and doesn't plan to make money on. But it's not okay to put that film with Radiohead music on a DVD included in a book sold worldwide with the expectation of income.

In changing the music I've tried awfully hard to be faithful to the mood and apparent purpose of students' original music. In the few cases when I couldn't find appropriate music, I went with music that, at the very least, was true to the intent of the film as a whole, as I understood it. I used two royalty-free Apple music programs, GarageBand and Soundtrack, plus music from PrimeAudio, and half a dozen uncopyrighted songs that my student, Joe Moffitt, downloaded from the Internet.

I'm pleased with the audio fidelity of these films. However, one film, *Above All Else*, has several brief but annoying sound dropouts. I've lost contact with the filmmaker, so I couldn't get a clean copy from her original.

The best way to see these films is to read what I have to say about each film first, then watch them with my comments in mind.

Starter Films

Lucky Guy (page 48), Courtney Fontes
Lucky Guy (page 50), David Lennon
Gotcha! (page 49), Veronica Roscoe
Snatch (page 54), Nick Kitchen
Macho Walk (page 54), Tim Tsurda
Proud Warrior (page 53), Sam Gill

Story Films

Planta's Suicide (page 191), Hannah Rae
The Silence Between Us (page 175), Sarah Hagey and Katherine Jose
Little Star (page 6), Kathy Verzosa
Generations (page 20), Irvin Benut
Crack is Wack (page 188), Ian McAlleese

Documentary Films

Start Walking (page 61), Bob Warkentin
The 7 Wonders of Fresno (page 208), Dave Hall
Free-Style Walking (page 207), David Bayouth and Craig Bolton
Bonsoir My Love (page 207), Hannah Rae
Above All Else (page 1), Anoush Ekparian

Art Films

Virtually Lonesome (page 224), Ryan Scarbery
Fast Food Abstract (page 220), Greg Piper
Man Research (page 241), Marcelo Moriega
Americans' Stuff (page 224), Lianne Neptune
When My Feet Get Bored (page 224), Vanessa Waring
Buckshot (page 229), Raphael Couret

Minimalist and Long-Take Films

Woman (page 7), Travis Leeper
Some Mornings I Smoke (page 29), Rachel Irvin
The Train (page 222), Anoush Ekparian
Priceless (page 158), Steve Haines
Turn Off (page 93), Jared Dodds
Fluid (page 94), Sarah Morris
Untitled (page 95), Scott Donaghe

Animated Films

One Tough Cookie (page 251), Hannah Rae
Abduction (page 251), Joe Moffitt

Frames and Clips from Chapter 12, "Special Effects"

Frame from *Blue Midway*, blue acetate on camera lens (page 203)
Frame from *Kit Kat Kid*, fish-eye lens (page 235)
Six in-camera digital effects (page 236)
Frame from *Waking Life?*, solarization (page 237)
Frame from *Woman,* color shift (page 238)
Clip from *Lucky Guy*, ripple and dissolve (page 239)
Clip *from People Eating Silently*, slow motion (page 240)
Clip from *Bonsoir My Love*, fast motion (page 240)
Frame from *Soft Life*, bright low contrast (page 241)
Frame from *Man Research*, bright low contrast (page 242)
Frame from *Canal Banks*, blue sky over black and white (page 242)
Frame from *Run*, high contrast black and white (page 243)
Frame from *Super Runabout*, high contrast color shift (page 246)
Frame from *Vraginromono*, phone conversation (page 249)
Frame from *Vraginromono*, credit made with Adobe Premiere (page 250)

Some of these films are discussed more than once in the book. Refer to the index of films and filmmakers for other discussions.

Index

Index of Films and Filmmakers

Books from Allworth Press

Allworth Press is an imprint of Allworth Communications, Inc. Selected titles are listed below.

GET THE PICTURE?: THE MOVIE LOVER'S GUIDE TO WATCHING FILMS
by Jim Piper (paperback, 6 × 9, 240 pages, 91 b&w illus., $18.95)

MAKING REAL-LIFE VIDEOS
by Matthew Williams (paperback, 6 × 9, 256 pages, $19.95)

DOCUMENTARY FILMMAKERS SPEAK
by Liz Stubbs (paperback, 6 × 9, 240 pages, $19.95)

TECHNICAL FILM AND TV FOR NONTECHNICAL PEOPLE
by Drew Campbell (paperback, 6 × 9, 256 pages, $19.95)

JUMPSTART YOUR AWESOME FILM PRODUCTION COMPANY
by Sara Caldwell (paperback, 6 × 9, 208 pages, $19.95)

THE FILMMAKER'S GUIDE TO PRODUCTION DESIGN
by Vincent LoBrutto (paperback, 6 × 9, 216 pages, 15 b&w illus., $19.95)

THE HEALTH AND SAFETY GUIDE FOR FILM, TV AND THEATER
by Monona Rossol (paperback, 6 × 9, 256 pages, $19.95)

SHOOT ME: INDEPENDENT FILMMAKING FROM CREATIVE CONCEPT TO ROUSING RELEASE
by Roy Frumkes and Rocco Simonelli (paperback, 6 × 9, 240 pages, 56 b&w illus., $19.95)

MAKING INDEPENDENT FILMS: ADVICE FROM THE FILMMAKERS
by Liz Stubbs and Richard Rodriguez (paperback, 6 × 9, 224 pages, 42 b&w illus., $16.95)

HOLLYWOOD DEALMAKING: NEGOTIATING TALENT AGREEMENTS
by Dina Appleton and Daniel Yankelevits (paperback, 6 × 9, 256 pages, $19.95)

DIRECTING FOR FILM AND TELEVISION, REVISED EDITION
by Christopher Lukas (paperback, 6 × 9, 256 pages, 53 b&w illus., $19.95)

CREATIVE CAREERS IN HOLLYWOOD
by Laurie Scheer (paperback, 6 × 9, 240 pages, $19.95)